ROUTLEDGE LIBRARY EDITIONS:
PRISON AND PRISONERS

I0124464

Volume 16

PRISONERS' CHILDREN

PRISONERS' CHILDREN

What are the Issues?

Edited by
ROGER SHAW

Routledge
Taylor & Francis Group

LONDON AND NEW YORK

First published in 1992 by Routledge

This edition first published in 2024
by Routledge
4 Park Square, Milton Park, Abingdon, Oxon OX14 4RN

and by Routledge
605 Third Avenue, New York, NY 10158

Routledge is an imprint of the Taylor & Francis Group, an informa business

British Library Cataloguing in Publication Data
A catalogue record for this book is available from the British Library

ISBN: 978-1-032-55549-2 (Set)
ISBN: 978-1-032-57281-9 (Volume 16) (hbk)
ISBN: 978-1-032-57286-4 (Volume 16) (pbk)
ISBN: 978-1-003-43871-7 (Volume 16) (ebk)

DOI: 10.4324/9781003438717

Publisher's Note
The publisher has gone to great lengths to ensure the quality of this reprint but points out that some imperfections in the original copies may be apparent.

Disclaimer
The publisher has made every effort to trace copyright holders and would welcome correspondence from those they have been unable to trace.

Prisoners' children

Justice, it is said, is about acquitting the innocent and punishing the guilty. Why then, asks Roger Shaw, are the children of imprisoned parents often penalised the most? The abuse, stigma and neglect experienced by many of these children raise serious questions about the nature of criminal justice. *Prisoners' Children* provides the first in-depth look at these hidden victims of crime and examines ways in which the harm can be reduced.

The contributors – a wide range of leading practitioners and academics in the field – address such diverse issues as the psychological impact of parental incarceration on children, the added problem of racism facing black children and their families, and the particular needs of mothers and babies in prison.

Prisoners' Children is a major resource for anyone who needs to know what can be done to confront these and other issues within prisons, the probation service, and schools.

Roger Shaw is Research Fellow at the Institute of Criminology, University of Cambridge and Chief Probation Officer for Powys.

Prisoners' children

What are the issues?

Edited by Roger Shaw

London and New York

First published in 1992
by Routledge
11 New Fetter Lane, London EC4P 4EE

Simultaneously published in the USA and Canada
by Routledge
a division of Routledge, Chapman and Hall Inc.
29 West 35th Street, New York, NY 10001

Typeset by Selectmove Ltd, London
Printed and bound in Great Britain by
Mackays of Chatham PLC, Chatham, Kent

British Library Cataloguing in Publication Data
Prisoners' children: what are the issues?
  1. Children effects of imprisonment of parents
  I. Shaw, Roger, 1935–
362.7086

Library of Congress Cataloging in Publication Data
Prisoners' children: what are the issues? / edited by Roger Shaw.
  p.   cm.
Includes bibliographical references and index.
  1. Children of prisoners — Great Britain. I. Shaw, Roger.
HV8886.G7P75 1991
362.7—dc20   91–9630
                                          CIP

ISBN 0–415–06067–2

Contents

vi   *Contents*

Part II   The response of society

Tables

Contributors

Ya'el Amira is a criminal justice/media and cultural studies student at Liverpool Polytechnic and is the wife of a prisoner with three children. She has been a co-ordinator of a prisoners' family support group and is involved as a volunteer with several such ongoing projects in the inner-city of Liverpool.

Dan Anderson is Senior Counsellor, Open University (Scotland). He has special responsibility for students in Highland and Central Regions and Lanark Division, and a special interest in access developments and training in adult education.

John Basson is Principal Medical Officer, Scottish Home and Health Department. He has particular responsibility for psychiatric services in Scottish prisons. He was formally consultant psychiatrist in the Intensive Care Unit and Forensic Service, Royal Edinburgh Hospital, and HM Prison Edinburgh.

Kay Blackstock is tutor in the education unit, Barlinnie prison. She has recognized the special importance of listening skills and has trained in counselling, groupwork, and gestalt therapy. She takes a 'holistic' view of education work with offenders, that it should include personal and social development as much as remedial work.

Tom Buyers was HM Chief Inspector of Prisons for Scotland from 1985 to 1989 and a founder member of the Scottish Consultative Group on parents and children affected by imprisonment. He is Vice-Chairman of the Scottish Association for the Care and Resettlement of Offenders (SACRO).

Liza Catan is Senior Research Officer in the Home Office Research and Planning Unit. She is a developmental psychologist who first encountered prisoners' children while working as a Research Fellow at the University of Sussex on Home Office-commissioned research into the development of babies in prison mother and baby units. Since moving to HORPU, she has continued research into topics which mix criminology with developmental psychology: on prisoners' families, child care in prison mother and baby units, juvenile offenders, and female prisoners.

Fiona Clarke is a probation volunteer. She works with the Butler Trust to establish staffed crèches inside prison visiting areas.

Angus Creighton is social worker at Barlinnie and Low Moss prisons. He has worked as a prison social worker for eleven years. Prior to social work training he was in industry.

Ann Davis is Director of Social Work Courses, University of Birmingham. She has worked as a social worker in the health and social services. Her publications include *The Residential Solution* and *Women, the Family and Social Work* (co-edited with Eve Brook), both published by Tavistock.

Kate Gill is a voluntary worker with the Prison Play Schemes. She is a former teacher and residential care worker. She is the longest serving member with the Scottish Children's Panels and member of a local review committee of the Scottish Parole Board. She had a significant role in the increasing availability of 'Toybox' prison play schemes for visiting children in Scottish prisons.

Roisin Hall is Principal Clinical Psychologist, Douglas Inch Centre, Glasgow, where she works with offenders. She also undertakes sessional work at Cornton Vale women's prison and at Barlinnie prison. Previously she was a lecturer in clinical psychology in Manchester University and she has also worked with the Open University in Scotland.

W. James Hughes was Chaplain of HM Prison Maze from 1982 until his death in 1989. He was born in Belfast and, after studying in Montreal and Dublin, followed his father into the Presbyterian Church. Throughout his ministry he moved periodically between pastoral work and the teaching of religious education in schools. It was while at Maze that he developed a keen interest in the plight of prisoners' families and, despite ill health and a heavy workload, extended this interest into the field of research. He had just completed his thesis for the University of Ulster when he died.

Roy D. King is Professor of Social Theory and Institutions and Head of the School of Sociology and Social Policy at University College of North Wales, where he is also joint Director of the Centre for Social Policy Research and Development. He has researched widely on prisons in Britain and the United States and has been an adviser to both the Home Office Prison Department and the US Federal Bureau of Prisons. He is the author of several books, including *Albany, Birth of a Prison – End of an Era, The Future of the Prison System*, and numerous articles.

Eva Lloyd is Research Officer in the Policy and Research Unit of Save the Children UK. She has a background in psychology and was previously at the Thomas Coram Research Unit, University of London as researcher in the area of social policy issues concerning young children and their families.

Kathleen McDermott is Assistant Dean of Students at Columbia University in New York City. Previously she was Research Fellow at the Centre for Social Policy Research and Development, University College of North Wales. Together with Professor Roy King she has conducted extensive research on prisons in England and Wales, and most recently on the impact of imprisonment on prisoners' families, the findings from which will shortly be published by Oxford University Press. She is also the author of articles on prisons and penal policy published in professional journals.

Moira Maclean is the original convenor of the Scottish Consultative Group which was set up to co-ordinate developments addressing the needs of parents and children affected by imprisonment. A former teacher, she writes on the needs of children and was a council and executive member of the National Children's Bureau. She is a voluntary worker in Scottish prisons aiming to reduce the damage to families caused by imprisonment.

Margaret McTaggart is Development Worker with SACRO. She started working with prisoners' families in 1984 with the 'Families Outside' project. She is a member of the Federation of Prisoners' Families Support Groups and the McAulay Working Party.

Stephen Moore works as a special education needs support teacher for Oldham MBC. He is secretary of the Partners of Prisoners and Families Support Group which helps prisoners' families in the Greater Manchester area and which consequently presented firsthand evidence to the Lord Justice Woolf Enquiry following the events at Strangeways. In 1986 he completed a study of the progression of prisoners' children through the education system. Although the number of such children is twice the population of special schools, he was the only known educationalist in the English-speaking world at that time to research the subject.

Tim Newell is Governor of HM Prison Winchester. His previous posts include Governor of Medomsley Detention Centre, Deputy Governor of HM Prison Leeds, and Assistant Regional Director in the south west region of the prison service. He is a member of the education committee of the Institute for the Study and Treatment of Delinquency.

John Pearce is Governor of HM Prison Edinburgh. His previous posts included Governor of Low Moss Prison and Deputy Governor of Peterhead. He has also served in the Scottish Prisons Inspectorate. Prior to his career in the penal system he held management posts in banking and industry.

Alan Rayfield is Governor of HM Prison Long Lartin. He has also governed Gloucester and Parkhurst and held positions in Wormwood Scrubs, Strangeways, The Verne, and Hollesley Bay Borstal. He has worked in Prison Department headquarters and in staff training.

Martin Richards is Reader in Human Development in the University of Cambridge where he heads the Child Care and Development Group which carries out research on parents, children, and family life. His books include: *Integration of a Child into a Social World* (ed.), Cambridge University Press, 1974; *Infancy: The World of the Newborn*, Harper & Row, 1980; *Children in Social Worlds* (ed.), Polity Press, 1986; *Divorce Matters* (with Burgoyne and Ormrod), Penguin, 1987; and *The Politics of Maternity Care* (ed.), Oxford University Press, 1989.

Roger Shaw is Research Fellow at the Institute of Criminology, University of Cambridge and Chief Probation Officer for Powys. He has practical experience of the criminal justice system gained as a probation officer, as senior probation officer in a prison, and as HM Inspector of Probation. He has served on a parole local review committee and was chairman of Leicester Prison Visits Centre Trust. He has published on a number of criminal justice issues, particularly on the subject of prisoners' families, including *Children of Imprisoned Fathers*, Hodder & Stoughton, 1987.

Ian Thompson is Principal Professional Development Officer with the Scottish Health Education Group. He has national responsibility for inservice training programmes for staff in the health and social services in Scotland. He was adviser to the Secretary of State on the revision of the Scottish Mental Health Act (1960). He is a philosopher and educationalist and his publications include *Dilemmas of Dying*, Edinburgh University Press, 1979.

Richard Vogler is a solicitor who has practised criminal law in England since 1977. In 1984 he completed his doctoral research at the Institute of Criminology, University of Cambridge, and is currently a lecturer in law at the University of Sussex. He has published work on European criminal justice and penal systems, summary justice and bail, and in 1991 his work on the role of the magistracy in civil disorder will be appearing.

Nigel Walker was formerly Professor of Criminology and Director of the Institute of Criminology, University of Cambridge. He has chaired or been a member of committees concerned with crime and sentencing. He is the author of many papers in professional journals and his books include *Why Punish?*, *Public Attitudes to Sentencing*, *Punishment, Danger and Stigma*, *Sentencing in a Rational Society*, and *Crime and Insanity in England*.

Linda Wilson-Croome is Chief Probation Officer in Leicestershire. She has worked in two penal establishments and held senior management responsibility for probation staff seconded to institutions. For two years she ran training courses for officers seconded to institutions in the south east region and has contributed to the training of prison staff. She maintains her interest in the probation officer's role with prisoners and their families through links with the five penal establishments in Leicestershire and the visits centre at Leicester Prison. Her paper 'Probation responses' was published in *Prisoner's Families*, ed. Light (1989).

Jane Woodrow is currently at the Institute of Criminology, University of Cambridge, where she is undertaking research into the dependent children of imprisoned mothers. She also writes comedy and drama for television and the stage.

Preface

The difficulties and problems experienced by prisoners' families were first brought to serious attention by the work of Pauline Morris in the early 1960s. However, while many changes have taken place in criminal justice since that time, little has changed for the children of prisoners. The unintended punishment inflicted on children by sentences of imprisonment imposed on their parents is not easy to nullify. The justice system is based on the principle of acquitting the innocent and punishing the guilty, consequently those who uphold it cannot afford to accept that by imprisoning a mother or father they may punish the innocent child more than the criminal parent. Nevertheless, some efforts are now being made to research the extent of the problem and to do something to try to reduce the negative, unintended consequences of parental imprisonment on the tens of thousands of children who experience it each year in the United Kingdom.

The purpose of this book is to bring together, in one volume, the findings of recent research and the ideas being put into practice by those who work in different parts of the criminal justice system. It presents a challenge to those retributivists who attempt to ignore the unintended effects of an incarceration policy by arguing that the offender should have thought about the consequences. Such an ideology implies that it is acceptable for guiltless children to suffer if that is necessary for maximum general deterrence and public protection. But today there are more than half a million children in Britain who have experienced the imprisonment of their parent. Can that still be justified? What are the effects? What can and should be done to reduce the harm? What are the issues?

The editor wishes to express his thanks to all the contributors for their co-operation and for agreeing to share this volume with authors from a wide range of disciplines and backgrounds. No attempt has been made to make the various contributions conform to a common pattern of ideology or style. Each addresses the issues from the special knowledge and experience of its author. This interdisciplinary approach will, it is hoped, help develop an awareness of the plight of prisoners' children and move them closer to the centre of the penal debate.

Introduction
Defining and addressing the issues
Roger Shaw

This is the first book to address comprehensively the issues surrounding the children of prisoners in the United Kingdom. Many of the contributors are noted academic researchers, others are leading practitioners in the criminal justice system, members of other professions, or voluntary workers. The diversity of styles and approaches reflects this. Such variety enhances the complete book and helps render it readable and informative to academic and practitioner alike; all have a part to play if the issues associated with prisoners' children are to be recognized and addressed.

In his introduction, Nigel Walker points to the dilemma which faces the justice system once the problem of prisoners' children is posed. He also suggests that some of the difficulties are of our own making. As an example, he points out that the declared purpose of home leave is to give prisoners opportunities to 'maintain links with family' – yet in reality home leave is reserved until shortly before release. Consequently it does not work to maintain links, only, possibly, renew them. Thus, one means of enabling a child to continue a relationship with his or her father is excluded. In Sweden the advantages of more liberal and early home leave have been recognized. Whatever the difficulties, and there would be many, Sweden must have tackled them; we should find out how.

For imprisonment of a parent to be a serious issue in relation to the well-being of the child it is necessary to show that the child suffers as a direct result. In the opening chapter, Martin Richards considers the evidence of the effects of child/parent separation and concludes: 'Certainly the evidence from psychological research should give no comfort at all to those who might wish to continue to ignore the effects of imprisonment for the families of prisoners.'

Although women constitute less than 5 per cent of all persons imprisoned in the United Kingdom and the number of children affected is consequently far smaller than is the case with men, the children of imprisoned mothers constitute a particular problem. The next two chapters of the book address this subject. Liza Catan describes the findings of her research on infants with mothers in prison and the impact of prison mother and baby units on child development. Jane Woodrow explores what happens to children left outside when their mother is sent into custody. The findings are bleak.

The following four chapters are concerned with children and families of male prisoners. Roger Shaw looks at the size of the problem and considers the implications of tens of thousands of children experiencing the incarceration of their father, Kathy McDermott and Roy King publish the report of their research on the impact of penal policy on the families of prisoners, while Ann Davis, drawing on her own research, describes the financial cost of men's imprisonment to women and children. The children of black prisoners, whose problems are compounded by racism, are discussed by Ya'el Amira, who has considerable experience of working with prisoners' families support groups and whose partner is in prison.

The contributors to the first section of the book draw out the issues associated with prisoners' children, the second part considers what could be or is being done to address the problems. Richard Vogler sets out the law in this area, explains the regimes in other comparable jurisdictions, and explores the disparity between the approach adopted by the courts in relation to the family life of children whose parents are at liberty and those whose parents are in prison.

The role of the prison service in England and Wales in relation to these children is described by Fiona Clarke who is a volunteer crèche organizer, and Tim Newell and Alan Rayfield who are prison governors. The encouraging work being undertaken in Scottish prisons to minimize the harm to the children of inmates is described in a chapter written by the people directly involved, who are from widely different disciplines. The emphasis is on education, information, parenting skills, and creating the right environment for visits. The chapter is edited by Ian Thompson from the Scottish Health Education Group. The situation in Northern Ireland poses particular problems. These are set out by Jimmy Hughes who was chaplain at the Maze prison, as he develops an argument for using the family to help produce change in the terrorist and planned, early release to enable the prisoner to influence his children away from para-militarism. While such a radical suggestion will meet with scepticism from many, it may offer a light in an otherwise very gloomy situation and therefore merits consideration and thought.

The penultimate three chapters address the roles of the probation service, schools, and prison visits centres as Linda Wilson-Croome, Stephen Moore, and Eva Lloyd show that the plight of the prisoner's child can be ameliorated if the political will exists and the right approaches are adopted.

In his conclusion, Roger Shaw identifies the political and practical obstructions to the recognition of prisoners' children and postulates two ways forward. One improves the facilities and delivery of services to these children, the other explores the macro picture and the links between crime, victimization, and social situation.

Not all children whose parents are imprisoned suffer as a result. Indeed some benefit when a violent or uncaring parent is removed. Researchers reported some families flourishing when a severely negative influence was incarcerated, bringing relief and the opportunity to escape to a new life. Unfortunately such instances were in the minority in all the reported research. Imprisonment of a parent remains a punishment to the child who had no part in the crime. By identifying the issues and moving towards some practical remedies this book puts the subject on the criminal justice agenda.

Introduction
Theory, practice, and an example

Nigel Walker

Offenders with dependants present a moral problem of a special kind for the sentencer who is contemplating a sentence of imprisonment. Occasionally he can be fairly sure that he will be relieving a family of a burden. More often he will be depriving them of material and emotional support. They may even suffer more hardship, stigma, and distress than the prisoner himself.

The welfare state recognizes the financial needs of these families. The social services – and especially the probation service – have begun to tackle their need for psychological support. What lawyers and penologists have been slow to acknowledge is the moral dilemma.

In the never-ending debate between retributivists and utilitarians it is taken for granted that any philosophy which entails or allows the punishment of the innocent is defective. Retributivists accuse utilitarians of being prepared – in theory at least – to see guiltless people penalized if this would maximize general deterrence (for instance by improving the apparent detection rate). Utilitarians have been at great pains to argue that this would not be a very far-sighted kind of utilitarianism.[1]

What utilitarians could point out – but for some reason have not – is that the retributivist is in an even weaker position as regards the penalizing of the innocent. It is not only in theory that he is prepared to accept this: his philosophy means that it must happen in everyday practice. The reason is that the thoroughgoing retributivist regards punishment as a duty. Whatever penalty seems appropriate for the offence and the offender is what *ought* to be imposed. To inflict less would do less than justice. The fact that in certain cases it will impose as much or more distress and hardship on guiltless dependants is a regrettable but not a mitigating circumstance.

The utilitarian is less often in this dilemma, and when he is it is not a moral one. If he has humanitarian as well as utilitarian principles he will want to cause as little suffering as seems possible without seriously weakening the deterrent effects of custodial sentences.[2] If faced with a case in which imprisonment would be the normal sentence but the offender has vulnerable dependants, he will ask himself whether a non-custodial measure is likely to receive enough publicity to undermine general deterrence, and whether the offender is likely to do serious harm if left at liberty. Unlike the retributivist he does not have to worry about consistency: only about the possible reaction of a consistency-minded public, which is a political, not a moral, worry.

For the retributivist, however, the punishment of the family infringes a moral principle: no punishment without desert. Yet paradoxically another of his principles – that desert makes punishment obligatory – infringes that principle every day. If his tariff prescribes a custodial sentence for a given type of offence, or for an offender with a certain number of previous convictions, and there are no mitigating considerations, the substitution of a non-custodial sentence constitutes a kind of discrimination which runs counter to his third principle, consistency.

In this situation he is apt to console himself in two ways. He may tell himself – and even the offender too – that he should have thought of his family before doing what he did. This relieves the conscience by piling on the blame. A more sophisticated consolation is that the family are not really being punished because the harm done to them is unintentional. The distinction is a fine one, since the harm is a consequence which the sentencer must have, or at least should have, foreseen. I am not arguing that sentencers should share the blame: simply that academic consolations are not practical solutions.

Few penal codes offer any guidance in such cases. In the era of capital punishment the English common law forbade the execution of pregnant women in order to prevent injustice to the unborn child, but that was a mere historical curiosity. Today the Italian code forbids short[3] sentences of imprisonment for women who are pregnant or have children of their own under 3 years of age living with them (but with exceptions for women involved in organized crime). The substitute for imprisonment in such cases is 'home arrest' (*arresto domiciliare*). I cite this not as a model but as an example of a provision which acknowledges a problem even if it takes only a small step towards a solution.

In any case it is arguable that hard and fast rules of this sort are needed only in codes which oblige courts to apply a tariff, and that more flexible systems which allow sentencers the discretion to 'individualize' sentences to fit situations as well as offenders are better able to deal with the problem posed by dependants. This may well be so in theory:

the question is how often it happens in practice. It may not be too difficult to persuade a sentencer to think twice before imprisoning a mother of toddlers; but a father of teenagers, or even 6-year-olds, is another matter, especially when his record makes it unlikely that he will respond to a fine, probation, or community service. Courts hesitate to deprive children of fathers only when they are motherless, and not always then.

These are the principles and the realities. They point to yet another principle: a moral obligation to do whatever is practicable to alleviate the material and emotional stress from which many prisoners' families suffer. The obligation is not confined to the social services or the probation service: it lies on the Prison Department too.

Indeed, it is arguable that once an offender has been committed to prison the most effective psychological help that can be given to his family lies in arranging face-to-face contacts with them (I am of course excepting some, though not all, cases in which he has done them harm). Some prisons take a great deal of trouble to make family visits as relaxed as possible, especially low security establishments. Others are prevented from doing so by overcrowding, architecture, staffing problems, and experience of abuse of visiting privileges.

What has received far less attention is a much more promising expedient: home leave. It seems worthwhile to outline the Prison Department's present policy, as set out in Standing Order 7E of 1989. The first point to be made is that there are certain classes of prisoner who, in most cases understandably, never become eligible for home leave (or indeed any other form of temporary release):

a. the unsentenced;
b. those awaiting further charges;
c. detainees under the Immigration Act, 1971;
d. those subject to extradition proceedings;
e. those due for deportation when released from their sentences;
f. those considered mentally disordered;
g. Category A inmates;
h. inmates on lists of escapers.

Governors are also advised not to grant temporary release of any kind unless satisfied that the prisoner can be trusted to abstain from further crime and to return to prison.

Even so, there are further restrictions. Their effect is that even a prisoner who does not belong to one of the 'barred' categories, and is not regarded by staff as likely to re-offend on leave or fail to return from it, does not become eligible to apply for a weekend at home until he has served a substantial fraction of his sentence. The longer the sentence, the longer the period in which his only face-to-face contacts with his family must consist of visits by them.

Yet one of the declared purposes of home leave (in paragraph 12) is to give prisoners opportunities to 'maintain links with family'. It would be more realistic to acknowledge that one of the aims with which home leave was initiated was the *renewal* of links with families: hence the wait until release comes over the horizon. If *maintaining* links were a genuine aim, home leave would be regarded as something that ought to be granted soon after the start of a sentence, and at regular intervals thereafter. In Sweden 'regular short-term home leave' is normally granted after a short qualifying period,[4] unless the prisoner is serving less than two months, is in high security, or is thought likely to re-offend or misbehave on leave. The first home leave allows 48 hours at home, and subsequent leaves allow 72 hours, once a month (two months in the case of closed national institutions). Prisoners in the 'free labour system' are allowed 36 hours' leave once a fortnight (once a week in the last three months of sentence). Even lifers and prisoners serving sentences of eight years or more are allowed leave in the third year of sentence.

Home leave has obvious advantages over family visits to prisons, and would greatly reduce their number. Equally obvious are the disadvantages. Staff would have to cope with more departures and receptions. Governors would need 'home circumstances reports' to help them to decide whether a prisoner should be regarded as eligible. Some prisoners would fail to return punctually (but this happens at present, and Northern Ireland's practice of granting Christmas leave to most categories of prisoner does not result in many failures). A few would re-offend on leave; but 48 hours does not give much time for this, and it is noteworthy that the news media, so ready to feature crimes by parolees, hardly ever report crimes committed during home leave. A more serious problem would be prisoners without homes and families, who would complain of discrimination if denied the privilege, and would not be consoled by the argument that home leave is intended to benefit families rather than prisoners. Yet Sweden must have faced and solved this problem; and we should find out how.

In short, if 'maintaining links with families' is meant to be more than mere lip-service, a relaxation of Standing Orders to allow governors to grant regular home leaves at an early stage in a prisoner's sentence would be more effective than any conceivable improvement in facilities for family visits to prisons.

NOTES

1 See, for example, Chapter 1 of H. L. A. Hart's *Punishment and Responsibility* (Oxford: Clarendon Press, 1968).
2 The sensible utilitarian believes that they deter *some* offenders and *some* potential offenders; and the evidence is on his side.
3 That is, of two years or less. The same protection is extended to offenders whose ill-health requires constant attention, and to those aged 65 or older who are partially disabled. Fathers of motherless children are not mentioned.
4 Qualifying periods (which include time spent in custody on remand) are one quarter of a sentence, but with a minimum of one month in custody (two months if the sentence exceeds a year) for prisoners in open institutions.

Part I

The impact of parental imprisonment upon children

1 The separation of children and parents

Some issues and problems

Martin Richards

INTRODUCTION

There has long been a belief that a satisfactory home life and, in particular, good parent–child relations have an important positive influence on the intellectual and social development of children. Or conversely, that delinquency and a variety of psychological and social problems may be attributed to deficiencies in parental care and control. As a character in *West Side Story* put it, 'I am depraved on account of I was deprived'.

In the period immediately after the Second World War when there was an understandable emphasis on rebuilding domestic life after the separations and upheavals of war, attention was particularly focused on the mother and the quality of her relations with her children. In a monograph written for the World Health Organization, John Bowlby made the rather startling claim that a satisfactory mother–child relationship was *essential* for adult mental health (Bowlby 1951; see also Bretherton and Waters (1985) for a more recent discussion of this theoretical position), and the scene was set for a long and active period of research on these issues. Despite remaining areas of ignorance and continuing debates about the interpretation of evidence and theoretical issues, some broad principles seem clear. Some childhood experiences can have both immediate and long-term consequences for some children. While some of the most consistent and powerful effects result from disruptions of mother–child relationships, a whole range of upheavals of social relationships and in domestic life have been shown to have consequences at least for some children in some circumstances. Effects cannot be attributed to a single process: while some may result directly from a break in one of the parent–child relationships, others may stem from associated features of changing domestic circumstances – the poverty that may follow divorce, for example, or the frequent changes of school and breaks in childhood friendships that may accompany parental unemployment and homelessness. Psychological factors may be very important too. A child's feeling of self-esteem, which may be closely linked to a number of aspects of development, seems to be very much a product of the quality of a child's relationship with those in the immediate family and social network and their understanding of the reasons for domestic changes and the actions of others who are socially important to them. If, for instance, a parent walks out of a marriage, a child may feel very rejected and self-esteem can plummet. But a father who leaves home for a job that a child may see in positive terms may have quite the contrary effect.

So, in order to assess the effects of separations and other changes in domestic life for children, it is necessary to understand the meaning of the events for the child, the quality of the child's relationships with those in their immediate social circle, and how these may alter consequences for their material well-being and wider social world, as well as many other factors such as the child's age, gender, and personality (see Rutter 1981 for a general discussion). Clearly with such variety and complexity one needs to be very cautious about making any simple broad generalizations.

The imprisonment of a parent will have profound effects for their relationships with their children and is likely to have all sorts of other indirect effects on their children's lives. In recent years there has been a growing series of descriptive studies of the consequences of imprisonment for families (e.g. Morris 1965; Matthews 1983; Shaw 1987; Light 1989), though we still lack systematic follow-up studies of children. Indeed, despite the recent work which has begun to highlight the plight of the 'hidden victims' of imprisonment, we still know a great deal less about its consequences than those of other much better studied domestic upheavals such as divorce or the death of a parent. To some extent, these very different kinds of situations will share features in common as well as each having their own specific consequences. To illustrate this I will consider some of the recent research on the consequences of divorce and parental death before returning to the discussion of imprisonment.

In the 1960s and 1970s divorce became a prominent feature of family life in Europe, N. America, and most other industrialized societies. In Britain, after two decades of rising rate, the incidence has steadied at a level that probably means that slightly over a quarter of all children are likely to experience divorce before they reach school-leaving age. Death rates in young adult life are now very low in the industrialized world but the loss of a parent through death is still the experience of about 4 per cent of children. At divorce the usual situation is that the father will leave home and the children will remain with the mother. Studies show that, within a few years of the initial separation, only a minority of children are in regular contact with their father. So, at first glance at least, the consequences of divorce might look rather similar to those following the death of a father. Indeed, in the early post-war years, both these categories of family disruption tended to be lumped together under the general rubric of 'broken families'. But by the 1960s it became clear that the outcome was rather different for children after the death of a father than after a divorce (see Richards 1987). To many people's surprise the longer-term consequences of divorce are often more severe than those following the death of a father. By comparing these two situations and their consequences we have a means of understanding how events that disrupt families and break social relationships can influence children.

CONSEQUENCES OF PARENT DIVORCE AND PARENT DEATH FOR CHILDREN

There is now a considerable body of work to show that most children exhibit some disturbance of behaviour when they become aware that their parents' marriage may end and, typically, this will persist for some months at least (e.g. Burgoyne, Ormrod, and Richards 1987; Emery 1988; Hetherington and Arasteh 1988). However, the form this disturbance may take and its severity will depend on many factors, including a child's gender, age, and the particular circumstances. Younger children often suffer from separation anxiety: having lost one very important person in their life they may fear that they will lose others. In the middle childhood sadness, anger, or depression may predominate. Children often feel very angry at their parents for separating. They – and this is most common in boys – may act out this anger and their behaviour becomes difficult and hard to control. Or children may feel that expression of the anger may drive away parents so it is turned inward and this may lead to depression.

Teenagers have more freedom of action and may choose to get out of a difficult home situation. Girls, especially, are likely to leave home at an earlier age after a parental divorce. Not surprisingly, school work tends to fall off as children try to cope with the consequences of a parental divorce. Indeed, overall children of divorced parents tend to leave school with fewer qualifications than those whose parents remain married.

As I have already emphasized, the impact on a particular child will depend on many factors. Not very surprisingly, there is evidence that children fare best if they are able to maintain a good relationship with both parents. On the other hand a move of house, a change of school, or the advent of new partners for the remaining parent are all likely to add to children's problems. Divorce is almost always associated with a very significant drop in income for households with children. Indeed, the evidence suggests that a majority of divorced women with children are dependent on state benefits, at least for a period of time. For a significant minority, poverty and homelessness follow divorce. The great majority of those maintained by the state in squalid bed and breakfast accommodation are separated mothers and their children. As has been amply demonstrated, poverty in itself has very negative effects for the development of children.

Recently researchers have been examining the longer-term consequences of parental divorce using data from the large-scale British cohort studies. These three studies include the children born in one week in 1946, 1958, and 1970. Analysis of data shows that the effects of parental divorce may still be seen in young adults with lower than expected occupational status (given parental social class position), increased incidence of psychiatric and other medical problems, and an increased propensity to divorce (e.g. Maclean and Wadsworth 1988).

All in all the outcome for children after a parental divorce seems to be rather gloomy, though it is very important not to over-emphasize the bad effects – we are talking of differences in prevalence between groups so not all children will show effects. And there can be positive results. Divorce can free a child from the presence of a disruptive or abusive parent. Or a move into a stepfamily, especially when a child is young, can make for a much happier childhood in some circumstances. And we should not forget that domestic adversity can lead to the learning of social skills and emotional resilience that provide benefits in later life.

Turning to the effects of a parental death: here again some consequences for both behavioural measures and school progress have been reported but the effects are much less than those seen after a parental divorce (Rutter 1981). Indeed, many studies find that educational achievement, for example, after a father's death is not significantly different from that of children who grow up with both their parents in the home. Of course, many children are deeply upset by the death of a parent but the consequences of such sad events seem less serious than following a divorce. Why should this be? In both situations children lose an important relationship (though not invariably so after divorce), the household may well be faced with a move, and there is usually a drop in income. However, the meaning of the two events is very different for those immediately involved. Both are likely to be deeply unwelcome to children, but in the case of divorce a child often feels that a parent has chosen to do something that the parent should know will be hurtful to them. This gives the child a sense of powerlessness and a feeling that the very people who should be most concerned to protect their interests are against them. Hence children feel hurt, angry, rejected, and neglected and these feelings in turn lead to feelings of low self-worth – if a parent does not value you enough to protect your interests, who else will? Or perhaps you are not worthy of anyone's concern. Death does not usually provoke this feeling that a parent has deliberately acted knowingly against a child's interests. Feelings are predominantly of loss and sadness but not of rejection.

Feelings are often reinforced by the actions of others in the family. After divorce, anger and bitterness between parents is usual and, sadly, this frequently leads to a child being given a very negative picture of their absent parent. After a death the reverse is usually the case. A dead parent is often idealized and held up as an example to a child. For boys, especially, they can identify with the dead father. They can aspire to grow up as he was. It is a very different situation for a child who constantly hears how awful his father was and how much better the remaining family is without him. In this case too a son may believe that he will grow up like his father – but a father who is despised and disliked by his mother as he himself might be. Hardly a situation in which self-worth is likely to blossom. It is interesting and probably significant to note in this context that there is some evidence that post-divorce, children do somewhat better if they reside with the same gender parent. Presumably in such situations they are somewhat insulated from a negative view of the parent they will identify with.

In the anger and bitterness that surround divorce, children's interests may become neglected, while after a death the remaining parent may find greater comfort and support from the most tangible reminder of the dead spouse. In one study the degree of parental involvement in a child's school work was measured by the frequency of visits to the school to see teachers. The frequency of such visits dropped off sharply after a parental divorce but, if anything, the reverse was true after a death. The remaining parent seems to become particularly protective of the child's interests.

Parallel effects may be seen in the wider family. Divorce often splits a whole kinship network so that a child may lose not only a parent but all the relatives on that side of the family. But after a death the opposite is often the case and the relatives of the dead parent are drawn in and provide help and support. There are parallels at the level of the state. While widowhood will usually mean a drop in income the effects are not as severe as after divorce. Pensions and other state benefits are at least marginally better for a widow.

A final aspect of the situation that should be mentioned is remarriage. Most divorces are followed by a remarriage or a cohabitation. For many, the wish to marry someone else (or at least live with them) may be a major reason for the divorce. Others actively seek new partners once their marriage has ended so, especially for the younger divorced parents, the great majority are married again or are cohabiting within a year or two of a divorce. Remarriage may do much to improve things for the parent and household income usually rises significantly, but children may have much more mixed feelings. Indeed, the follow-up studies suggest that children, in terms of behavioural and educational measures, are often better off with a parent who remains on their own than after the arrival of a stepparent. One reflection of the different dynamics of death and divorce is that, after a death, the average interval before remarriage is much longer.

Before we leave this discussion it is worth at least briefly considering one other situation before we turn our attention to the families of prisoners. These are households where the father is absent through work. Patterns vary widely from those who simply leave the house early in the morning and return later, perhaps after the children have gone to bed, to those who are away for months or even years at a time. An example in the latter category are men in the Navy who may be away for nine months or more at a time. For some of these, those on nuclear submarines, for instance, no communication with those ashore is permitted while they are at sea. Studies of naval families (e.g. Totterman 1989) suggest these patterns of absence have significant effects on both the wives and their children. Children often felt sad during their father's absence but, interestingly enough, even some of the youngest children tried to hide their feelings from their mothers. There are some suggestions that school work may sometimes suffer and that there can be behavioural disturbance but these difficulties seem much less marked than after a marital separation. Of course, the situation is very different. While children may be saddened by their father's absence and families may find the transition between the times when he is away and when he is present stressful, the father's job is generally seen in quite positive terms. Children are able to understand why he is away and often have the support of other families and children in the same position.

In trying to understand the situation of families where there is a periodic absence of the father because of work, it is important not to assume all differences that may be found are a direct effect of father absence. There is usually at least some degree of choice over occupation. Men join the Navy knowing that they will be at sea for long periods. In most cases they marry after joining the Navy, so their potential brides know they will be spending long periods on their own. Therefore, we need to consider the possibility that these couples may have different expectations and perhaps different styles of relationships than couples who marry with the assumption that they will be living together more or less all the time. In turn, this might be associated with different styles of child rearing and so behaviour in the children. In other occupations where there are periodic absences, such as North Sea oil-rig work, it has been suggested that apparently high rates of divorce and marital difficulty might be at least partially explained by a selective process. Men with shore jobs whose marriages run into difficulties might seek a new job which takes them away from home in order to avoid the marriage problems. What is certainly well established is that occupations that involve absence from home tend to have higher divorce rates (Burgoyne, Ormrod, and Richards 1987).

THE FAMILIES OF PRISONERS

Given what we know about other situations which involve separation of parents, how might we expect imprisonment to influence the prisoners' children? Though there are obviously some important differences, I would suggest that the effects might have several similarities with those of a parental divorce. A child loses contact with a parent for a period of time or, at best, contact is reduced to infrequent brief visits. The departure of the parent is likely to be sudden, unexpected, and stressful for a child. Family income is usually sharply reduced and there may be the sorts of housing problems and other practical difficulties of the kind that so often accompany divorce. The remaining parent may well be depressed, confused, and feeling unable to cope with the situation. As the studies of divorce have shown, parents who are preoccupied with their own problems or depressed are less good at providing the support and extra attention that children who are feeling insecure will need. Studies of prisoners' families, just like those at divorce, show that parents are not good at providing children with straightforward information about what is happening so their worst fears and fantasies can grow unchecked and may well be much more frightening than the reality of the situation. Some parents go to great lengths to hide the truth of the situation from their children but, as children usually know much more than the parents believe, the children may become very confused by the mixed messages they receive. Insecurities they may be feeling about their parents may be fed and encouraged by accounts of what is happening which a child finds inconsistent or quite simply unbelievable. But a child may find it very hard to challenge a parent whom they want to believe and trust. Of course, these kinds of dynamics are very dependent on a child's age and their ability to understand what is happening and the significance of events.

On the whole, families of prisoners may receive little help or support from their kin or friends. Much may depend on the nature of the offence and how much others know about what has happened. As with telling the children, some go to great lengths to hide the true reason for the absence of the spouse from friends and family, perhaps fearing very negative reactions. But whether or not the attempts at deception succeed, parents are likely to feel isolated and unsupported. Public attitudes do not help and knowledge is not widespread of the difficulties that prisoners' families may face nor is there a great deal of sympathy for their situation. This is perhaps best illustrated by what seems to be a very different situation where prisoners do have strong community support as for many in Northern Ireland. Here is the rather special situation in which the families of some prisoners receive a good deal of support and practical help from friends and relatives and escape the stigma and negative attitudes that imprisonment of a family member attracts in most situations.

Because of their usual role as the main caretaker, and society's expectation of this, it is mother with whom most children have their closest relationship, and so separation from a mother is likely to be much more upsetting for a child than separation from a father. For these same reasons the imprisonment of a mother may well lead to a child being looked after, not by the father, but by another female relative or perhaps in a situation arranged by the state. So, both because of the loss of what will often be the primary relationship and because of the kind of caretaking arrangements that may need to be made, the children of female prisoners seem likely to suffer more than those of male prisoners. When it is the father that is imprisoned, his absence may be more upsetting for a son than a daughter because of the child's identification with him. However, some of the recent work of the children of divorced parents does suggest that, particularly in adolescence, daughters who have lost contact with their fathers may have had more difficulties in establishing social relationships with peers.

In this discussion, I have been describing the possible effects of parental imprisonment as if they were similar to divorce. But because of the strains imprisonment may impose on a marriage, imprisonment may also lead to divorce. So then a child may suffer from both kinds of upheavals. But even if a marriage survives the imprisonment of a spouse, this may well engender bitterness and conflict in the marriage. Behaviour problems in children are associated with conflict in the parents' marriage (e.g. Rutter 1981).

When a prisoner completes the sentence and returns home there may be a long period of readjustment of domestic life and it may be some time before a child may re-establish a good relationship with the returned parent. A child can feel a deep anger with and resentment of the parent for what they have done or a child may continue to feel insecure, perhaps fearing that further periods of imprisonment may occur.

CONCLUSIONS

As I pointed out at the beginning of this chapter, we lack good studies of the longer-term effects of parental imprisonment for children. But I have tried to show the experience of many children while a parent is in prison bears some similarity to other kinds of domestic upheaval which have been shown to have very significant effects for children. Certainly the evidence from psychological research should give no comfort at all to those who might wish to continue to ignore the effects of imprisonment for the families of prisoners.

In a more positive sense, we can use the research on other separation situations to devise programmes to minimize the effects for children. This would emphasize the need for regular contact – visits, phone calls, letters, and for children to be given clear information about what is happening in a way that they can understand given their developmental age. The feelings that children may have about the absence of a parent need to be understood and they should be given opportunities to express them and to speak about what is happening. We cannot expect societal attitudes to change overnight, but we may be able to improve some situations for children by encouraging the wider family and friends to offer more practical help and support.

REFERENCES

Bowlby, J. (1951) *Maternal Care and Mental Health*, World Health Organization: Geneva.

Bretherton, I. and Waters, E. (1985) 'Growing points of attachment theory and research', *Monograph of the Society for Research into Child Development* 50:29, University of Chicago.

Burgoyne, J., Ormrod, R., and Richards, M. P. M. (1987) *Divorce Matters*, Penguin Books: London.

Emery, R. E. (1988) *Marriage, Divorce and Children's Adjustment*, Newbury Park, Calif: Sage.

Hetherington, E. M. and Arasteh, J. D. (eds) (1988) *Impact of Divorce, Single Parenting and Stepparenting on Children*, Hillsdale, NJ: Erlbaum.

Hinde, R. A. and Stevenson-Hinde, J. (eds) (1988) *Relationships with Families: Mutual Influences*, Oxford: Clarendon Press.

Light, R. (ed.) (1989) *Prisoners' Families*, Bristol: Bristol and Bath Centre for Criminal Justice.

Maclean, M. and Wadsworth, M. E. J. (1988) 'The interests of children after parental divorce: a long term perspective', *International Journal of Law and the Family* 2:155–66.

Matthews, J. (1983) *Forgotten Victims*, London: NACRO.

Morris, P. (1965) *Prisoners and Their Families*, London: Allen & Unwin.

Richards, M. P. M. (1987), 'Children, parents and families: developmental psychology and the re-ordering of relationships at divorce', *International Journal of Law and the Family* 1:295–317.

Rutter, M. (1981) *Maternal Deprivation Reassessed*, second edition, London: Penguin Books.

Shaw, R. (1987) *Children of Imprisoned Fathers*, London: Hodder & Stoughton.

Totterman, N. (1989) *Intermittent Father Absence and the Development of Children*, unpublished PhD dissertation, University of Cambridge.

2 Infants with mothers in prison

Liza Catan

When the mother of a young child receives a custodial sentence the immediate concern is: who will take responsibility for the baby while she is in prison? This is no light question, for most young children are cared for mainly by their mothers. When a mother goes to prison, who will – or can – adapt their life to give round-the-clock care and supervision, adapt their home, and provide the playmates, toys, and equipment that are part and parcel of home for a young child? Although Social Inquiry Reports, which record family circumstances, are available to the court, child-care issues rarely play a part in the choice between a custodial or a community-based disposal. Nevertheless, it is the first problem confronting the woman herself, her family and friends, the social, probation, and prison services.

There is no firm, up-to-date information on the numbers of infants affected by a mother's imprisonment in Britain. A spot census of women in penal establishments in 1982 (Nooney, Eastwood, and Ray 1984) recorded that 471 women (i.e. 48 per cent of the female prison population for that year) had between them 1,158 children under the age of 16, 129 of whom were under 2 years old. A later census (Prison Department 1986) recorded 340 women in custody (28 per cent of the average population in 1986) with 455 children under the age of 5. However, it is frequently claimed that many women conceal the existence of young children for fear they may be taken into care, and that the numbers of young children with mothers in prison may be considerably higher (NAPO 1989).

For most young children the first consequence of a mother's imprisonment is that they are separated from their mothers and leave the family home to be cared for by relatives, friends, or taken into care and fostered. Few fathers attempt to maintain the family home after their spouses go to prison and, even when they do, the youngest children are the most likely to be sent out to female relatives – their grandmothers and aunts. However, for a few, there is the possibility of entering prison with their mothers and staying with them in one of three mother and baby units at HMP Styal, Holloway, and Askham Grange. Together, these units provide places for up to thirty-nine babies aged up to 9 months in Styal and Holloway and up to 18 months in Askham.

Both these alternatives have generated widely voiced concerns about imprisoned mothers' babies; many have claimed that babies will be affected negatively by the experience both of prison life and of separation from their mothers. On the one hand, it is argued that any separation of mother and baby is traumatic for the child and likely to cause long-lasting damage to the child's development and to the prisoner's view of her role as a mother. The policy implication of this view, which is frequently proposed by child-care professionals, is that prison facilities for children should be expanded, to cater for many more children, a wider age range, and for longer stays. Such a facility already exists in Germany, as an annexe to the women's prison in Frankfurt-Preungesheim. On the other hand, it is argued that, like all institutions, prisons provide restricted and impoverished environments in which young children will not develop satisfactorily. These beliefs lead to the argument that there should be no children in prison. Thus it appears that 'the Prison Department cannot get it right, whatever happens' (Blom-Cooper 1978/9).

A review of literature relevant to these alternatives led to the conclusion that there is little solid evidence for or against any of these views (Catan 1988a) and, at that time, there was no systematic empirical research directly on babies in prison, or on children separated from an imprisoned mother. The various arguments were often supported with citations from research carried out on children in situations deemed analogous to those of the unit or the separated babies. However, these arguments were invariably faulty. Some were based on research, like Klaus and Kennel's theory of maternal–infant bonding, that is now discredited. Others used over-simplified or period-piece versions of the child development classics (e.g. John Bowlby's attachment theory). Yet others cited research on development in situations that were not comparable to the situations of the unit babies (e.g. Spitz' foundling home or Dennis' Lebanese crèche) or of those left outside (e.g. Harlow's monkeys). Thus, before the research was conducted, issues about women prisoners' babies were formulated by applying child development theories in a rather general, and inaccurate, way.

In this climate of public interest and debate, the Home Office began a review of policy on babies in prison and a research study on the development of babies in the units was commissioned from the University of Sussex. Its purpose was to provide evidence that would help determine whether a period spent in a prison mother and baby unit is indeed in the interests of a child whose mother must be held in custody. The question that motivated the research was: how is the physical and psychological development of babies affected by a stay in a mother and baby unit? The development of unit babies was compared with that of babies of a similar age and background left outside during their mothers' imprisonment, and this provided the opportunity to study the effects on development of separation from an imprisoned mother.

The research found that it is not being in a prison mother and baby unit *per se* that raises issues, nor being separated from an imprisoned mother, but that issues arise concerning the preventable experiences that frequently attend or follow on from these alternatives. Thus, it enabled the hitherto negative and rather general expectations about the effects of separation and institutionalization to be refined, filled out with detail, and more closely focused on practical issues.

These themes will be developed in the rest of this chapter. First, there is an account of the research findings on unit babies, followed by the findings on separated babies. The final section examines issues for women prisoners' children arising in the post-release period and in the longer term.

METHODOLOGY

The research was undertaken between April 1986 and October 1988. The unit group was composed of the seventy-four babies who resided in the units during that period. The comparison group consisted of thirty-three similarly aged children, two-thirds of whom were looked after by members of the extended family and one-third by social services foster parents during their mothers' imprisonment. The babies' development was monitored using the Griffiths Mental Development Scales, a standardized baby test which provides developmental norms for locomotor, social, linguistic, fine motor co-ordination, and cognitive development over the first two years of life (Griffiths 1954a). The Griffiths Scales were administered monthly during the babies' stay in the units or separated from mother and, where possible, for a three-month period after the mothers' release. Monthly physical growth measures were also taken. Information on aspects of the babies' experience deemed likely to affect their performance on the Griffiths Scale was also collected by time-sampling and interview methods and, for the more institutional aspects of unit babies' experience, comparisons were made by observing babies and staff in the University of Sussex crèche.

In addition to the common factor of an imprisoned mother, the groups were alike in several important respects. Both had larger proportions of single-parent families, unemployed and non-home-owning parents than is found in the general population. However, these indices of socio-economic deprivation were more prevalent in the comparison group, which is possibly due to the fact that it contained a higher proportion of younger, Afro-Caribbean mothers. Despite these differences, the two groups of babies embarked on the events that followed their mothers' imprisonment with comparable developmental assessment scores.

BABIES IN MOTHER AND BABY UNITS[1]

Contrary to popular expectation the unit babies performed very similarly on the Griffiths Scales to those left outside, indicating that the environment of the units did not impair their overall developmental progress. Their development was normal, also, in relation to a larger group, representative of all contemporary British babies. There was thus no evidence of severe, generalized developmental delay, such as was found in the classic studies of institutionalized babies (e.g. in the work of Spitz 1945, 1946; Goldfarb 1943; Provence and Lipton 1962).

There are two explanations for the unit babies' normal progress. First, it is probable that severe retardation of basic development occurs only in babies reared in the type of institution that furnished the settings for the classic institutionalization studies. These were orphanages and foundling homes where babies were reared in conditions of extreme environmental restriction coupled with extreme deprivation of human contact and relationships – conditions which are no longer to be found in modern children's institutions in developed countries. Thus prison mother and baby units are not comparable to the children's homes in which severe institutionalization effects were originally studied. A second explanation may be derived from research on babies in institutions with their mothers, which has been largely ignored in debates about the units (e.g. Spitz 1945, 1946; Skeels *et al*. 1938; Skeels and Dye 1939). These studies found that, when babies in even comparatively bleak institutions were looked after by their mothers or by stable mother substitutes, they developed normally because the caretakers created an immediate environment with more variety and stimulation than was available in the institution itself.

However, while no severe and general developmental effects were found, the test scores of babies who spent longer than average in the units revealed a gradual developmental decline over a four-month period, compared with those separated from mother for a similar length of time. The decline occurred in two areas of development only – locomotor and cognitive; while the developmental levels of the babies left outside did not change over the four-month period from the start of their mothers' sentence, unit babies' scores declined gradually. By the fourth month, there was a statistically significant difference between the scores of the two groups. Thus, even though most of the babies' stay in a unit was brief (average lengths of stay during the research were: thirteen weeks in Holloway, seventeen weeks in Styal, and nineteen weeks in Askham Grange), it appears that, over time, some aspects of unit regimes and environments cause a small and gradual developmental decline. Significant downward linear trends were found between the fourth-month score and those for the preceding months. Thus the indications were that the developmental decline may continue over longer times spent in the units.

To explain these findings, information was gathered on many aspects of the unit environment and regimes, the facilities and their use.[2] It was felt that, while the unit environment was sufficient to support the development of basic skills, it did not offer sufficient opportunity for babies to practise and elaborate them. For example, after mastering the art of sitting up, babies need to be left unrestrained on the floor, in order to practise moving into the crawling position. After mastering crawling, they need freedom of movement and a varied terrain in which to practise crawling, e.g. up steps or low ledges. After they can walk, they need the space and freedom to practise walking longer distances, to lift their feet over small obstacles, and so move on to running.

Many aspects of the unit environment and regimes, the facilities and their use were found to restrict this type of free movement and elaborative exercise. In general, the observation of unit babies' experiences yielded the picture of their spending extended periods of awake time physically confined. Long lock-up hours in Holloway, coupled with the lack of comfortable, spacious, and varied floor space for the babies in both Styal and Holloway, and unimaginative use of the more adequate indoor and outdoor facilities in Askham, led to their spending long waking hours strapped in prams, chairs, and bouncers. This restriction was caused as much by the misuse of the facilities as by inadequate facilities *per se*, and, although there were many positive aspects of the babies' experience, such as constant close contact with others, the fact remains that they were physically restricted in ways that gradually affected their locomotor development.

Explanation of the decline in cognitive scale scores is more complex. This scale tests the integration of a range of developmental skills in practical problem-solving tasks 'that call upon the child's ingenuity and readiness to respond' (Griffiths 1954b). Depending on the child's age, these tasks take the form of 'find the sound', 'find the toy under the handkerchief', fitting together a set of seriated cups, or an elementary pre-jigsaw. Many young children are provided with such challenges at home, in playgroups, or at nursery school, where there are a large variety of educational toys and adults who introduce challenging tasks to the children by unobtrusively structuring their play with such toys. It was observed that there were few educational toys in the units, and that neither mothers nor staff presented the children with novel and challenging problems in toy form. For the older babies, there were no action sing-alongs, or messy exploration with sand and water, playdough, or finger paints. Most of the adults' activities with the babies were classified as care, comfort, social interaction, and loving, while educational, guided, and exploratory play were comparatively infrequent. While the absence of this resource may not be so vital in the more varied home environment, it is probable that a prison unit, however good, is unlikely to provide similar amounts of novelty and stimulation to developing children. Therefore, a lack of playgroup-like educational toys, exploratory and structured play may well be the missing ingredients underlying the decline in unit babies' cognitive scale scores.

The researchers felt that the most salient difference between the prison units and the university crèche was that the crèche was managed and staffed by qualified child-care workers. The units are staffed by medical nurses, some of whom have midwifery qualifications, and by uniformed prison staff. However, many of the differences in organization and in the consequent structuring of infant experience in the two institutions may be attributable to the different types of expertise available in them.

For instance, child-care workers know how to structure and enrich the child's physical environment. Given the tendency for even the best-intentioned of adults in an institutional setting to revert to neat, ordered, and relatively bare environments, and to restrict inmates' movement around the various locations within the institution, it is likely that the richness and variety of the babies' physical environment are better protected by someone who has sole responsibility for it.

Child-care workers in many settings, such as work-place nurseries and hospitals, find that a vital part of their work involves limiting the encroachment of other institutional concerns on their regimes and facilities – a task that is sustained by their specialist knowledge of environmental supports to child development.

As a result of their training, child-care workers also possess a variety of skills that enrich the object environment of the young child. For example, if left to their own devices, babies tend to play with toys and objects at the lowest developmental level that is available to them. Throughout the first year, they tend to suck, chew, shake, and bang objects. However, through sensitive adult intervention they may be introduced to more skilful activities – for example, building, nesting, and pretend play. Such activities enrich both the object and the social world of the child and are thus both entertaining and educational. Alternatively, if babies are not being watched over in an interactive, playful way, with an understanding of what in a situation is of interest to them, they do tend to be kept in situations where they can be relatively self-entertaining and safe from harm, i.e. in walkers or bouncers, to watch the world and be kept safe from falling, disappearing, being walked on, or any other of the common fates of unaccompanied babies.

In contrast, the professional expertise of nursing and prison staff predisposes them to attend to the medical and custodial necessities of life in the unit and gives them the competence to understand and act in these areas. Consequently, as we have seen, children's developmental needs are accommodated within these other priorities, rather than being given equal weight and consideration.

Thus, a new set of issues arose from the research. It indicated that prison mother and baby units do have the potential to support normal, healthy development and this finding counts in favour of providing child-care facilities in prisons and offering mothers the choice to have their babies with them during the sentence. The issues are now more practical and concern the means of improving conditions in the mother and baby units. The practices identified as adversely affecting unit babies' development are problematic, also, in other types of controlled, institutional settings such as primary-school classrooms and children's hospitals. However, considerable progress has been made in these institutions towards creating more natural conditions for young children and it is no longer felt that child-centred practices conflict with the educational or medical purposes of the institution. Prison mother and baby units have lagged behind this general reform of children's institutions, and thought must now be given to accommodating child-care needs within the custodial and rehabilitative purposes of the penal establishment.

BABIES SEPARATED FROM IMPRISONED MOTHERS

There were no developmental decrements in the separated babies and this indicated that the quality of care given by relatives and foster parents compensated for the experience of separation from their mothers. However, the research uncovered several areas of difficulty that, in less fortunate circumstances, could affect care givers' ability to provide such high quality child-care. These concerned the stresses on care-givers, the *ad hoc*, unstable nature of the child care arrangements, and infrequent contact between children and their mothers in prison.

In the Sussex research, the care arrangements made for babies left outside indicated a situation where already stressed families struggled to cope with the difficulties involved in taking over the care of a young child. Ten of the thirty-three babies studied were taken into care, some because no one in their family could take over, a few because social services were seeking to take the child more permanently into care. These babies went to the homes of social services foster parents. However, even in these cases the transition was rarely smooth:

A 16-month-old girl and her sister, aged 2½, both highly intelligent but somewhat hyperactive, continued to live with their parents while both were remanded on bail. The mother's case was tried first, and she received a custodial sentence. The father cared for his daughters until his case came up and on the day left the girls with a cousin of his wife's, together with a sum of money. He was also imprisoned. The girls, always excitable and very active, became increasingly upset when their parents did not return. They were sufficiently mature to understand that their parents had gone, but did not accept the (possibly inadequate) explanations given. Bedwetting, sleepless nights, desperate clinging to their aunt when she tried to leave them with a child minder to go to work, quickly reduced the aunt to a state of nervous exhaustion. She had no-one else to help her. At ten o'clock one night she took the children to the local police station and asked for help. The children were taken into care and fostered in the same home.

The rest of the children were looked after by female relatives. Fourteen children were taken in by their grandmothers (including one great-grandmother) and nine by their aunts (one of them a great-aunt). Thus, responsibility for the majority of children who were not taken into care fell upon late middle-aged and even elderly women. Five of the younger women – the aunts – were themselves single mothers. Thus care of children left outside fell mainly to representatives of two notably powerless and highly disadvantaged social groups, who are unlikely to have sufficient financial resources and social support to ease the additional responsibilities involved.

The difficulties and strains experienced by substitute care givers were further illustrated by a marked lack of stability and continuity in care arrangements. In less than a year, many of the babies experienced several changes of home and care giver. Half the babies experienced a change of substitute care giver after their mother went to prison; three babies had received care from three different care givers and fourteen from two. Care of 72 per cent of the babies was shared between two or more women. Thus many adults were involved in the care of the babies left outside, often simultaneously, but also serially. This pattern was also discernible in the babies who were temporarily separated from their mothers before entering the units. Thirty-two unit babies were born before their mothers' sentence and eleven of these had received care from at least two substitute care givers before entering the comparative stability of the units.

The babies left outside also experienced major changes of home environment after their mothers' imprisonment. Fourteen babies changed home; three babies did so four times, four experienced three changes, and seven babies changed home twice. Again, these changes took place over less than a year. However, of the thirty-two unit babies born before their mothers' imprisonment, four had also experienced three changes of home and seven had changed home twice before changing for the last time to a mother and baby unit. Thus maternal imprisonment initiates an unsettled period for babies, whether they are taken into the units or left outside. However, babies left outside experience more changes and a lengthier period of disruption as families reorganize to cope with an extended period of care or social services intervene with fostering arrangements.

Such lack of continuity and stability can cause temporary but severe distress in children and the research included two older comparison group children who had developed nervous eczema and displayed the compulsive and indiscriminate friendliness to strangers that are text-book hallmarks of the insecure child:

Two months after they had been fostered, the researcher visited the two sisters described above, who had been abandoned at a police station. There was an unsettled air in the house, with many large packages lying about the hall and sitting room. The foster mother explained that two months looking after the girls had exhausted her too, and that they were to be moved to another foster home that afternoon. The girls ran up to give kisses to the researcher, whom they had never met, and called her 'Mummy', then ran off on a frantic circling of the house, randomly grabbing and pulling at objects. Everything caught their attention and nothing held it. The developmental test was administered on the run to the 16-month-old. Towards the end, there was a ring at the doorbell and two Social Services men entered to pack the girls' cots, toys and clothing into a van. The foster mother tried to explain the things were being taken to their new home, but the girls were too restless to listen. When she accompanied the men to the van, they ran out into the road after her, grabbing her hands and kissing her cheeks when she picked them up.

Over an 8-month period, the sisters had two more foster homes and remained in the last one for several weeks after their mother's release, when she gave birth to a third daughter. The 16-month-old developed eczema, the older girl began to wet her bed and the sleep patterns of both girls became highly erratic.

An important aspect of prison regimes and practices concerns the maintenance of ties between mother and children, and by their very nature the prison units fulfil this function. By contrast, imprisoned mothers and their babies left outside had very little contact. Seventy per cent of the babies were taken to visit their mothers in prison at some point, but prison-visiting rules permit only two visits a month and this maximum is clearly insufficient for young children to become familiar with the prisoner. Also, since women prisoners often serve their sentences far from home, and due to the difficulties involved in travelling long distances with young children, only 30 per cent of the babies paid the maximum number of visits to their mothers in prison. Some families may be additionally constrained by the expense of travelling long distances for visits and the assisted visits scheme provides financial assistance for only one monthly visit. As a result, 70 per cent of the babies visited their mothers once a month or less – which, from the child's point of view, is a total separation. The research did not examine the implications of such infrequent contact from the mothers' point of view, but there were signs that it may lead to continuing separation after the sentence; all the unit mothers said they expected to remain with their babies after release but only eighteen out of the thirty-three mothers separated from their babies had firm plans for reuniting with them.

There was evidence that, for some women, mothering skills became rusty while in custody and that, for a while at least, children no longer viewed their mothers as primary care givers.

The babies left outside were also frequently separated from other familiar relations; none were looked after by their fathers within the nuclear family and siblings were frequently separated by the new care arrangements. This may simply reflect the high number of single-parent families in the sample and, in those with two parents, a conventional allocation of child-care responsibilities to female relatives. However, it may also indicate the need to examine the extent to which fathers need additional advice, training, and support to hold the family unit together and thus minimize disruption for the children.

Thus the issues for children left outside concern the provision of support, both financial and practical, to relieve the difficulties facing female relatives when they take over the care of women prisoners' children. There is also a need to examine the possibility of providing more visits and a more imaginative array of visiting schemes for the children left outside. A variety of schemes have been pioneered in Canada and the US for keeping mothers and children in touch during the sentence and mothers responsibly involved with their children, which as yet have no equivalent in Britain (see Boudouris 1985; Cannings 1990).

THE LONGER-TERM PROGNOSIS FOR IMPRISONED MOTHERS' CHILDREN

The Home Office-funded research followed the babies for three months after their mothers' release and found that their experiences during their mothers' imprisonment appeared to have had no measurable impact in the short term. The test scores of unit babies rose during the first month in the community and remained stable over the second and third months. Thus the developmental decline observed in unit babies appeared to be temporary and the separated babies' development remained stable over the whole follow-up period. However, questions about the effects of maternal imprisonment are most frequently cast in terms of the longer-term effects on children during the post-release period and even further ahead, into adolescence and adulthood. Other research provides clues about these longer-term outcomes.

The post-release period is clearly crucial for the future of an imprisoned mother's family, for during this time the overwhelming majority of women try to re-establish the home and reassemble the family under its roof. The success of this effort and the smoothness with which it is accomplished must affect the children's immediate and eventual prospects for a stable family life. Wilkinson (1988) has conducted the one research study on the post-release period of women prisoners and found it to be a time of considerable turmoil for most women and their children. She found that the majority of women leave prison to an overwhelming mix of problems connected with debt, lack of employment, homelessness, damage to the home, the breakdown of personal relationships, and the extrication of children from care. Help from the probation service was limited to assisting the women's contact with agencies that offer limited practical help with such problems and preparing claims for assistance. Many women whose children were taken into care during the sentence were experiencing difficulties regaining them six months after their release. Wilkinson argued that many of these problems were not caused solely by the disruption of imprisonment but rather than imprisonment exacerbated the women's already disadvantaged and difficult situations that were due, in the last analysis, to their social and economic marginalization.

This account echoed a much earlier study of imprisoned mothers (Gibbs 1971), which found extensive homelessness, marital breakdown, and separation from children that pre-dated the sentence. A similar picture emerged from a recent study of women in Holloway (Posen 1987), which found that two-thirds had never been in paid employment before entering prison and the rest had been in low-paid employment such as hotel and domestic cleaning, shop work and auxiliary nursing. Half the women either definitely had no home to return to after release or feared they were losing their homes. A similar proportion had been the victims of violence, rape, or incest, mostly perpetrated by male family members.

This sombre picture of the family lives of female prisoners suggests that the help available to them after release must be completely inadequate. It may be that the support from female members of the women's families that was available during the sentence is slowly withdrawn in the months after release, leaving the women alone to refound their families with only minimal support from local authority provision and state benefits.

Questions about the longer-term effects of maternal imprisonment are more difficult to address. It is not sufficient to say – although it is true – that there is no research that bears directly on the issue. The main difficulty lies in the fact that the question has been framed in a misleading form: whether there is a causal connection between an event – maternal imprisonment – and a complex set of outcomes – e.g. delinquency, broken marriages – many years later.

Research is unlikely to produce a plausible answer to the question in this form. The events surrounding a mother's imprisonment are unlikely to act singly and there may be ameliorating factors which, in particular cases, counteract adverse experiences. Also, over time, the number of interacting influences accumulate and produce a blend of positive and negative influences that, as it becomes more complex, also becomes more individual. Thus in one case, a stable family, with an adequate income, and a child of average intelligence may operate jointly to overcome the adversity experienced as a result of the mother's sentence. Another child may benefit from none of these and suffer family breakdown, poverty, and lack of success at school. Fall-out from a mother's imprisonment will add further stress to this accumulation of disasters. Thus, while it seems plausible to expect that a significant number of children of imprisoned mothers will have disadvantaged and even deviant futures, research addressing the question of a causal connection between such futures and maternal imprisonment is unlikely to confirm the hypothesis.

For these reasons, research on the origins of disturbed, offending, and delinquent behaviour now uses more complex models of environmental influences. This suggests that the outcome of single events is unpredictable, but that potentially stressful events occur in familiar clusters which operate cumulatively to produce the expected negative outcomes:

> No one factor reliably differentiates the delinquent from the non-delinquent, nor the more seriously anti-social from the less seriously so. Rather, delinquents seem to suffer from a greater number and severity of adversities than do their non-delinquent peers.

> (Hoghughi 1983)

This model was used to study adverse family influences by Rutter and Quinton (1977). They identified six family variables that are consistently associated with conduct disorder in children – severe marital discord, low social status, large family size, parental criminality, maternal psychiatric disorder, and admission into care – and demonstrated a steady rise in the likelihood of childhood conduct disorder with the accumulation of each additional variable. Rutter (1985) argued that these, in conjunction with other commonly associated factors, such as family discord, weak family ties, and the existence of persistent social difficulties like alcoholism, a poor work record, and reliance on state benefits, were associated with serious conduct disorders and delinquency in the children, mainly because they increase the difficulty of good parenting. West (1982) also identified a similar array of family factors indicating a high risk of delinquency in children. That such characteristics, often in the absence of compensating forces, cluster together in generations of families that are economically marginalized and socially disadvantaged, has led some commentators to talk of a 'culture of poverty' that characterizes the early milieu of the majority of delinquents and young offenders.

Thus, if we wish to know whether the infants of imprisoned mothers are likely to be similarly at risk of future delinquency or offending, we should not ask about the effects of maternal imprisonment *per se*, but rather examine whether the families of women prisoners possess the characteristics that comprise the 'culture of poverty', increasing the difficulty of good parenting. While the research reviewed in this paper is insufficiently systematic or broad in its scope to prove these links, it has indicated that this is a distinct possibility. Parental criminality is one of the most important factors, and many of the infants of imprisoned mothers have, also, fathers who have offended, often more seriously than the mothers. Poverty, unemployment, unstable relationships and living arrangements with spouses or co-habitees, and children in care were prevalent in all the studies of female prisoners reviewed. The possibility of family breakdown is increased under such circumstances and may be still further increased by the wider consequences of imprisonment or the post-release period. While some studies also suggest the presence of strong, supportive relationships in the women's own families, there is as yet no evidence that these offer longer-term support to the women or guidance and supervision to the children as they become adolescents. Thus it may well be that in the long term, the infants of imprisoned women are at risk of conduct disorder, delinquency, and even offending and are consequently an easily identifiable high-risk group of children and families whose multiple disadvantages require a broad array of co-ordinated social and economic policies.

NOTES

1 The full report of this research is available in Catan (1988b).
2 A full account of this part of the research is available in Catan and Lloyd (1989).

REFERENCES

Blom-Cooper, L. (1978/9) *Minutes of Evidence on Women and the System*, Parliamentary Papers: National Income and Expenditure Committee, vol. XVI.

Boudouris, J. (1985) *Prisons and Kids: Programmes for Inmate Parents* Maryland: American Correctional Association.

Cannings, K. L. (1990) *Bridging the Gap: Programs and Services Facilitate Contact Between Inmate Parents and their Children*, Corrections Branch, Secretariat, Ministry of the Solicitor General of Canada.

Catan, L. (1988a) 'What are the issues about the children of women prisoners?', in A. Morris and C. Wilkinson (eds) *Women and the Penal System*, Cropwood Conference Series No. 19. Cambridge: Institute of Criminology.

Catan, L. (1988b) *The Development of Young Children in HMP Mother and Baby Units*, Occasional Papers in the Social Sciences, No. 1, University of Sussex.

Catan. L. and Lloyd, B. (1989) *Habitats, Play and Social Relationships of Young Children in Prison Mother and Baby Units*, unpublished report to the ESRC.

Gibbs, C. (1971) 'The effect of the imprisonment of women upon their children', *British Journal of Criminology* 11(2):113–30.

Goldfarb, W. (1943) 'The effects of early institutional care on adolescent personality', *Journal of Experimental Education* 12:106–29.

Griffiths, R. (1954a) *The Griffiths Mental Development Scales*, Amersham: Association for Research in Infant and Child Development.

Griffiths, R. (1954b) *The Abilities of Babies*, Amersham: Association for Research in Infant and Child Development.

Hoghughi, M. (1983) *The Delinquent*, London: Burnett Books.

NAPO (1989) *Women, Children and Custody*, National Association of Prison Officers briefing.

Nooney, K., Eastwood, L., and Ray, I. (1984) *A Census of Mothers in Penal Establishments*, Prison Department, Directorate of Psychological Services Report, Series II, No. 132.

Posen, I. (1987) *Holloway Reception Survey*, Holloway Psychology Department, unpublished report.

Prison Department (1986) *Census of Mothers in Penal Establishments*, unpublished paper.

Provence, S. and Lipton, R. C. (1962) *Infants in Institutions: A Comparison of their Development with Family-Reared Infants First Year of Life*, New York: International Universities Press.

Rutter. M. (1985) 'Family and school influences: meanings, mechanisms and implications', in A. R. Nicol (ed.) *Longitudinal Studies in Child*

Psychology and Child Psychiatry, Chichester, Sussex: John Wiley.

Rutter, M. and Quinton, D. (1977). 'Psychiatric disorder – ecological factors and concepts of causation', in H. McGurk (ed.) *Ecological Factors in Human Development*, Amsterdam: North-Holland.

Skeels, H. M. and Dye, H. B. (1939) 'The study of the effects of differential stimulation on mentally retarded children', *Proceedings and Addresses of the American Society of Mental Deficiency*.

Skeels, H. M., Updegraff, R., Wellman, B. L., and Williams, H. M. (1938) 'A study of environmental stimulation: an orphanage pre-school project', *University of Iowa Studies in Child Welfare* 15:4.

Spitz, R. A. (1945) 'Hospitalism: an enquiry into the genesis of psychiatric conditions in early childhood', *Psychoanalytic Study of the Child* 1: 53–72.

Spitz, R. A. (1946) 'Hospitalism (follow-up report)', *Psychoanalytic Study of the Child* 2:113–17.

West, D. (1982) *Delinquency: Its Roots, Careers and Prospects*, London: Heinemann.

Wilkinson, C. (1988) 'The post-release experience of women prisoners', in A. Morris and C. Wilkinson (ed.) *Women and the Penal System*, Cropwood Conference Series No. 19. Cambridge: Institute of Criminology.

3 Mothers inside, children outside
What happens to the dependent children of female inmates?

Jane Woodrow

A LACK OF ATTENTION; A LACK OF CONCERN?

While we do now have some knowledge on the subject of children of male inmates in this country (Shaw 1987) and of children who are with their mothers in mother and baby units in English prisons (Catan 1988), still very little is known about dependent children who live in the outside community while their mothers are in prison.

Research that has been conducted in this field is negligible and, with a single exception (Stanton 1980), does not focus directly on such children's experiences, but relies heavily on mothers' perceptions of what they believe or fear to be the case for their dependent children, and as such is empirically unsound. The largest body of such literature is American and, while illustrating problematic areas for children in the US, gives only pointers to what may be happening in Britain.

Studies conducted in Britain which focus on other aspects of women's incarceration, such as Wilkinson's (1988) research on the post-release experiences of female inmates, Casale's (1989) study of female remandees in Holloway, and Carlen's (1983) study of women in prison in Scotland, give some small indications of what may be happening to dependent children of mothers in British penal institutions, while Catan's (1989) comparative sample group of infants left with substitute carers in the outside community gives us a little more direct insight into the plight of such children as well as, like Gibbs (1971), identifying who their substitute carers are.

However, such few publications on or around the subject as exist are not always easily accessible to the public, and tend to be written in academic or practitioner jargon. With little research and information available in this area, the lack of public concern regarding such children may be seen as a reflection of a lack of public awareness rather than a callous disregard by commission. But until their plight receives attention little will be done to alleviate problems faced by them and those responsible for the children in their mothers' absence.

HOW MANY MOTHERS? HOW MANY CHILDREN?

Women in England and Wales make up a very small proportion of the total number of prison receptions each year – approximately 5 per cent (Home Office 1989). The number of those who are mothers is not known, nor the number of any dependent children they may have.[1]

Heidensohn (1981: 130) illustrates the difficulties of trying to put a figure on the numbers of mothers in prison: quoting Home Office Statistics (1967) for the year 1965, where 70 per cent (530) of the total female prison population in England and Wales had children (over 1,000 in all), she compares this to the findings of Gibbs (1971) that only 35 per cent (223 women) of her Holloway sample had dependent children (totalling 504 in all). However, the ratio of children to mothers is broadly similar, averaging out at two children per mother.

This figure compares to a spot census carried out in all female establishments in 1982 (Nooney, Eastwood, and Ray 1984) which recorded that 645 women in prison had a total of 1,649 children, averaging out at approximately 2.5 children each. The largest number of these children, 1,158, were minors and under the age of 16.[2] The number of women who were mothers represented 40 per cent of the annual average female prison population in 1982.

The female prison population in 1988 averaged just over 1,700 on any one day (Home Office 1989); using the 1982 census figure of 40 per cent as a conservative course between the earlier figures quoted as the total number of women in the female prison population with dependent children, and taking the generally held average of two children per mother as previously demonstrated, this would mean 1,360 dependent children are thus affected in any one day.

However, information derived from spot censuses presents a snapshot rather than an overall picture of a specific situation as censuses look at a given population over a limited period of time, usually on one day as in the above survey. The 1988 Prison Department statistics (Home Office 1989) recorded approximately 7,700 female receptions that year.[3] This figure includes double-counting on categories of remands and sentenced women, and of women who may be received into prison more than once in a year; thus it is not possible to judge the absolute numbers of women involved. But it can be crudely estimated that if 40 per cent of this figure are mothers then there will be approximately 3,000 incidences of families with dependent children affected annually when mothers go to prison; and it may be surmised that, where mothers are counted more than once, their children may be subjected to multiple disruptions. Alternatively, if the remands for the year 1988 are completely removed, this leaves approximately 3,800 female inmates under sentence of whom 40 per cent may be taken as mothers with two children, totalling in excess of 3,000 dependent children thus affected per year.

However, as inmate mothers in both the US and Britain are often reluctant to divulge the existence of any children they may have for the fear (often not groundless) of losing their children into care[4] (Stanton 1980; Carlen 1983; WEG 1987), censuses and indeed reception surveys used to estimate numbers of inmates' children involved err on the conservative side. Those who are no longer regarded as children but who may for reasons of mental or physical ill health still be dependent upon their mothers will obviously also be excluded from this type of survey or census.[5]

What is significant from Home Office prison statistics is that the majority of women going into prison are young, the bulk being under 30. This is reflected in the high numbers of young children in research samples. For example, 70 per cent of mothers had no children over the age of 16 in the 1982 census, and almost a third of the children in this group were aged 4 and under; while an unpublished Home Office (1987) census of 1986 recorded that 340 women (20 per cent of the annual average prison population of 1986) had 455 children under 5.

Thus separation from the mother often happens very early on in a child's life. This is at a time when females are being subjected to longer prison sentences, when remands imposed on them have become more frequent and longer in duration (Home Office 1989), and when the likelihood of female offenders going to prison for indictable offences has almost doubled over the past decade (NACRO 1990).[6]

As women in prison have already reached the ultimate tariff the criminal justice system can dispense, so the chances increase whereby any subsequent re-offending may result in further separation from older children and new siblings becoming affected for the first time.

THE NATURE OF THE PROBLEM

Although fewer children are affected by maternal imprisonment than by paternal imprisonment, in excess of 100,000 children (Shaw 1987) to 3,000 annually in England and Wales, this does not mitigate the nature of the individual child's experience, nor this group's more general situation which may be described as complex and more serious than that of most male prisoners' children, the majority of whom are looked after by their mothers and stay within the same family home (Shaw 1987).

Women prisoners' children who are looked after by their mothers prior to imprisonment are frequently subjected to many major disruptions throughout the mothers' imprisonment, including at least one change of care giver, and often involving a change of home environment (Catan 1989; Wilkinson 1988). Such disruptions, which also involve a change of area for the child, may mean too a change of school, health visitor, and the like, as well as a loss of friends and family, often continuing even after the mother's release.

Where mothers are not caring for all or some of their children prior to imprisonment they are often still in contact with them (Dobash, Dobash, and Gutteridge 1986; Casale 1989) and may continue to play an important part in their lives; thus, as research in the US demonstrates, many such children will still be subjected to disruptions including changes in care givers as a result of their mothers' imprisonment (Zalba 1964).

When mothers go into prison, most children not only lose their principal care giver but many will become parentless, as research shows female offenders are often single parents (Casale 1989; Catan 1988; Carlen 1988; Gibbs 1971). In cases where fathers/cohabitees exist prior to the mother's imprisonment, they do not appear to take responsibilty for the children's care (Catan 1989; Dobash, Dobash, and Gutteridge 1986), even, as Catan's (1988) evidence suggests, where fathers/cohabitees are not working.

Sometimes children lose both parents (mother and her cohabitee) simultaneously, as when both are jointly accused and imprisoned at the same time, or occasionally where the father/cohabitee has been killed by the mother. Children may also lose to prison a mother who has abused them or other child/ren.

When mothers go into prison the majority of children stay within the extended family. Substitute carers of such children are generally female, usually grandmothers on the maternal side or aunts, sisters of inmates (Catan 1989; Gibbs 1971; Henriques 1982). Sometimes both may simultaneously share the care of the children (Catan 1989). A smaller but significant number of children go immediately into care, and a few to live with neighbours and friends.[7]

Research demonstrates that the majority of women in prison come from the disadvantaged end of the socio-economic spectrum, with poor housing, debt, and a lack of employment opportunities, child care arrangements, and the like (Catan 1988, 1989; Casale 1989; Posen 1988; Carlen 1983, 1988; Wilkinson 1988). Thus, it is perhaps inevitable that their network of friends and relations should be similarly placed. Henriques (1982) in the US and Catan (1989) in Britain found carers tend to be late middle-aged to elderly, or if young then frequently single parents themselves; most are likely to be on benefits. Henriques (1982) recorded a range of problems experienced by substitute carers including infirmity, illness, financial concerns, and organizational problems experienced by younger carers trying to fit the inmate mother's children's routines around their own. Many substitute care givers were unable to cope, and resentful at having to try to do so with the sacrifices this often entailed; this in turn must negatively affect the nature of the care experience for the inmate's child.

Carers also have to deal with any emotional and social problems children may bring with them or present as a result of their separation from the mother. Again, there is no one statutory channel through which carers can seek help.

The high number of placements that break down during the mothers' imprisonment demonstrates the many difficulties faced by carers as well as by children themselves who may be subjected to a whole series of care givers.[8] Yet carers unable to cope are faced with the dilemma whereby if they ask for support, financial or practical, from the statutory services they may lose the children into care. (Mothers may also not wish this for the same reason.) Carers of inmate mothers' children also appear to lack the kind of informal support network Shaw (1987) found to exist among communities where imprisoned fathers are a common occurrence. Mothers of such children received practical help from friends and neighbours with daily tasks such as school duties and shopping.

As well as being separated from mothers, dependent children both in Britain and the US are often separated from other siblings at the time of the mother's imprisonment or as subsequent placements break down (Dobash, Dobash, and Gutteridge 1986; Wilkinson 1988; Zalba 1964). Such children may be separated between foster care, different members within the extended family, or with natural fathers where several exist in the same family. This may mean children not only lose regular contact with the mother and other siblings, but also with the extended family and friends.

Elder children deserve special attention as they often bear a greater burden of the parents' imprisonment. Shaw (1987) in Britain and Henriques (1982) in the US found elder children often take on the role of the missing parent in looking after younger siblings. They are more likely to be aware of the imprisoned parents' actual situation while having to keep up a pretence with younger children who are often fobbed off with an excuse for the parents' absence, or are too young to understand.

Older children of previously sentenced women are more likely to be living with other relatives, or to be already in local authority care, before the mothers' most recent term of imprisonment (Dobash, Dobash, and Gutteridge 1986; Gibbs 1971; Wilkinson 1988; Stanton 1980; Zalba 1964).

When mothers go into prison they are not given the opportunity to explain the situation to the children (where indeed, children are old enough to understand), let alone to reassure them or make preparations for their care; often it is those looking after the children who are faced with the task of what to tell the children, where this question is addressed at all.[9]

What children are told is arbitrary, but appears to be linked to such things as the age of the child, the carer's attitude to the mother and her crime, and the length of the sentence. For example, in the latter case Shaw (1987) found a correlation between shorter sentences and hiding the truth from the child. In such cases, explanations for absences are generally given as due to the parents' hospitalization or working away (Shaw 1987; Stanton 1980; Zalba 1964). However, in 'protecting' children from the truth in this way, children's anxieties may be increased rather than alleviated, where, for example, they believe the mother to be ill – and are left wondering when she is likely to get better and return home, and, when she does, is she likely to be 'sick' and go away again?[10] Moreover, children may be subjected to further confusion by learning the truth from neighbours or from news reports (Shaw 1987; Stanton 1980), or by simply reading the sign over the prison gate. Some kind of intervention and counselling at an early stage between mother, child, and carer is obviously necessary in order to decide what and how to explain the situation to the child to try to ease any further confusion and anxiety for them.

Mothers are frequently arrested in the child's presence, even during drugs raids.[11] There are no British police guidelines or code of practice on the arrest of parents with dependent children, and treatment of any children is dealt with on an arbitrary basis by the arresting officer. Consequently some mothers are able to make temporary child-care arrangements, while others may have their children accompany them to the police station. At the station children may be subjected to police procedures along with the mother, including accompanying mothers in police cells.[12] Alternatively, children may be taken away to be looked after by strangers at the local social social services department.

Where children are not present when parents are arrested and detained, the problem may be even more serious. Shaw (1987) gives two alarming but not uncommon accounts of young children thus affected: one of a 5-year-old left on his own in the house in front of a gas fire after his single-parent father was arrested while out at the shops and another of a child coming home from school to a find a boarded-up house; neither were aware of what had happened to their parents.

Conversely, despite police guidelines in New York since the early 1970s, McGowan and Blumenthal (1978) still found examples of children who were left unattended overnight when mothers were arrested. The authors suggest mothers are reluctant to tell the police for fear of the authorities being alerted and of losing their children into care. As many imprisoned mothers in Britain and the US have already lost some children into care at some stage during their lives, there is every reason to suspect that, if such guidelines were introduced into Britain under such circumstances, they would prove as redundant as in New York.

Mothers often arrive in prison unsure of their children's whereabouts (Casale 1989) or with no knowledge at all of what has happened to them (Posen 1988);[13] there is no easy method of passing on information once inside the system. Conversely, worried relatives outside are sometimes unable to trace mothers immediately (Casale 1989).

The small number of female offenders in the system is reflected in the number of female penal institutions in England. In total there are only twelve which include five remand centres. These are scattered around the country and tend to be sited in remote areas where public transport is very infrequent. Thus travelling is often a long and tiring trek for both children and their often elderly carer, or for young carers accompanied by children of their own.

Obviously the remand situation makes long trips impractical for many carers and children, but even where children and carers make the trip the visit may sometimes not take place for, as Casale (1989) found in Holloway, prisoner management methods may mean other considerations take priority over visits and children may arrive to find the mother has recently been moved to another establishment but has not been allowed to alert her family enough in advance to prevent a wasted journey.

Children appear to be treated like adults at some institutions where they are expected to sit at a table and not move during the visit (Dobash, Dobash, and Gutteridge 1986). This is difficult for many small children, especially after sitting still in a car or bus for several hours beforehand.

But, without special play areas, many custodial establishments lack the facilities to enable children to let off steam safely.

Ironically, men's prisons and some remand centres boast visiting centres while women's prisons do not.[14] Such centres located within female establishments would give carers a chance to relax while allowing children time on their own with their mother. Visiting centres and/or children's play areas, within or just outside prisons and remand centres, would also give the mother and carer a chance to discuss family-related matters without children being present.

Crowded and noisy visiting conditions often provide the only chance older siblings get to see new arrivals to the family, born during the mother's sentence. Mothers may have had no chance to prepare older siblings for the new arrival beforehand.

Visits in any case are not easy; mothers and carers in the US and Britain frequently reported tearful and traumatic visits, the effects of which, as expected, continued for some time after (Carlen 1983; Henriques 1892). Children who have a day off school to visit mothers are faced with the prospect of having to explain their absence to their peers.

Visits where children in care are brought by social services to visit their mothers tend to happen infrequently (Dobash, Dobash, and Gutteridge 1986), probably reflecting case-work loads and other commitments of social service staff. However, during the visit the social worker often needs to discuss family business with the inmate which may take up valuable visiting time.[15]

Often children visit their mothers only infrequently, or visits do not take place at all where carers or mothers do not wish it, or where cost and time involved is too great (Catan 1989; Carlen 1983; Wilkinson 1988).[16]

When mothers leave prison it is not simply a process of picking up where they left off with the family. Women often leave custodial institutions in even greater debt than when they went in, often with rent arrears piled up, poor or no accommodation at all, and a lack of possessions (Wilkinson 1988; Carlen 1983; Casale 1989). Such women are often ill equipped to find reasonable paid employment. Without child-care facilities, but in receipt of a prison record, they lack the means with which independently to secure alternative accommodation or more generally to 'get back on their feet'. Some women also experience delays and difficulties in obtaining benefits on release (Wilkinson 1988).

Mothers who are unable to solve these crushing problems, including those with children in local authority care who must obtain accommodation in order to appear 'settled' to have children returned to them

(Wilkinson 1988), may not be reunited with children in the immediate future or on a more permanent basis. Others appear to be forced back into relationships with violent and alcoholic men, or are compelled to accept appalling housing conditions (Wilkinson 1988; Carlen 1983).

Thus children are often reunited with mothers in very poor environments and thrown back into relationships with mothers who may well be under a great deal of stress; they may also have to adjust to a new step-father and step-siblings. In some circumstances this may mean moving to another area. Alternatively, some children may be happily settled with carers only to be abruptly uprooted again.

Mothers in the US and Britain reported various problems of readjustment on release including incidences of children who became more clinging, began bed-wetting, and dropped behind in school work after mother's release (Stanton 1980; Wilkinson 1988), while Catan (1989) found evidence to suggest children may not initially view mothers as their primary care givers on their return.

The children of female inmates have neither the status of a victim of crime, who may receive help from the organized victims' scheme, nor of children with divorced or deceased parents who have access to support and counselling.[17] Yet children of violent offenders and others who attract long sentences may not see their mothers again, while many of these children are frequently subjected to the stigma of having an imprisoned parent (Shaw 1987; Henriques 1982).

Conversely, such children do not enjoy the same rights and privileges as the imprisoned parent. For example, it is both the mother's right and privilege as a prisoner that entitle her to visits where she may see her children. The child has no such entitlements to visit the mother.

CONCLUSION

Children affected by mothers' imprisonment are neither seen nor heard. A collusion appears to exist between governments and inmate mothers and those looking after the children. This conceals their very existence and enables governments to uphold notions of justice and individual punishment for the law breaker that recognition of such children would destroy. It prevents carers (or mothers on their behalf) from seeking help and support from outside agencies, or from applying for such things as temporary foster-care status or extra benefits, for fear of losing the children into care. However, a system of foster-care payments for carers whether officially fostering children or not would cost less than local authority care for such children, while allowing the child to stay within the extended family (where this is appropriate) and thus subjecting the child to less disruption.

A progressive programme of fostering children near to the mothers' prisons has been successfully undertaken in the US for children who would normally go into care on mothers' imprisonment (Baunach 1985). Children have greater contact with their mothers than is normally the case and mothers share in the decision making on children's care.

However, research in the US shows that children of female offenders suffer less when their mothers are given probation. Certainly they do not face disruption on a par with that of jailed mothers' children, and the whole experience is less negative for them in terms of home, school, stigma, and self-esteem (Stanton 1980). Given that the majority of women in Britain are sentenced for non-violent and often victimless crimes, and that a high proportion of female offenders who are remanded do not subsequently receive prison sentences,[18] there is an obvious case to be made for the greater use of bail and alternatives to custody for women.

But it is important to look beyond penal and sentencing policy in order fully to understand the implications of what may be happening to the children of female inmates. It is apparent that children of inmate mothers appear to suffer a similar pattern of disadvantage to that which female offenders have often experienced themselves as children, e.g. homelessness, poverty, dislocation, separation from parent/s, and a history of institutional care (Carlen 1988; Zalba 1964).

Shaw (1987: 48) states that 'the children of imprisoned fathers can be identified at the bottom of the "pecking order", as one of the most deprived if not the most deprived group in our society'. However, children of female inmates must lay claim to the latter status.

NOTES

1 A voluntary Home Office spot census took place in women's penal institutions in England in autumn 1989. However, for problems with censuses see p. 30.
2 It is not possible to work out the total number of minors/dependent children in this census as a breakdown of the under 18s is not given.
3 This figure includes non-criminals, fine defaulters, young offenders, remandees, and sentenced females.
4 Many women in prison already have some children in local authority care or living within the extended family prior to their incarceration. For example, Gibbs (1971) found 42 per cent of dependent children in her sample were not living with their mothers prior to their imprisonment; while Dobash, Dobash, and Gutteridge (1986) found dependent children of 17 per cent of

the women in her sample were looked after by close relatives while a further 36 per cent were in local authority care before the mothers' incarceration. Such figures are indicative of the previously disruptive life-styles of many inmate mothers and their children.

5 Additionally, mothers may have chronically sick or disabled dependent children: Shaw (1987: 72) found an 'alarmingly high' number of children of inmate fathers in his study thus affected.

6 Sentences have particularly increased in the eighteen months to three years sentence band, and again, though to a lesser extent, over all bands in the three to ten years categories; while untried remands have doubled over the last ten years both in number and length.

7 For example, Gibbs (1971) found 44 per cent of dependent children were living within the extended family, while 26 per cent went immediately into local authority care and less than 5 per cent were with neighbours.

8 Of the thirty-three infants in Catan's (1989) comparative sample, three had three care givers and fourteen had two care givers in less than one year of the mothers' imprisonment.

9 Shaw (Light 1989) found one-third of children in his sample were told nothing at all about their fathers' absence.

10 In the US, Stanton (1980) reported a case of a child who feared his mother had died in hospital and had to be taken to the prison to be reassured she was alive, while Zalba (1964) found incidences of children who had been told their mothers were dead.

11 Such situations are not uncommon, and mothers reported doors being knocked down and premises searched by police officers while children were present (in personal communication with female offenders).

12 In personal communication with female offenders.

13 Posen (1988) found this a particular problem among African women in Holloway, many of whom had no idea what had happened to their children in Africa. (These are usually drug couriers with long sentences.)

14 Although there are now plans for a visitors' centre at Holloway.

15 In personal communication with female offenders.

16 Catan (1989) found only 30 per cent of infants outside paid their mothers the maximum number of visits possible in prison, while another 30 per cent did not visit their mothers at all.

17 For example, teachers are frequently unaware that children have a parent in prison and there is no process by which schools are informed of the situation (Moore 1988), or health visitors, doctors, and others involved with children.

18 Only one-third of women who are placed on remand subsequently receive custodial sentences (Home Office 1989).

REFERENCES

Baunach, P. J. (1985) *Mothers in Prison*, New Brunswick, NJ: Transaction Books.

Carlen, P. (1983) *Women's Imprisonment: A Study in Social Control*, London: Routledge & Kegan Paul.

Carlen, P. (1988) *Women, Crime and Poverty*, Milton Keynes: Open University Press.

Casale, S. (1989) *Women Inside: The Experience of Women Remand Prisoners in Holloway*, London: Civil Liberties Trust.

Catan, L. (1988) *The Development of Young Children in HMP Mother and Baby Units*. Working Papers in Psychology Series–No. 1, Brighton: University of Sussex.

Catan, L. (1989) *Young Families of Female Prisoners*, unpublished, University of Sussex.

Dobash, R. P., Dobash, R. E., and Gutteridge, S. (1986) *The Imprisonment of Women*, Oxford: Blackwell.

Gibbs, C., (1971) 'The effect of imprisonment of women upon their children', *British Journal of Criminology* 11(2):113–30.

Heidensohn, F. (1981) 'Women and the penal system', in *Women & Crime*, Cropwood Conference, December 1980. Cambridge: Institute of Criminology.

Henriques, Z. W. (1982) *Imprisoned Mothers and Their Children*, Washington, DC: University Press of America.

Home Office (1987) *Mothers and Babies in Prison*, unpublished Report, P4.

Home Office (1989) *Prison Statistics: England and Wales, 1988*, London: HMSO.

Light, R. (ed.) (1989) *Prisoners' Families*, Bristol: Bristol and Bath Centre for Criminal Justice.

McGowan, B. G., and Blumenthal, K. L. (1978) *Why Punish The Children*, Hackensack, NY: USA National Council on Crime and Delinquency.

Moore, S. (1988) 'Teachers and prisoners' children', *Childright* 43:16.

NACRO (1990) *Women in Prison*, NACRO Briefing 33, January.

Nooney, K., Eastwood, L., and Ray, I. (1984) *A Census of Mothers in Penal Establishments*, Prison Department, Directorate of Psychological Services Report, Series II, No. 132.

Posen, I (1988) 'The female prison population', in A. Morris and C. Wilkinson (eds) *Women and the Penal System*, Cropwood Conference, March 1988, Cambridge: Institute of Criminology.

Shaw, R. G. (1987) *Children of Imprisoned Fathers*, London: Hodder & Stoughton.

Stanton, A. M. (1980) *When Mothers Go To Jail*, Lexington, DC: Heath.

Wilkinson, C. (1988) 'The post-release experience of female prisoners', in A. Morris and C. Wilkinson (eds) *Women and the Penal System*, Cropwood Conference, March 1988, Cambridge: Institute of Criminology.

Women's Equality Group/London Strategic Policy Unit (1987) *Womens Imprisonment: Breaking the Silence*, London: Spider Web.

Zalba, S. R. (1964) *Women Prisoners and their Families*, Los Angeles: Delmar Publishing Company.

4 Imprisoned fathers and the orphans of justice

Roger Shaw

It is a sobering thought that, in spite of the increasing attention being paid to the children of broken and bereaved families, no government in Europe, North America, or elsewhere appears to know how many children within its jurisdiction are affected by the imprisonment of a parent. The Cambridge study set out to throw some light on this in England and Wales by investigating imprisoned fathers. The initial findings were first published in Holland (Shaw 1986a) and England (Shaw 1986b). This chapter explores the England and Wales statistics further and considers also the situation in Scotland where the use of imprisonment is higher than in England and Wales. The article differentiates for the first time between fathers who had lost contact with their children before the start of the sentence and those who were living with them as an integrated family until imprisonment caused separation. These latter children are rendered orphans by the justice system.

During two separate three-month periods in 1984, men aged 21 and over who were received into a prison in the Midlands with a sentence of up to six months were interviewed and asked to complete a questionnaire about their family circumstances. A little under half of all the men in each of the two samples were found to be either married and living with their wife or else in what they considered to be stable cohabitation at the time of their imprisonment (see Table 4.1).

These men had responsibility for more than 378 children who were with the wife or cohabitee. The exact number is not quoted since, in respect of family sizes of five children or more, men were required to answer 'more than four'. There were no children in about one-fifth of the families but a wide spread of family size in the remainder (Table 4.2).

Four prisoners were known to be single parents whose partners had either died or deserted, thereby leaving the fathers with all or

Table 4.1 Marital status of men at time of sentence

Marital situation	Sample A n=202 %	Sample B n=213 %
Married and living with wife	22.2	28.0
Living with cohabitee	22.5	19.8
Married and not living with wife or cohabitee or unmarried and not living with cohabitee	55.3	52.1

Table 4.2 Responsibility for children at time of prison sentence by men with wives or cohabitees

Number of children n=>378	Sample A fathers n=92 %	Sample B fathers n=102 %
0	23.9	19.6
1	22.8	19.6
2	20.7	25.5
3	10.9	18.6
4	13.0	12.7
5 or more	8.7	3.9

some of the children. In one of these cases the two children were taken into care and separated from one another when their father was imprisoned.

In addition to those children for whom the father had responsibility, there existed a further group who were no longer with him due to divorce or separation or his desertion or who were in the care of the local authority. These children totalled more than 196. Unlike responses to other questions in the study, this one produced a high number of 'no answers', 14 per cent and 27 per cent in samples

A and B respectively from prisoners who failed to respond to the question inquiring about children they had fathered and for whose well-being they no longer had responsibility. It is likely, therefore, that the real number of children in this category is significantly higher than that shown in Table 4.3. Additionally, there were ten children in motherless families either with their single-parent fathers or with father/grandparent families. Thus 415 prisoners in the two samples were found to have produced at least 584 children prior to their imprisonment on this occasion, and possibly considerably more.

Many prisoners whose children were not living with them immediately prior to the prison sentence were in regular contact through access visits where the parents were separated or divorced, or by visiting the child if in the care of the local authority. Some of these relationships were considered by residential child-care workers to be meaningful to the children concerned. Therefore it must be said that the punishment meted out to a father may impinge on some of these children too and not only on those where the family was together prior to the sentence.

The exact number of separate individuals received into Prison Department establishments in England and Wales in a year is not known and cannot be arrived at by adding together the different groups identified in tables in prison statistics. There are several reasons for this, the most significant being that a large number of people are received into prison more than once in any one year and often under different classifications, such as fine default or remand.

Table 4.3 Children fathered by prisoners but who were not living with wife or cohabitee at time of sentence

Number of children n=>196	Sample A fathers n=202 %	Sample B fathers n=213 %
0	58.4	52.6
1	13.9	5.2
2	6.9	9.9
3	4.5	2.3
4	1.0	2.8
5	nil	0.5
6 or more	1.5	nil
Refused to answer/ unable to answer	13.9	26.8

Taking these factors into consideration and together with what was discovered about the men in the samples, it is possible to suggest that approximately 75,000 separate adult males were received into prison in England and Wales in 1984.

The men in the two samples were not markedly different from national receptions in terms of age (Table 4.4). If their production of children is not greatly dissimilar, then on the basis that 415 men produced more than 584 children, a figure which does not take account of pregnancies and the high proportion of 'no answers' to the question about children elsewhere, 75,000 receptions in England and Wales could produce more than 100,000 children. This figure would be swollen by the children of prisoners aged under 21, a not inconsiderable number according to health visitors and prison chaplains who co-operated with the study (Shaw 1987, 1989).

It was established that 31 per cent of sample A and 33 per cent of sample B had not been in prison before. Year on year figures would therefore suggest that the number of children in England and Wales whose father is imprisoned at some time during their childhood is quite high. Not far distant from the period of the study, Farrington (1981) and the Home Office (1985b) demonstrated the prevalence of convictions of males for non-motoring offences. However, the proportion of the population which is composed of former inmates of penal institutions is not known, so a reliable statistic in regard to

Table 4.4 Age range of men over 21 as percentage of receptions

Age	Sentences of up to six months including fine defaulters		All sentences and remands but excluding fine defaulters
	Sample A	Sample B	National Figures England and Wales One Year 1984 (Home Office 1985a)
	n=202	n=213	n=69,000
	%	%	%
21–24	33	35	35
25–29	19	16	23
30–39	31	25	25
40–49	11	17	11
50–59	5	5	4
over 60	1	1	1

their children is even harder to acquire. However, on the basis of the figures referred to here, it seems reasonable to suggest that in excess of half a million children under the age of sixteen have experienced the incarceration of their father on one or more occasions. This represents more than 5 per cent of the ten million children in England and Wales in 1984 (Central Statistical Office 1985).

Historically Scotland has been profuse in its use of short prison sentences. During the period of the English study Scottish courts gaoled considerably more people for fine default in proportion to the population than did England and Wales (Scottish Home and Health Dept. 1985; Home Office 1985a). As with elsewhere in the United Kingdom, it is impossible to say how many of these people are sent into custody more than once in any one year. Thus it is difficult to make comparisons between the Scottish and the English and Welsh prison populations. There are obvious differences in some of the figures which caution against simple comparisons. Nevertheless, it seems probable that the proportion of Scottish children who experience their father being imprisoned is a great deal larger than that in England and Wales due to the proportionally greater use of short periods of custody, especially for fine default and remand.

Notwithstanding the decline in the numbers of persons received into prisons in England and Wales and Scotland evident from the 1988 statistics (Home Office 1989; Scottish Home and Health Dept 1989), influenced possibly by government efforts to reduce the use of custody and demographic and other factors, increasing use of imprisonment by the courts over the years has led to a great many children being brought up in an environment wherein the most severe penalty that the state can impose is neither a rare event not restricted to serious crimes (Shaw 1987, 1988). Children in the poorest districts, even if they have not experienced their own father being imprisoned, are likely to know of friends, neighbours, or peers who have. An acceptance of prison as normal is evident in this comment from a teacher in an inner-city school with a poor catchment area: 'We've got more kids who have had their dad in prison at some time than we have O-level successes. Kids with families with no prison tainting are as rare as hens' teeth round here.'

The work of Sparks (1971), Blackler (1968), and the Home Office (1978) supports observations of contributors to other chapters in this book that prisoners tend to come from the lower socio-economic groups. It is not surprising, therefore, that this research shows children of imprisoned fathers to be mostly socially, financially, and educationally deprived. Thus the incarceration of a father frequently adds emotional trauma and further economic hardship to existing gross disadvantage.

The position of the prisoner's child has steadily worsened. Increasing use of custody in the 1980s and earlier led to more and more children experiencing the incarceration of their father. From time to time, overcrowding in remand centres has led to more prisoners being held far away from their families, thus making it increasingly difficult, and sometimes impossible, for a parent and child to maintain any sort of relationship. In reply to a question in the House, the Home Secretary stated that 1,917 prisoners were held in police cells on 4 October 1988 but that the number had fallen to 1,223 by 10 November following the suspension of industrial action by the Prison Officers Association (Hurd 1988). Serious disturbances in local prisons and remand centres current at the time of writing this (April 1990) will add to the problems of the prison system – at least in the short term – and will inevitably cause more fathers to be held far away from their children, so exacerbating the problems of maintaining meaningful relationships. The problem is not helped by the United Kingdom having less liberal home leave and fewer and shorter visits than most other European jurisdictions (NACRO 1985a, 1985b, 1988).

When a remand in custody is ordered or a sentence of imprisonment, especially a short one, is passed on a father, there is a tendency for the parents to explain his absence in some other way. However, the child may discover the truth at school or from neighbours or the press – with disastrous consequences in some cases (Shaw 1987). A third of the sample were told lies to explain the absence and a further third were told nothing at all. Morris (1965), Monger and Pendleton (1981) and Wilmer, quoted in Monger and Pendleton (1981), found similar proportions. Many children were left to worry why father had suddenly vanished without explanation. Those who learned of his whereabouts from other sources were left to dwell on what terrible thing he had done that their mother was unable or unprepared to talk about it. In reality he may only have been sent to prison for a few days for an unpaid fine, or some other relatively minor transgression, or even for unpaid rates (Stoke-on-Trent CAB 1988).

A sample of families from one particular area was followed up in the study and, where the woman consented, the school teacher and health visitor were also interviewed or questionnaired. From this it was learned that, while for some mothers the father's incarceration was her first experience of such an event, for about two-thirds of the sample it had happened previously on one or more occasions.

Some women had experienced a previous partner imprisoned but this had not deterred them from taking a new man with a known prison record.

It is important to make the point that occasionally a man's influence on his family can be so damaging and negative that his incarceration is quite likely to be beneficial to the children. Imprisonment can also provide a respite in an unsatisfactory marriage or give a woman the opportunity to escape with her children from a damaging or perhaps violent relationship which she was fearful of doing while he was at liberty. Marriages apparently broken by imprisonment should not, therefore, always be seen as an undesirable consequence of incarceration. This point must be made forcefully; too often the anti-custody lobby cites imprisonment as the cause of family breakdown without examining the background in the necessary depth. In reality, numerous marriages are at breaking point at the time custody is imposed and the sentence only precipitates the event or provides the woman with a much needed escape route. However, such cases were in the minority in the study and imprisonment of a father must generally be viewed as an event likely to be painful and detrimental to any children involved.

Many fathers sent to prison for fine default, remanded, or sentenced to short periods for minor offences leave unsupported children, sick, invalid, and pregnant wives or mothers whose coping and parenting abilities and low social skills mean they are unable to manage unaided. In relation to imprisonment for fine default the situation is made worse by the activities of fines loan sharks. These latter seek out and put pressure on women whose partners have been locked up for failing to pay a fine, to buy their man out 'for the good of the children' and similar reasons. It is of course true that if the necessary sum of money is taken to the prison the fine defaulter can be released. However, these loan sharks charge an extortionate rate of interest which damages the woman's economic state further or places yet another barrier in the way of the man when he is released.

The study showed that health visitors in poor districts tended to have a number of families where the father had prison experience. In many instances they listed a catalogue of problems and tragedy common to the same family – father in prison or about to go in; damaged child or loss of a child; drug, alcohol, or solvent abuse; health, employment, and money problems (Shaw 1989). To health visitors in such areas, as with probation officers and social workers, the pattern is familiar. Although some of these families were survivors and successfully played the system for all it was worth, a far greater number were unable to obtain their rights because of poor education and a lack of confidence and social skills; they were crushed beneath the weight of officialdom and bureaucracy, victims of ignorance and lack of interest, and occasionally, it seemed, even vindictiveness and spite.

Residential workers gave examples of children taken into care following imprisonment of fathers who were single parents or where the mother was unable to cope in the absence of her partner because of her low IQ, poor social skills, or because she was sick or disabled (Shaw 1989). Since almost 3 per cent of the children in the sample were already motherless when their father was imprisoned, the number of children nationally left without either parent following sentence may be at least as large as it is in the case of imprisoned mothers, who are known frequently to have no partner to take care of the children (Woodrow, chapter 3).

Nearly a quarter of a century ago Morris (1965, 1967) drew attention to prisoners' families in England and more recently Matthews (1983) and Light (1989) highlighted their problems. Shaw (1986a, 1987, 1988) has described children running away from home when their father was locked up or truanting persistently from school. Others displayed disturbed behaviour, started to mix with delinquent groups, and became involved in crime for the first time. Invalid mothers, devoid of social skills, were left alone or their children were taken into care as if they were the delinquents. Depression, bed wetting, lack of concentration, and deep-seated unhappiness are commonly reported by teachers and health visitors. The research showed that less than 40 per cent of prisoners' wives felt they had support from professionals such as probation officers, social workers, health visitors, or members of voluntary agencies (Shaw 1987). Study of children of imprisoned fathers shows clearly that many of these youngsters suffer more as a result of the sentence than do their fathers in prison – or in some cases even the victims of their crime. This issue raises fundamental questions since the justice system is believed to operate on principles of right and wrong, the acquittal of the innocent and the punishment of the guilty. When children are caught up in the punishment meted out to their father this concept of 'justice' becomes confused. No doubt a significant number of the half million children in Britain today whose fathers have been incarcerated at some time are also confused. Many have been made 'Orphans of Justice'.

REFERENCES

Blackler, C. (1968) 'Primary recidivism in adult men', *British Journal of Criminology* 8 (2):130.

Central Statistical Office (1985) *Annual Abstract of Statistics*, London: HMSO.

Farrington, D. P. (1981) 'The prevalence of convictions', *British Journal of Criminology* 21 (2):173.

Home Office (1978) 'A survey of the south east prison population', *Research Bulletin* 5:12.

Home Office (1985a) *Prison Statistics, England and Wales 1984*, London: HMSO.

Home Office (1985b) 'Criminal careers of those born in 1953, 1958 and 1963', *Statistical Bulletin* 7.

Home Office (1989) *Prison Statistics, England and Wales 1988*, London: HMSO.

Hurd, D. (1988) Commons statement, 14 November.

Light, R. (1989) *Prisoners' Families*, Bristol: Bristol and Bath Centre for Criminal Justice.

Matthews, J. (1983) *Forgotten Victims*, London: NACRO.

Monger, M. and Pendleton, J. (1981) *Throughcare with Prisoners' Families*, Social Work Studies No. 3, University of Nottingham.

Morris, P. (1965) *Prisoners and their Families*, London: Allen & Unwin.

Morris, P. (1967) 'Fathers in prison', *British Journal of Criminology* 7:424.

NACRO (1985a) 'Visits to prisoners', *NACRO briefing*, October.

NACRO (1985b) 'Home leave', *NACRO briefing*, July.

NACRO (1988) 'Home leave', *NACRO briefing*, October.

Scottish Home and Health Dept. (1985) *Prisons in Scotland*, Report for 1984, Edinburgh: HMSO.

Scottish Home and Health Dept. (1989) 'Prison statistics Scotland 1988', *Statistical Bulletin* 6/1989.

Shaw, R. G. (1986a) 'Kinderen van gedetineerden' in D. H. de Jong, J. L. van der Neut and J. J. J. Tulkens (eds) *De vrijheidsstraf*, Arnhem: Gouda Quint BV.

Shaw, R. G. (1986b) 'The prevalence of children of imprisoned fathers', *NASPO News* 6:4.

Shaw, R. G. (1987) *Children of Imprisoned Fathers*, London: Hodder & Stoughton.

Shaw, R. G. (1988) 'A neglected consequence of imprisonment – the inmates' children', *Justice of the Peace* 152 (39):17.

Shaw, R. G. (1989) 'The health visitor and the prisoner's child', *Health Visitor* 62 (8):248.

Sparks, R. F. (1971) *Local Prisons: The Crisis in the English Penal System*, London: Heinemann.

Stoke-on-Trent CAB (1988) *Jailed for Debt*, Stoke-on-Trent: Citizens Advice Bureau.

5 Prison rule 102: 'stand by your man'

The impact of penal policy on the families of prisoners

Kathleen McDermott and Roy D. King

There are now officially 101 prison rules made by the Secretary of State under the authority of the Prison Act 1952 s. 47(1) (Plotnikoff 1988). They are laid before Parliament in the form of Statutory Instruments and they govern the work of the prison service in England and Wales. Part of the task of the prison service, as stated by the Prisons Board, is to use the resources made available to it by Parliament, '[to enable prisoners to retain links with the community and where possible assist them to prepare for their return to it' (Train 1985)]. The service must do this in accordance with the relevant provisions of the law, including the prison rules. It is our contention in this chapter that there is a further, albeit unwritten, prison rule without which the prison service could not hope to meet this objective. It is a rule which does not have the status of law although it is sanctioned with all the pressures that the penal system can command at virtually every stage of the penal process. Above all, it is a rule that is largely unsupported by public resources. Indeed it is sustained in no small measure by the mechanism currently most beloved by politicians of a certain persuasion – self-financing by those least able to pay. It applies not to prisoners but their families and it says: '*Stand by your man*'.

We reached this conclusion after spending the last five years in continuous research on both sides of the prison walls. Between 1985 and 1989 we conducted a series of studies in five representative prisons in Midland Region – at Birmingham, Ashwell, Featherstone, Nottingham, and Gartree, after lengthy pilot work at Stafford. The research explored the relationship between security, control, and humane containment in the prison system through an examination of the ways in which these prisons implemented their given tasks and how their efforts were evaluated by staff and prisoners.[1] In our extensive interviews with adult male prisoners most testified to the importance of maintaining contact with their families in helping them to cope with their sentence and time in prison. The family provided a sense of history and a hope for a future life beyond the wall. Placed within this context prisoners could cling to an alternative identity to that of 'inmate'. That prisoners' accounts of their past, present, and future relationships were not always realistic, indeed frequently self-serving, only drew attention to the extraordinary unreality in which any kind of contact was supposedly maintained. For the great majority of our prisoners the maintenance of contact had proved to be beset by difficulties. Given the paucity of provisions that constitute the best endeavours of the prison service to fulfil this element of its stated task we sought and obtained funding for a second study that would allow us to examine this from the outside as well.[2] Since April 1989 we have been engaged on an investigation of the survival strategies adopted by the families of prisoners, including several of those whom we had known in the first study.

Our aim was to understand how families cope with imprisonment, not so much as victims but as members who have had to make sense out of their personal tragedies; and how they create strategies and make decisions that affect the very survival of the family unit.[3] We also wanted to look again at what role the prison service plays in the family's struggle for survival, and so far as possible to experience that for ourselves, by playing a more active participant role in the research than is often adopted. At a forum for prisoners' families in March 1990 at Feltham Youth Custody and Remand Centre, the Director General reiterated his personal commitment and that of his staff to the tasks of the prison service, laying particular emphasis for the occasion on the maintenance of community links. But by then it had already become apparent to us that, on the ground at least, in spite of some recent improvements, this amounts to little more than lip service – a recognition that the existence of families outside can be valuable for the maintenance of good order and discipline inside; and that if they stand by their man there is somewhere to send him when he is finally released. As things stand at the moment all parties – staff, prisoners, and their families – learn as the sentence progresses to maintain the unrealities of their situation, often to the evident detriment of all concerned. Without a massive change of priorities and injection of resources the damage inflicted by the process of imprisonment on those who get caught up in its path simply cannot be addressed.

This is the first report on our research. Our data are based on several interviews over a period of eighteen months with some forty families. Half of the families live in Greater London while the remainder come from Birmingham, Manchester, Liverpool, Peterborough, north and south Wales, Belfast, and south east England. In twenty-eight cases our main interviewee had a partner in prison, and in all but one of these families there were dependent children – a total of sixty-two children in all. The remaining twelve families had sons or brothers inside. A quarter of our families are from ethnic minority backgrounds.

All of the prisoners were male. They were aged between 17 and 60 years and 25 per cent were serving life sentences, 40 per cent sentences of over four years, and 25 per cent sentences of up to four years. The remaining 10 per cent were on remand. Ten of the men were released during the course of the study, although two were re-arrested and remanded in custody on new charges. Over four in ten of the men had never been in prison before and for nearly six in ten of the families this constituted their first experience of having a relative in custody.

An ideal research design for the analysis of the process of coming to terms with imprisonment would have been longitudinal, with long periods of follow up of a random sample of the families of prisoners. In the absence of the level of resource that would have made such research possible we sought to find ways that would enable us to glimpse at least something of that process within a cross-sectional design. Accordingly, the choice of our families was not random. Nor was it intended to be representative. Rather we wished to make sure that we included families with no previous experience of custody as well as those whose lives had been dominated by it; families confronting remand in their local prison for the first time as well as those used to trekking all round the country to distant training prisons as their partners came towards the end of long sentences; and families from minority groups as well as the indigenous population. In these limited objectives, that might enable us to anchor some of our findings to key points in the process, we clearly succeeded. But we also hoped to make up for lack of breadth by developing close links with families that would contribute depth to our materials. Our recruitment of prisoners and their families was therefore achieved through word of mouth, indeed almost by recommendation from the prisoners we already knew from our previous research and from the contacts we made through the proliferation of groups for prisoners' families on the outside. In this way we effectively had contact with some of our respondents over a period of five years through two research projects, and we were witness to some dramatic changes in circumstances and prospects.

From the outset it became clear that having made contact with families the research would have to play an active role if real relationships were to be sustained. This included playing child minder, taxi driver, sympathetic listener, and periodic negotiator as much as interviewer or observer, but it brought us very close to the everyday experiences of these families: children being ill, difficulties with school, appliances breaking down and no money to replace them, jobs being sought after, the humiliation of DSS interviews, as well as the joys of marriages and births, the support of neighbours and friends, even the fun and frustration of a day at the seaside. But all of this was within the context of the not so everyday experience of having a member of their unit in prison. At this level the families in our study also experienced their partners or sons being sentenced, transferred from prison to prison without any explanation, receiving deportation orders, or even being on the roof of a prison and then watching it on TV.

It was always our intention to talk to the prisoners either on a visit to the prison using a visiting order so that as far as possible we experienced the prison rules and facilities as outsiders and not as privileged researchers, or at their home when they were on home leave or after release. In most cases we achieved this and for a short while, at least, we were able to share these families' attempts to negotiate a way of reintegrating their lives. But, having taken all this on, the difficulty for us was always one of stopping our slender resources for fieldwork from being swamped.

Although some of our 'best' contacts were, for a variety of understandable reasons, reluctant to have the research extended to include their families, sufficient took the risk for us to gain some insight into the progressive impact of imprisonment over a substantial period of time. In this chapter we try to present the experiences of our families not just of imprisonment itself but of the whole penal process. We begin at the beginning, with the circumstances of arrest. At this stage outcomes are uncertain, but for many of our families it marked the abrupt, and as it turned out final, separation from their partner in a situation for which there could be no preparation.

ARREST

The arrest is usually the first family contact with the criminal justice system and the circumstances in which this takes place often influence how they cope with what is happening to their relative. For all of our families the arrest was a traumatic experience. How well they handled it seemed to depend less on whether they had any previous experience with the police and more on the actions of the police themselves. In two-thirds of the cases the arrest took place at home. We do not know how typical these cases are but an extremely high proportion of the home arrests (seven out of ten of them) involved two or more of the following features: the arrest was accomplished by several policemen who were either armed or accompanied by Alsatian dogs; the house was ransacked; partners were taken into custody; and threatened with having their children taken into care.

> They told me that I had to go down to the station with them but I should leave my child. I don't know why but I just couldn't let go of her. They put me in a cell with her for three hours and then they questioned me for another couple of hours. They kept on saying that it was my fault, that I knew what my husband was doing. They said I should tell them everything or else I might lose my child. I didn't know anything to tell them! I just kept holding my daughter and crying. Finally they let us go but they shouldn't have treated us like that. You weren't a person to them.

Not surprisingly those families in our study who had this kind of experience felt themselves to have been used as a lever to produce a result against their partner.

As only one in eight of the men in our study received bail the vast majority of our families were immediately faced with the prospect of their relative being held in custody either at the police station or in prison.

ON REMAND

Once a man is remanded in custody the family may have some difficulty in finding out exactly where he is. The problems of overcrowding and industrial relations in the local prisons of England and Wales can create a kind of musical chairs for prisoners; some find themselves transferred from one prison to another or even from one police station to another (McDermott and King 1988).

> You know I was following him all over the bleeding country. First he went to Brixton, then to police cells in Lambeth, then to police cells in Norfolk, then to Ashford and then to the Scrubs. I never felt sure that I knew where he was especially after the first time I showed up in Brixton and they told me he wasn't there!

The remand phase is an extremely stressful time for all concerned. Our respondents told us that they felt their lives were 'turned upside down' or 'held in suspension' until the time of the trial. It was a time when communication and information are essential but difficult to obtain. There are bills to be paid, people to notify, jobs to be held down, children to deal with, a hundred things to sort out. Often, though, little actually gets done: our families felt helpless as the immediacy of imprisonment overshadowed everything else. Often they lived in the vain hope of getting bail – a chance to talk and make arrangements. The knock back often came as a bitter blow. Meanwhile they clutched at straws.

> Remand was the worst time because everything was so uncertain. You just didn't know what was going to happen. You didn't have time to think because you were always going to the jail for visits or calling solicitors and other people to help you. You didn't really deal with the kids because you were always thinking of him inside. It was easier to borrow money than stand for hours at the social. Only weeks later did you realize the hole you were in.

Many of our families had been on income support at the time of arrest. In all cases, however, it had been the man who was claiming benefit as head of the household. Once he was sent to prison the family found to their consternation that their benefit was cut off. The DSS requires that claimants report any change in circumstances immediately. Failure to do so results in loss of payment unless there is good cause for not reporting (CPAG 1989). Our families found this to be strictly interpreted; illness was good cause, but disorientation following husband's arrest was not. None of the women in our study had notified the DSS for at least two weeks after their partner was remanded into custody. It was the last thing on their mind and they could not believe that the DSS would deny their claim. All of the women lost those two weeks' payment.

The financial strain, though, was not just due to loss of income from the partner's job or income support. Imprisonment itself involved major new expenditures for the family.

> I would go every day to see him at Risley. Sometimes I just didn't have any money left so I would hitch with my daughter. I was a little foolish at first and spent all my money on him. My little girl and I were eating potatoes in order that he could have his magazines and stuff. I won't do that again but then I just felt so badly for him and that *he* was the one to be protected.

The greatest financial strain for families during the remand period was visiting. Under the Assisted Prison Visits Scheme (APVS), close relatives of prisoners may have the cost of their visits to establishments paid for them by the government, provided that they are on sufficiently low income. But the scheme will pay for only one visit a month.

Remand is a time when communication for both the prisoner and the family is essential. Yet visits to remand prisoners are a draining and exhausting procedure. Once the visitor arrives at the prison there is a wait often of half an hour or more, usually outside and exposed to the vagaries of the British climate. There is then another wait inside the prison while the prisoner is brought over for the visit. In most local prisons there are no crèches for children. There are no books. There are no craft materials. It is rare for there to be toys. The visiting rooms, even in the newly refurbished local prisons, are neither inviting nor comfortable. Walls, still painted in drab institutional colours, are bare except for official signs which communicate basic information about prison rules and the penalties for infringing them. Families 'march' in to take their places on one side of a long table while prisoners 'march' in on the other side, only to find themselves sitting closer to the stranger next to them than to their relative across the table.

When the visit finally takes place, it lasts a mere fifteen minutes. In some circumstances the visit could take longer – but in the experience of our families this was rare and the existence of the possibility only served to keep them tantalizingly on edge. Of the families we interviewed, the average length of time it took them to accomplish that quarter of an hour of grossly restricted contact – from leaving home to returning home – was three and a half hours. Nine parts travel and waiting time to one part actually visiting. And this was for remand visits in local prisons – the main virtue of which is their convenient location.

> Going there every day with the kids and all was sheer hell and all that hassle for fifteen minutes! Also the cost of it. It was getting there, feeding the kids to keep them happy and supplying him inside.

Given the pressure of numbers and limited time, prison officials are often abrupt and impersonal to visitors. Their demeanour tends to exacerbate the visitor's feelings of alienation. Children especially are distrustful of staff whom they may see as personally responsible for keeping their father inside. One little girl on a visit tried to take an officer's keys so she could let her father out. Visits are sometimes so stressful and incomprehensible for children that they refuse to go again. 'The boy doesn't want to go any more. He's angry at his Dad because he won't come home so he just doesn't want to go.'

While the prison service has declared its intention to build more visit centres and to improve visiting conditions (Home Office 1990), the visit centres will be only in new prisons and the improvement budget amounts to only £150,000 over the next three years. Only twenty of the 130 prisons in England and Wales yet have visit centres (PRT 1989). Although most of these are properly in local prisons where they are most needed, the provisions in them vary from the good to the appalling. Meanwhile, probably the majority of prisoners on remand are visited by their families in something like the circumstances we describe.

Apart from the notices referred to above, and in spite of publicly expressed policy statements, the families of prisoners are given remarkably little information concerning rules and procedures. There are some rules, for example concerning the type of transistor radios permitted, which appear to be the same for all prisons. But there are others where local practices differ. Most of our families learned what is or is not permitted through experience on a case by case basis. In a world which is totally rule bound, and where the rules, couched in a whole new lexicon, often seem petty and arbitrary, one might be forgiven for thinking that good communication and explanation would be at a premium. In fact it seemed to our families, many of whom had had no previous contact with prisons and who had difficulty in coping with uniforms and officialdom, that the control of essential information was a mechanism for keeping them at a disadvantage. Could one hand in money at remand visits? 'Yes', they were told at Wormwood Scrubs, but 'no' at Winson Green where it had to be sent in. Many found the process of asking and being turned down needlessly frustrating and embittering.

We conducted an informal review of the information found at the prisons we visited as 'visitors'. Each prison is expected to publish a booklet about its facilities and rules and regulations for visitors; and to display notices about the assisted visits scheme, the mission statement of the prison service, and the race relations policy statement. In the fourteen prisons that we visited during the last year, only one had fulfilled all of these expectations, and half had fulfilled *none* of them. Most displayed the mission statement, but this seemed somewhat hollow given the absence of the others. When we enquired of officials why this should be so, it transpired that there were no explicit instructions for communicating information to prisoners or their families, such details being left to the discretion of individual governors. We think these procedures should be clarified, with an explicit obligation placed on governors to communicate rules and regulations and privileges in plain English to all who need to know.

Information and advice desks run by voluntary groups in a few prisons have helped to fill this void – one of us sat in on one of these on a regular basis throughout the research, both as a means of gathering additional data and as a way of reciprocating the co-operation extended to the research – but the responsibility for providing accurate and up-to-date information for all visitors remains squarely with the prison service.

SERVING THE SENTENCE

The second phase, that of the sentenced prisoner, is a time when both prisoners and families have to come to terms with being apart, and during which they find that the prison world completely permeates their lives. The length of a prisoner's sentence obviously limits the coping strategies that are possible and conditions the response of all parties. But even short sentences can be devastating in terms of the adjustments required – which may continue long after the sentence has been completed. Sometimes families had not allowed themselves to contemplate a custodial outcome and had not been prepared for the possibility by solicitors: in such cases it is difficult to describe the sense of shock.

> He [the lawyer] never ever told us that custody might actually be an option. We just weren't prepared for it. I didn't really talk about it with people before because I hoped it would all just be cleared up. It was all so confusing. A probation officer came up to me at court and said something but I could only see his lips moving, I had no idea what he was saying.

Numbed by the initial shock of sentencing, another partner told us how she was quite unable to contemplate living with any further raising of hopes, even when advised to appeal.

> The judge told the lawyers to appeal but I don't want to hear that he'll get his appeal. They told me he would never be found guilty and now he's got life. I can't go through any more disappointment. I am prepared for him to do a long stretch. If he gets out well then that's a bonus but I don't want to know. I have to take it a day at a time.

It is a commonplace of the prison literature that prisoners do their bird a day at a time: we found it was just as important for families.

> In the beginning I was in bad shape. I went down to six stone. The doctor had me on tranquillizers and all. But once he got sentenced I knew he was in for possibly a very long time and

I knew I had to cope. It's been hard as I had to move with the kids but now we have our routine and we're getting on with our lives.

Allocation

Many prisoners serve the whole of their sentence in the local prison. But, if not, the most crucial decision made by the prison service, not only for the prisoner but for the family also, is the allocation to a particular prison. The service has a policy of trying to locate a prisoner near to his or her home. All things are relative. In practice a prisoner is normally allocated within an administrative region but, once considerations of security and available vacancies have been taken into account, 'close to home' it is not! In neither of our studies did anyone – prisoner or partner – report that it took the visitor less than an hour just to reach the prison; in most cases it took up to three hours and in many it took even more. Prisoners typically underestimated both the amount of time, and the amount of organization and planning, it took for their families to accomplish a visit. Their partners told us that a visit to the prison took up their whole day. The average round trip for families in our study took seven hours of which not much more than a quarter was actually spent with their relative. Some visitors, an elderly mother and a young wife with toddlers in tow, had harrowing tales to tell of complex journeys which ended with a long wait, or worse a long walk or an expensive taxi, as connections with poorly timetabled prison transport failed to materialize. Of course, the prison service is constrained by the location of existing prisons and by the resistance from communities to having a new prison in their neighbourhood. But there is much that could be done to make the final stages of the journey more convenient and less expensive.

Transfers

The problem of initial location of prison can be compounded when a prisoner is transferred. Often this occurs without adequate notification to the family; sometimes this can be justified on grounds of security risk but it is always a cause of stress to both families and prisoners.

I didn't know he was moved until I got his letter from the new prison. He said that it was very strange that for two or three days no one knew where he was. He said that it was very frightening because if anything had happened to him no one would know where he was.

The stress caused by prison transfers is most acute when the family finds out that a prisoner has been moved only when they visit the prison from which he has already been transferred. According to Circular Instruction 5/87 the prison is supposed to notify the family when a prisoner is transferred but this does not always happen. One mother in our study lived in Belfast and could only afford to travel by boat. She had to travel overnight in order to get to her son's prison in time for a visit.

> I had called the prison three days before saying that I was coming over and wanted to have a morning visit. They said that it was no problem. I then arrived at the gate only to find that he was transferred to Ashwell the day before! I then travelled another two hours to get there and then they weren't going to let me in to see him. I told them no one was going to stop me and in I went!

Some families have fought tooth and nail to have their relative transferred because of the hardship it caused them to visit. Sometimes this has been successful but it was not always achieved with good will.

> When he was at Parkhurst it was very hard to visit him. I had to leave at 6 a.m. in order to catch the train to London and then transfer to another train and then a bus before actually getting there. Our son was only a baby then and it meant dragging the buggy and all his things. I complained to the Home Office to move him because it was so hard. They moved him all right, to Albany next door! When I called back the Home Office this jerk said, 'Well, we moved him didn't we!'

Other families have tried to have their relative transferred without either success or explanation.

> My main problem is having my sons in different prisons. Why can't they both be in the same prison? I just can't afford to travel to both places. I hadn't seen either of them for four months when they had the inter-prison visit. And then they call giving me one day's notice. He indoors goes mad over it and refuses to drop everything and go. I do drop everything and go because I'm their mother. I have petitioned to get them transferred for the past two years and still I get no answer. Both boys are model prisoners and don't cause any trouble. So why don't they transfer them?

The stress of not knowing why a prisoner is *not* being transferred is exceeded only when the family learns that a prisoner *is* being transferred, but on grounds of punishment. A prisoner who is considered a 'nuisance' to staff or labelled as a 'troublemaker' and a threat to good order and discipline (King and McDermott 1990) may find himself transferred to the opposite side of the country. While staff may view this as teaching a lesson to the prisoner, part of the tuition fee is paid through the effects on the family. Families of prisoners who have been 'ghosted' feel particularly vulnerable, that somehow their relative is unsafe and the more frequent the moves the more victimized they feel.

> My husband has been in thirteen prisons in seven years. I never feel settled any more because just when I think well, this is it and start feeling settled, he gets moved again. I'm really worried about him as he is deteriorating. You know, I have been fighting the prison system the whole time he's been in to get him treated fairly. I could never have a job because I spend all my time fighting for him or visiting him.

For the families of these men, of course, it now costs more time and money to visit. But the families may feel that they too have been labelled. It can be stressful getting used to new rules and new staff at the best of times – even in prisons people find it reassuring to see familiar faces, and get to know whom they can call on for help – but families may feel additionally marked out if the person they are visiting has been transferred as a 'control problem'. We recognize that transfers, including disciplinary transfers, are necessary from time to time. But it is sometimes hard to distinguish on behavioural grounds those incidents which result in transfers from those which don't (McDermott and King 1988; King and McDermott 1990). The effects on families make it still more important that prisons should become better at 'consuming their own smoke'.

Staff

The prison staff constitutes the 'human face' of the prison to those on the outside. Families gain their impressions of what it must be like inside in large part from the interaction they have with staff. Sometimes this is reassuring and sometimes it is alienating, but either way it is an impression of extraordinary power.

I hated Wandsworth, the prison was really hard on me and treated me like I was a slag. It would take me two hours to get there and they would only give me fifteen minutes because they didn't like my husband. But Maidstone is much better for him and for me. I've met his case officer. He's just an ordinary bloke really who comes from Peckham and drinks in the pub across the road. But he took the trouble to explain things. It really reassures me that there is someone there I can trust and who cares.

Not all families ended up with such positive experiences. Several recounted how staff had made rude remarks to them or refused to help when asked questions. In the course of our fieldwork we witnessed scenes where ordinary courtesy or help was withheld – for example a family having problems starting their car after a visit and being refused assistance from the staff. Perhaps the most sensitive interaction between staff and families occurs during the search before a visit. On these occasions we saw both good and bad practice: in a difficult area some staff manage to treat families with dignity and tact but others do not. Some of our families felt they were subjected to unnecessary humiliation.

I went to Camp Hill to see my son and I was a bit late. There was a female officer on and she did a body search on me not only in front of a male officer but also in front of my 4-year-old grandson. I was so humiliated, I had to fight back the tears. I felt that I was the one inside prison and I felt dirty. I tried not to show anything when my son came in but he could tell I was upset. Now he's all upset and who knows what he's going to do.

Families reported to us what a huge difference it made to their peace of mind when they had a good rapport with staff. To feel that there was someone in the prison whom they believed cared and could be approached constituted a major relief. From what we could observe during our study inside prisons, what was good or indeed bad about staff behaviours towards families seemed to derive from the personality and initiative of individual officers rather than anything institutionalized in their role. We believe that a constructive stance towards families which emphasizes respect and sensitivity towards their needs should form a prominent part of the professional training of all prison staff.

The regime

Conditions inside prison can also be a source of either reassurance or distress for families. When prisoners are locked up for most of the day in unhygienic conditions with little to do families feel understandably resentful that their son or partner is being treated inhumanely. They may genuinely fear that he will deteriorate mentally or physically and that this will lead him to react with aggression directed either at themselves or the system. Many told us how powerless they felt as they watched their loved one become increasingly bitter.

> He's in Wandsworth waiting to be transferred to Downview and I'm so worried about him. He's locked up for twenty-three hours a day. I went to see him on Saturday and he was really rough. I asked him if he could have at least shaved and he said that they had no water! He sat there during the visit just glaring with anger and he couldn't even enjoy the children. I don't know what he'll do if he has to stay there much longer.

On the other hand, families can be exceedingly gratified when they find that a relative is in a prison that has a good regime.

> You know at least my son is doing something positive. He's not whining but getting on with his life. He is doing the OU and has won the Koestler award for writing a TV play. I'm really proud of him and it shows that he has brains but has just used them the wrong way. Now when he gets out he knows that he can accomplish something.

In many homes that we visited there were proud displays of jewellery boxes, paintings, and pottery that had been made in prison. Some even had diplomas for this or that course on the wall. These objects seemed to serve both as a constant reminder of the relative inside and a public demonstration that conviction and sentence had not been the final statement of his character.

Even where the facilities of the prison regime are reasonably good, however, there can be few prisoners who find that their sense of self-responsibility is enhanced by the experience of imprisonment. In our first study prisoners frequently complained that staff treated them like children, and that there were few real choices that were open for them to make. Even the most basic requirements had to be the subject of requests or formal applications. A kind of wilful, childlike selfishness becomes a condition of survival in these circumstances, and given the frequency of denials inside the system it is often the families outside that bear the brunt of the consequences. This aspect of imprisonment has rarely been given the attention it deserves. As we show below, the satisfaction of these needs by the family quickly becomes a part of a major financial burden.

Financial burdens

Sentenced prisoners, subject to various provisos, become eligible for certain privileges – radios, walkmans, training shoes, perhaps bed-spreads and curtains. While these help to 'normalize' the experience of imprisonment, they can create a major financial strain on families.

The prison service determines how much prisoners are paid for the work they do, what private cash they can have, and what they can spend it on. The average pay of prisoners is currently £2.46 a week (Ruxton 1989). Out of that pay a prisoner must buy tobacco if he smokes, stamps if he wants to send more than one letter a week or to send any letters first class, batteries, tea, and other items which he might need. It is hardly surprising, at these pay levels, that families are put under considerable pressure by prisoners both to send money in and to buy articles for them on the outside.

It easily costs me £50 a month. I'm worse off now that he's inside because I have to support him in there. You can't really refuse him because all they really want are normal things. So he gets everything – he wants for nothing. But I have to pay the bills too. He and the kids get all my money. I'm the only one who goes without.

We asked the families in our study to list everything that they had bought their imprisoned relative in the last year, how much money they sent in each week, and how much they spent on visits which was not covered by the Assisted Prisons Visits Scheme. On average it cost the families £545 a year to keep their relative in prison. As most of the families were already on income support, the effect of imprisonment has been to impoverish these families still more. In spite of this, partners of prisoners were allowed neither to claim single parent allowance nor to claim the prisoner as a dependant. This additional hardship could be eliminated or hugely alleviated if prisoners were paid a more sensible working wage. The ideal of renumeration for prison work that would allow a sensible contribution to prisoners' upkeep, the maintenance of their families, and some provision for release is clearly as far off as ever, in spite of the achievements for some groups of prisoners in some European and American prison systems (Ruxton 1989). But we regard it as imperative that the prison service be required to implement as a matter of urgency the recommendation of the Prison Reform Trust to increase prisoners' pay to the level of the 'personal expenses' element of Part III Accommodation payments under income support (Ruxton 1989). This would increase the average pay for prison work to £9.84 a week and increase the overall prison budget by one and a half per cent. Even so the additional £384.76 a year per prisoner would still leave families making a substantial contribution.

Communication problems

It was characteristic of our families that they felt unable to tell their partners of the extent of the financial burden they were carrying, or the sacrifices that it entailed. But this was part of a broader problem of communication between those inside and those outside the walls. The fact is that families felt obliged to cope alone with almost whatever problem beset them, partly because they feared that to share it with their prisoner would only increase his sense of impotence, and partly because they were afraid he might blame them as uncaring or incompetent to have allowed it to occur without resolution.

One recent initiative that has gone some way to improving communication between prisoners and their families has been the installation of payphones in lower security prisons. It is a policy development that is greatly to be welcomed for it offers an enormous potential benefit to all parties. But there is a long way to go before this potential is realized. Unlike in some American prison systems, the policy in England and Wales has excluded high security establishments. In those lower security prisons which do have payphones there is a considerable variation in access. The range is from one phone per fifty-one prisoners who have access from 8 a.m. to 11 p.m., to one phone for 465 prisoners with access for only two hours in the evening (*Hansard* 1989). As with so many matters in the prison system, parsimonious provision can serve to undermine the benefits by raising levels of frustration. In some prisons there is clearly a danger of telephones becoming the focus for tension as prisoners queue up to phone for a few precious moments only to find they are pressured to get off the line to allow the next man to make his call. And, in a familiar 'catch 22', as long as prisoners' pay is so low the cost of this privilege will be passed on to the families. Whenever we have asked staff, prisoners, or their families there has been unanimity about the value of telephone communication: installation of more payphones throughout the system would be a simple and cost-effective method of implementing a major contribution to both rehabilitation and good order and discipline.

Given the present limitations on the use of telephones, for most prisoners the only real time families have to talk over problems is on visits – an opportunity that arises, at best, twice a month. Throughout the visit the participants are watched, and they remain within the hearing of prison officers and other visitors. These circumstances are not conducive to any real sharing of experiences and many families find that they dare not 'upset' their partner by broaching a difficult subject which they will not have time to resolve. Prisoners are especially concerned not to have a 'bad' visit. To avoid the worst, all parties may conspire to say as little as possible.

> When I go on the visit I have to dress up and be cheerful for him no matter what is happening. He looks to me to lift his spirit. If I start to tell him some of my problems he gets so wound up and then the visit is ruined. A few times he was so upset that he argued with one of the officers afterwards and got nicked. It isn't worth it. There isn't enough time to go over everything and besides he can't really do anything about it.

Sometimes in a situation of crisis, either the family or the prisoner may seek a 'welfare visit' which may offer the opportunity for a more extensive discussion in the more sympathetic presence of a probation officer. However, this is necessary only because provisions have been inadequate to prevent the crisis from occuring in the first place. One of our respondents told us of a situation which seemed to demonstrate perfectly the lack of fit between a system governed by bureaucratic rules and the needs of families responding to problems that do not follow a schedule:

> I asked if we could have a welfare visit where the social worker comes up with me and we go into a private room and work out our problems. You just can't do that in the visits room with all these people around. How can you cry and yell with everybody watching? They told me we couldn't have one because I visit him every week. They seem to only go so far and don't recognize our needs.

It is not uncommon for an understanding probation officer, or even a wing principal officer, to allow a prisoner to use the office phone to call home to deal with a crisis, but such thoughtfulness seems to occur in spite of, rather than because of, the system.

Parenting problems

Some of the most difficult problems faced by prisoners and their partners, not surprisingly, concern their relationships with their children: imprisonment creates circumstances in which it is difficult to be either child or parent. Once again a principal difficulty is the lack of fit between the bureaucratic rules of the system and the changing human needs of the people caught up in it. Perhaps one of the most important needs for children is the warmth of physical contact with fathers as well as mothers and although this is now allowed in the maximum security prisons which we know, it is still the practice in many prisons to prohibit it.

> The visits are really hard on the little one. She always wants to sit on her father's knee but the staff get upset and tell her to get down. She just doesn't understand why she can't. He gave her a stuffed animal that is quite large and so she goes home and tries to sit on its lap.

Some of the women had asked if they could take a photograph of the child with the father only to have their request denied apparently on security grounds. The mothers complained that their young child often didn't realise that the person they actually visited was their father: a facility to take simple family photographs periodically would go a long way to reinforcing and maintaining family identities for all parties.

It has been estimated that at least 100,000 children a year have a father in prison in England and Wales (Shaw 1987), and the number of children who have mothers in prison is not even known (Catan 1989). However, we see little evidence of recognition that children should have the right of access to their parent and to maintaining a relationship. In fairness we must acknowledge that a few prisons have started fathers' groups and established crèches in the visits room. But so far these developments are no more than tokens. There is a need for programmes whereby children can visit their fathers in prison for weekends in circumstances that are more children-friendly than anything we have seen in this country.

As things stand at the moment one of the most pernicious and insidious aspects of the system is that the prospects for communication are so poor that virtually all of those we spoke to on the outside felt constrained to conceal the problems they had in bringing up the children from their partner inside, or else to give only the most sanitized account.

He worships Paul and in his eyes his son can do no wrong. He has such an ideal picture of who Paul is. So whenever Paul got into trouble, I either didn't tell him or made it out less than it was. I'll tell you though it's been hard having no one to share the hard times with and now that he's coming out, I'm worried that their relationship has no basis in reality.

The only time when the prisoner and family feel that they have a real opportunity for communication is when the prisoner gets home leave – but by then so many unrealistic expectations have been built up that it is often too late.

PRE-RELEASE

The first stage of preparing for release is the application for parole. It is a procedure that causes much distress partly because it is shrouded in so much secrecy and misunderstanding. Prisoners and families are told that prisoners can apply for parole after serving one-third of their sentence. Families understand that parole is granted if the authorities believe that the prisoner is no longer a threat to society and could benefit more by being under supervision in the community than being in custody.

Whatever anxieties many of our families felt about the eventual release of their relative, all seemed to hold out the hope that he would get parole as long as he behaved himself and had a home to go back to. Many families went to great lengths to secure him a job, believing this would also help ensure parole.

I have gotten him a promise of a job if he gets parole even though the probation officer thinks he should stay home for a while. Maybe he's right but I can't take the risk. I can't understand why they would say no as he has a home to go to, a job, and a family who'll help him. [He did not get the parole.]

The closed world of the prison never seems more impenetrable than when a relative is refused parole *without* any explanation, so it is to be welcomed that under the proposed new parole regulations reasons will be given for decisions. At present, families facing a knock back begin to doubt whether their relative has told them everything, and they feel powerless themselves because they do not know what else they could do to better his chances the next time. The rejection of a parole application nevertheless might still leave a prisoner eligible for home leave. Lower security prisoners are now able to apply for home leave after serving one-third of their sentence and thereafter can apply every six months (Home Office 1988a).

The widening of home-leave policy is another welcome initiative by the prison service, though it remains a modest development compared to what is offered elsewhere. According to Lakes (1990), in eighteen out of twenty-one Council of Europe member states, as well as Canada (CSC 1986) and parts of the United States (US Dept of Justice 1984), home leave is granted more frequently and earlier than in Britain without any major crisis in the criminal justice system.

As the home-leave policy operates now in England and Wales, it creates high expectations and even higher disappointments. It occurs too late in the sentence and too infrequently to achieve the intended objectives. By the time the opportunity occurs to exercise them, prisoners have lost the very skills they need. Imprisonment can be seen as a massive process of social deskilling. All too often it takes away or severely damages the capacity to interact with people in a normal, open, give and take manner: the ability to share in the responsibility for self and others has been largely replaced by a need to gratify selfish whims. It is not that they do not try; rather that, by the time they get a chance to try, the whole task is so daunting and so pressured that they are just ill equipped to cope. Nowhere does the effect of this process reveal itself more than when the prisoner goes on his first home leave.

> When I got my home leave I thought everything would be great. I'd be Robert Redford and she'd be Meryl Streep, but it wasn't like that at all. Everything had changed. I don't mean the outside – I got used to that right away. But here at home. The kids had changed, they had grown up without me. I'd had no input to their upbringing. And she, God had she changed! I was berserk the whole time. We did nothing but yell at each other and in a bizarre way I was glad to go back.

The families are only drawn into the process of home leave when a probation officer makes a home visit to see if the situation is appropriate for the prisoner to come home to. On the basis of our data this contact is perfunctory: indeed so disproportionate was it to the magnitude of the task that it could only be regarded as derisory. Of all the women we interviewed, not one probation officer or prison official had asked her if she had any problem with the prospect of a home leave or even the timing of the home leave. At no time did *she* get *any* advice or preparation for the forthcoming visit.

First time I see probation in over ten years is when they come to do a home report. They were not at all interested in how I was or how I was coping or whether his return was a problem for me. They just asked me if I was willing to have him back. Once I said yes, they were gone!

RELEASE

The stress of home leave merely foreshadows the stress of release. Release is, of course, the objective which sustains most prisoners through their sentences. But the closer it comes the more anxious they feel about it. Most are so badly prepared for it that its arrival precipitates them into crisis. It is not just that he has to relearn the skills he has lost while imprisoned: he has also to shake off the very attitudes and behaviours that enabled him to survive on the inside. And he has to do it all from day one.

You know time has stopped for me. I still think like I did when I went in and I'm trying to make up for all the time that I lost but I know I can't. I also have this bitterness, this inner rage that I don't know how to let go of. I've been treated as less than human for so long that I no longer know what to expect or what is expected of me.

However, release also creates a crisis for the family. During the time of imprisonment the family has grown and changed as it had to adapt to a changing situation, a situation which excluded the family member inside. The family now has to try and reintegrate someone who has also changed, but changed in response to an environment that mostly excluded them.

I thought I was pretty well prepared for his coming home but I wasn't. There was so much I resented about him and we never got around to talking about it while he was inside. I guess also I did change. I stand up to him now and tell him what I think and he doesn't like that but he's learning. I'm a lot more independent now. I've had to be. He hasn't been here to change the plugs and all. I've had to do it all.

Many prisoners, expecting their partners to continue in the more traditional and compliant roles they played before the sentence began, have difficulty in adapting to the women who have become used to exercising their own independence and responsibilities. The situation is often made more difficult as a man seeks to come to terms with his rage about his treatment in prison while the woman has to deal with her anger at what he has put her through – an anger she could not express as she helped him through his sentence.

> When he came home God it was hard. He just came barging into my life. I've made a life for myself here and it's quiet and mine. He comes in and lies on the sofa and *assumes* that I'll do everything for him. I know this sounds petty but it's the intrusion. I know a lot of this is prison but I am the one who has to deal with the consequences.

CONCLUSION

In our research we could not but be impressed by the extraordinary tenacity with which most of our respondents – spouses, partners, and mothers – 'stood by their man'. They did so for many reasons: many of course wanted to and would have done so whatever, but virtually all felt themselves also to be under pressure of expectations that they should do so. Most felt that not to do so would have let their family member down by prejudicing his chances of surviving the sentence or of getting early release. But most also felt that at every turn they got no thanks and precious little help. They felt used or abused by the police, by their own legal advisers, by prison staff, by probation staff, by the DSS, by officials of all kinds. It was not that there was no help, no kindnesses extended. It was that these were oases in a desert landscape in which most had to find their own way to survive. Deprived of proper opportunities of maintaining civilized contacts with their partners, problems are not discussed but put off, concealed, or glossed until it is all but too late to do anything about them.

There is no shortage of public statements about the needs. In addition to the fourth task of the prison service, which we quoted at the outset, Prison Rule 32 makes it clear that '[f]rom the beginning of a prisoner's sentence, consideration shall be given, in consultation with the appropriate after-care organisation, to the prisoner's future and the assistance to be given him on and after his release'. The trouble with the statement of tasks is that the prison service clearly takes a minimalist interpretation of what is 'possible'. And the trouble with Prison Rule 32 is that little attention is paid to giving effect to the results of any 'consideration' that might be given and 'consultations' which may take place. It is true that in 1986 the prison service issued guidance on prisoner 'throughcare' and published it in its 1987–88 annual report. Throughcare is the responsibility of probation officers, prison officers, and other specialists to meet the social and welfare needs of prisoners from sentencing through to release. The guidance states that throughcare should also include 'practical assistance in helping them to retain their links with the community and to prepare for their return to it' (Home Office 1988b). From the experiences of our families, at least, there seems as yet to have been little practical benefit flowing from this guidance.

The proliferation of prisoner families' support groups throughout the country in recent years is both an indication of the awakening consciousness and a testament to the void left by the prison service in putting into practice its fourth task. The newly formed national Federation of Prisoners' Families Support Groups, that is aiming to act as a network of support and information for groups throughout the country, can be expected to exert a pressure through which a more united family voice can be heard. If it can succeed in putting some teeth in Rule 32, then we look forward to the day when the system no longer relies on the unwritten Rule 102: '*Stand by your man*'.

NOTES

1 The research was carried out under Research Grant No. E06 25 0020 as part of the ESRC Crime and Criminal Justice Research Initiative.
2 The research on which this paper is based was carried out under Research Grant No. R000 23 1401. We would like to thank all those on both sides of the walls who participated in the research for sharing their experiences with us; and Stephen Shaw and Adam Sampson for their comments on the draft.
3 As our original research concerned only prison for adult males, we included only families of male prisoners in this study. Female prisoners and their families are, of course, also affected by penal policy and their needs and problems have been under-researched.

REFERENCES

Catan, L. (1989) 'Young families of female prisoners', paper given at the British Criminological Conference, Bristol, July.
CPAG (1989) *National Welfare Benefit Handbook 1989*, London: Child Poverty Action Group.
CSC (1986) *Correctional Statistics*, Ottawa: Correctional Service of Canada, Department of Justice.
Hansard (1989) 24 July, C.499.
Home Office (1988a) Circular Instruction 9 of 1988, Guidance on Home Leave.
Home Office (1988b) *Report of the Work of the Prison Service, April 1987–March 1988*, London: HMSO.
Home Office (1990) 'Briefing', No. 18, 26 January, London: Home Office.

King, R. D. and McDermott, K. (1990) 'My geranium is subversive: notes on the management of trouble in prisons', *British Journal of Sociology*, 41(4):445–71.

Lakes, G. (1990) 'Standard minimum rules for the treatment of prisoners', report to the 8th United Nations Congress on Prevention of Crime and Treatment of Offenders.

McDermott, K. and King, R. D. (1988) 'Mind games: where the action is in prisons', *British Journal of Criminology* 28(3):357–77.

Plotnikoff, J. (1988) *Prison Rules: A Working Guide*, London: Prison Reform Trust.

Prison Reform Trust (1989) *Prisoners' Information Pack*, London: Prison Reform Trust.

Ruxton, S. (1989) *Fair Pay for Prisoners*, London: Prison Reform Trust.

Shaw, R. (1987) *Children of Imprisoned Fathers*, London: Hodder & Stoughton.

Train, C. (1985) 'Management accountability in the prison service', in M. Maguire, J. Vagg, and R. Morgan (eds) *Accountability and Prisons*, London: Tavistock.

US Department of Justice (1984) *Sources of Criminal Justice Statistics*, Washington, DC: Department of Criminal Justice.

6 Men's imprisonment

The financial cost to women and children

Ann Davis

INTRODUCTION

The last decade has witnessed a steady increase in the number of children brought up in households headed by one parent. The vast majority (over 90 per cent) of these households are headed by women. These are households which are over-represented on all measures of deprivation. As Slipman states:

> Poverty is the spectre that haunts the one parent family. Put simply it is women's poverty tied to children's poverty. Together they make a formidable trap from which it is difficult to escape; which cuts off all aspects of life's opportunities . . . acute problems are experienced by the many lone parents who drop into poverty with a shocking rapidity upon relationship breakdown. They experience a spiral of poverty which removes their control over their lives and enforces a dependency upon state benefits and the welfare system, that determines both their future life chances and those of their children. It is the poverty trap that creates the problems of the one parent family.
>
> (in Becker and MacPherson 1988: 232)

Among the poorest of these households are those headed by the partners of prisoners. The numbers of households in this situation has risen as the number of male prisoners in the United Kingdom has reached an all-time high in the 1980s. Yet scant attention has been paid in prison research or poverty research to the women and children who are bearing the costs of male imprisonment.

Focusing on the financial costs of male imprisonment to women and children is not an easy matter. As Smith has noted, despite the marked increase in the number of women and children affected by men's imprisonment, official government statistics do not provide adequate information about the number involved and the circumstances in which they find themselves. A notable absence is any reliable information about the incomes of prisoners' households and the dependence which such households have on social security benefits. Smith has recently estimated that 85 to 90 per cent of prisoners' households are substantially dependent on social security income (Smith in Light 1989: 50). If this is so, it suggests male imprisonment sentences most women and children to lives of considerable poverty.

The 1980s in Britain witnessed an increased economic polarization between the majority who have benefited from increased prosperity and a small, growing minority of poor people (Pond in Hamnett *et al.* 1989: 76). Women are over-represented in that minority and women's distinct experience of poverty has taken on new dimensions in a decade of change and constraint in public welfare provision (see Glendenning and Millar 1987; Graham and Popay 1989). Critical to understanding the distinct features of women's experience of poverty and how it connects with child poverty is an analysis of the way in which women's relationships in households impact with their treatment in the external worlds of employment and state welfare provision to construct financial deprivation. The major reforms in the social security system, introduced in the late 1980s, have increased women's vulnerability to poverty (see, for example, Pahl 1990). However, their experience of poverty is not just a question of benefit dependency. When women find themselves managing on benefit income in the face of rising housing, fuel, and food costs, they do so in the context of competing demands from other household members. The outcome for many women in this situation is that they only 'get by' by placing themselves and their own needs as the lowest priority. As Land and Rose have argued, 'self-denial is still seen as women's special share of poverty' (Land and Rose 1985). For most women heading up single-parent households this consistently means putting the health and well-being of their children first. Women with partners in prison have to take into account an additional set of needs – those of their absent partner. This adds a further, complicating dimension to the financial costs of imprisonment and locks women and children into particularly difficult financial situations.

BEGINNING TO COUNT THE COSTS

At the beginning of 1989, I undertook a small study of the financial circumstances of prisoners' partners in the West Midlands. My interest in this was triggered by the changes which had been introduced by the

Social Security Act 1986, changes which have done little to ease the economic situation of one-parent households.

The study involved interviews with eight women who had partners in prison. I made contact with these women through the visitors' centre at Winson Green prison in Birmingham. The women I talked to were some of the poorest, most courageous, and most stressed benefit claimants I have ever interviewed. All of them had health problems related to their physical as well as their mental well-being. Few could afford to eat regularly after they had secured the most they could for their children. In a number of respects they share the situation of hundreds of thousands of other women who, as single-parent claimants, try to raise their children on social security benefits. But they were also clearly bearing some distinct personal, social, and economic costs associated with being the partners of prisoners.

The women interviewed in this pilot study were between the ages of 19 and 53, and had in total nineteen children who lived with them. All were British-born white, mixed race, or Afro-Caribbean women. For four of these women, their partner's imprisonment was a first-time experience; for the rest it had happened on at least one occasion before. One of the women I interviewed was married to a man serving a life sentence.

What emerged from these interviews was a common pattern in the way that each woman recalled the impact of her partner's imprisonment on her and her children's lives. This pattern was one which has been noted by other researchers (Light 1989). It has been characterized as having three stages: the period of separation following arrest and remand; the period of surviving the sentence; and the period just before and following release. At each stage women registered particular financial as well as personal and social consequences of trying to cope. These reinforced each other, and while this chapter explores financial costs there is a sense in which it is artificial to separate these out from the personal and social.

As they described their experiences of each stage, women also described particular issues which arose for them in respect to finances. Associated with the stage of arrest and remand was a disruption of income for the women and children involved. Sentencing marked a stage at which most women were forced to take decisions about financing. The period just before and after release raised issues about loss of control by these women of the households' finances.

DISRUPTION OF INCOME

For all of the women, the arrest and remand of a partner was a life-disrupting event taking them from the routine and pattern of a shared life, with associated financial arrangements, to a new world of loss and uncertainty. This was a time in which women's energies were absorbed in dealing with the shock of change and frantically searching, phoning, and asking questions as they tried to find out what had happened and where their partners were. In this whirl of trying to establish contact with their partners their financial circumstances became a low priority.

> I was so frantic I just begged and borrowed to see me and the kids through and pay for the phone calls I was making to find out where he was.
>
> (19-year-old woman, two children)

> Looking back I don't know how I would have managed without mum. She was feeding us and making sure the kids got to school looking decent. My head was somewhere else and I had nothing but Child Benefit. I didn't even know enough to tell the social I needed money.
>
> (28-year-old woman, three children)

When partners had been located and women began to piece together what had happened, money worries started to hit them hard. It was not just the immediate demands of creditors. Women also had to consider the overall management of their incomes. As one woman put it:

> He'd always managed the bills, because he earned the money. I had no idea how we were fixed, I didn't even know about how much mortgage we paid, and what was due. I didn't know where to start. I'd never had to face up to these things before. It was a nightmare.

This disruption to both household income and their role in relation to it was disorientating for most of the women I interviewed, and they did not know where to go for support. They felt unable to ask their partners for advice because they thought they had enough worries to contend with 'inside'. Most were also reluctant to share the detail of their money worries with family or friends. As one woman of 32 years with a child explained:

> I felt ashamed, silly really, not just ashamed of where he was but

that I didn't know the first thing about how to sort things out. I didn't say a word about the money to anyone and so it all began to pile up.

Most women found at an early stage that their household budgets had to spread beyond household costs. Visiting partners on remand is expensive. Men asked for treats and comforts, and the women felt they should supply them. The conflict, for these women was enormous. As one 19-year-old explained:

> When I look back now it seems crazy. I wasn't eating; he was moaning about the food inside and I was borrowing to buy him something each time I visited, and what I took him was never enough.

These conflicts about how to meet the needs of partners and children as well as themselves were intensified at this stage for most women because they had so little to manage on. None of the women I interviewed claimed their full social security entitlement at the outset. The reasons were unique in each case but all combined elements of ignorance of entitlement, a lack of time and energy to establish and pursue their claims for social security benefit, and delays in local social security offices processing claims.

Currently, a person who is detained as a prisoner and who has a partner is not entitled to claim social security benefits. His/her partner can claim as a single adult or parent with children during the period of detention. All the women I interviewed had to discover this for themselves, and some did not find out until their partner was sentenced. Of those who did find out at an early stage some did not know how to claim social security or what to claim for. Two women, who were employed in part-time work, thought (erroneously) that because they were working they were not entitled to any social security.

For the three women who did make a social security claim during this period, the official delays in processing (and in one case losing) the claim meant that they did not have any social security income for weeks. When they approached the local social security office in desperation they were advised to ask relatives and friends for help. Not one was offered any of the available Social Fund emergency payments.

Two of the women were unable during the trauma of this stage to organize themselves and 'spare the time' to sort out their social security. Their days were spent visiting partners and trying to keep a routine for themselves and their children. The shock they had experienced and the reaction of their family and their local community to their predicament made them fearful of outside contact and the reactions of others. Both found themselves turning to tranquillizers and sleeping pills. One, a 34-year-old woman with two children, described her feelings thus:

> I was a walking zombie, outside a brave smile telling everyone I was fine, inside I was dead, numb – I couldn't sleep without pills. I couldn't get up without pills. I didn't know the time of day or day of the week. I remember going down to the social one day, my sister had been nagging me to do it. I got to the door and turned round. I knew I couldn't face the questions.

For all these women and their children, it was help from family and friends, in cash and kind, which became the main source of financial support. Three had some earnings of their own and two turned to commercial finance companies for loans. The state's social security system did not offer a swift or major form of financial assistance at this stage of income disruption. Yet seven out of the eight women had an entitlement to income support, from the first day of their partner's detention.

MAKING A DECISION

By the time their partner was sentenced these women and children were facing considerable financial problems. Bills and housing debts were mounting. The tolerance (and resources) of family and friends were exhausted. For a number of these women a financial crisis like the threat of disconnection from the telephone or their fuel supplies led to them taking decisive action. For others, it was the prison sentence which ended any hopes they had of their partners' returning quickly and, as one woman put it, 'I realized I had to take things in hand'. What all these women experienced was considerable shame and anger at the way they were received by the range of agencies they approached in order to sort out their financial affairs. After hours of waiting in the social security offices, at the fuel board, in the telephone company offices, and building societies, they found themselves having to disclose, in earshot of many other customers and staff, the circumstances they were in. The reaction they received from staff was hostile, never sympathetic. As one 34-year-old woman put it:

I felt like a criminal. As soon as I said I'd come because my husband was inside their attitude changed. Whether it was claiming at the social or getting the gas to put my name on the bills, I could tell they thought I was to blame. I hardened myself to it, but it still hurt, I can't pretend it didn't.

Several of these women found themselves in very complex financial negotiations. They not only had to reach agreements to pay off accumulated debts, they had to try and cancel credit arrangements which they could no longer afford to keep up. Though they received no professional advice and very limited help from friends and family, some succeeded in organizing a new pattern of income and expenditure. Others did not. Several found their partners had not, in fact, made the regular past rent, rates, or fuel payments which they thought had been cleared, and there were arrears that they had not known about.

While managing was difficult, these women did find themselves with control of the household income for the first time in their lives. The experience was, for some, an empowering one, and it banished the uncertainty experienced in the earlier stages of their separation from their partners. These women felt it was improving the security they were able to provide for their children because they could now plan for them and deliver on the promises they made to them, without partners getting in the way.

However, it would be a mistake to see the positives of some of the women's financial circumstances as the whole picture. All struggled on their income and cut down heavily on their own expenditure on food and clothing. All felt they could not provide their children with the basics they needed. All referred to the fact that out of their weekly budgets they had somehow to put aside a sum for costs associated with keeping contact with their absent partner, for which they did not receive any extra benefit.

The only financial help, in addition to single-claimant or single-parent weekly benefit, to women with partners in prison is the Assisted Prison Visits Scheme. This was introduced in April 1988 when local social security offices stopped acting as agents for the Home Office. The scheme, which is administered by post from a national office, pays the 'close relatives' of prisoners who are on basic social security payments (such as income support and family credit) or income of an equivalent level, the basic travel costs of one visit every twenty-eight days. Payments are dependent on close relatives making detailed written application to the office. Close relatives of prisoners are not notified automatically of this scheme.

All the women I interviewed whose partners were in prison for the first time got to hear of the scheme by chance from other women after they had made at least one visit. The four for whom the experience was not new had been alerted to the scheme before. However, the April 1988 changes meant that two of them, finding that their local social security office would not process the claims, thought the scheme no longer existed and incurred considerable debts, for example, borrowing the fare, before they learnt of the change in the procedure for claiming. The local offices these women visited provided no information about the changes in the arrangements and staff employed there either knew nothing of the scheme, or said that they no longer administered the scheme and knew nothing of the new arrangements.

This failure to be notified of the scheme at the onset of visiting resulted in substantial debts for four women whose partners were in prisons some distance from their homes. When these women could no longer turn to their family for help they became involved with the local agents of financial companies which charged high rates of interest on loans, and this burden was a heavy one to bear on weekly benefit payments.

Even when women were claiming financial help under the scheme, they found it did not cover the full costs of prison visits. Travelling long distances with children is not just tedious, it is expensive. It was not only a question of making sure that everyone looked well turned out; there were the costs of feeding children on journeys or using cafés in order to get hot water to heat babies' feeds at regular intervals. When public transport connections were missed, taxis were the only available alternatives to the women and their children, desperate not to miss visiting times at remote prisons. The conditions in which the women and their children had to wait before being admitted to some prisons meant that clothes and other belongings were ruined by rain as families stood in the open.

The strain of these occasions clearly took a terrific toll on all the women I interviewed. These were not times to share troubles with a partner or to ask for help over financial pressures. The women felt they needed to be at their best in order to keep up their partners' morale and reassure them that all was well at home. In the words of one woman:

> I used to arrive so tired and psyched up. I just wanted to cry when I saw him, but I had to put on my brightest smile and

listen to his troubles as the kids ran wild after the journey. I'd come away and remember all the things I should have asked and never did, things which were worrying me. Visits used to tear me apart.

LOSING CONTROL

The imminent release of a partner brought home to these women how far they had come in their struggles to keep their heads above their financial troubles. For those who had discovered strength and abilities in themselves in the struggle to retain financial order in their lives, their feelings about the partners' return were tinged with apprehension about what they might lose financially and personally. They found they could not raise this on their visits because they had shared so little of the financial problems on the outside with their partners that they literally did not know how to begin. In the face of their partners' demands for reassurance that a welcome awaited them at home, women were reluctant to talk about re-negotiating their financial arrangements.

Women who had failed to keep their heads above their financial difficulties felt alarm at what their partners would discover on their release. One woman with three children, who had had to manage without electricity for over a year, found herself desperately trying to borrow money to pay the bill and the reconnection charge so that all would be well when her partner returned. She was the only woman in this group who reported turning to a social work agency for financial help, and she did so with considerable alarm:

> My pal told me that the council would help if you had kids and said you couldn't manage them. I was worried that they'd take them off me, but I was that desperate to get things right for when he came back I took the risk. They asked a lot of questions but said they couldn't help out with the electric. They told me to try probation.

In turning to the probation service she, like several other women, found no response to her financial concerns. The focus of probation officers was on the support that these women would provide for their partner on his return home not the financial circumstances that they and their children found themselves in.

For several women, the imminent release of their partners brought unexpected pressure from their family connected with finance. As one woman said:

My mum and dad were so good to me when he was inside. I never asked for help, they just gave it. My mum would say: 'Dad and I were thinking it's the new school term next week, we'll get the kids kitted out, don't worry.' When they knew he was due out, they changed. They'd been against me marrying him from the beginning. They came round and put it straight, 'If you're having him back don't expect us to bail you out when he lets you down again.'

For six of these women the return of a partner meant that they gave up their status as benefit claimants, and not one knew that there was another option. Indeed, two women who had disabilities lost the additional social security income paid to claimants with disabilities as a result of their partners' becoming the claimant. This loss was significant to the households concerned. For three women the personal, as well as financial, difficulties of their partners' return, proved too much for them. They found that they could not re-negotiate terms with them, and that the loss of their hard-won independence was too much to bear. One 25-year-old woman described it this way:

I had matured. I had to while he was away. I thought he had too, he said he'd learnt a lesson but when he came back he was back to where he'd been before and I'd moved beyond it. There was no going back for me. I moved out and took the kids I knew we would be better off without him.

For the others, the return provided a relief from the burdens of single parenting. But there were still costs and they proved painful for some, as the following comment shows:

I don't know, I just feel so guilty now. When he was away, Sharon [13-year-old daughter] and I were that close, friends say she took over some of the worrying for me. When he came back she lost out. There's less money for her now, he makes sure of that, and she has to share me with him. She's getting into trouble; he can't control her, and I've given up.

None of the women interviewed reported a feeling of increased personal financial security following their partners' release, even though for two women it meant coming off social security benefits because their partners found work. Their continuing financial insecurity was rooted in the fact that in both these households the women found themselves and their children in such a state of dependency.

CONCLUSION

This small study begins to explore some of the financial costs to women and children of men's imprisonment. It is an indictment of governments that this is such a neglected topic. Prisoners' partners and their children appear to be in a deeper poverty trap than most single-parent households yet their plight is not being responded to by state agencies ostensibly concerned about the welfare of children.

The reasons for the failure of the state to make adequate provision in this area are interesting to reflect on. One of the declared rationales of the recent social security reforms has been to 'wean' individuals from dependence on state income support and, in one sense, it appears to be delivering on that objective. However, this is a group of benefit claimants who cannot readily turn to alternatives for income such as employment, given the demands of child care which most of them face and the absence of both day care and well-paid jobs for women in their situation. The failure, therefore, of the social security service to respond in a timely fashion does not result in independence from the state. It results in increased financial pressure and indebtedness for women whose family agendas are full to overflowing. The immediate loss of a partner's social security benefit income on admission to prison contrasts markedly with the payment of full social security for six weeks on a partner's admission to hospital and the continued payment of a reduced benefit after this period, an arrangement by which the state acknowledges the continuing additional costs to a household in which a partner is receiving maintenance from a state service. Questions need to be raised about why prisoners' households do not receive the same treatment. The separation of limited help towards the costs of travelling to prison from mainstream social security payment arrangements segregates prisoners' partners from other claimants whose partners are absent. It also appears to add complications and delay in the payment of the only additional form of state help available for the families of prisoners.

There are tremendous and continuing costs attached to this treatment of women whose partners are in prison, costs which are not just borne by the women and children involved, but which are spread to their partners and to wider society. When the government introduced its 'New Approach' to social security in the mid-1980s it talked of aiming to establish a 'partnership between the individual and the state'.

Most people not only can but wish to make sensible provision for themselves. The organisation of social security should encourage that. It should respect the ability of the individual to make his own choices and to take responsibility for his own life. But at the same time it must recognise the responsibility of government to establish an underlying basis of provision on which we as individuals can build and on which we can rely at times of need.

(Department of Health and Social Security 1985)

The women I interviewed were taking their responsibilities towards their children and partners very seriously. The problem was the lack of a secure 'underlying basis of provision' on which they could rely as they struggled to survive their partners' imprisonment.

REFERENCES

Becker, S. and McPherson, S. (eds) (1988) *Public Issues and Private Pain: Poverty, Social Work and Social Policy*, Insight.

Department of Health and Social Security (1985) *Reform of Social Security*, Vol. 1, Cmnd. 9517, London: HMSO.

Glendenning, C. and Millar, J. (eds) (1987) *Women and Poverty in Britain*, Hemel Hempstead: Wheatsheaf.

Graham, H. and Popay, J. (1989) *Women and Poverty: Exploring the Research and Policy Agenda*, papers from a jointly organized conference, Thomas Coram Research Unit/University of Warwick.

Hamnett, C. *et al.* (eds) (1989) *The Changing Social Structure*, London: Sage.

Land, H. and Rose, H. (1985) 'Compulsory altruism for all or an altruistic society for some?', in P. Bean *et al.* (eds) *In Defence of Welfare*, London: Tavistock.

Light, R. (ed.) (1989) *Prisoners' Families*, Bristol: Bristol and Bath Centre for Criminal Justice.

Pahl, J. (1990) *Money and Marriage*, Basingstoke: Macmillan.

7 We are not the problem
Black children and their families within the criminal justice system

Ya'el Amira

There are studies of black prisoners (Gender and Player 1989; McDermott 1990) and of the children of prisoners (Shaw 1987; Catan 1988) but there has been no research in relation to black children of black prisoners and the differently defined needs they have. Therefore, in the absence of quantitative data, what follows represents a subjective evaluation of the experiences of the children and parents interviewed, and my interpretation of my own experiences.

The problems that children of black prisoners face (along with black children of any prisoner) are those of any child with an imprisoned parent. However, it is important to recognize that there are issues of particular relevance to this group of children, and special needs thus incurred. All black people in wider society are caught up in the complexity of institutionalized power relationships. These are designed to insulate and protect existing power structures which reinforce inequality at every level. These inequalities extend across race, gender, and class (Davis 1982).

ENVIRONMENT

In addition to being a product of all the aforementioned, environment is often a large problem for children having to adjust to the reality of an imprisoned parent. In an inner-city area, for example, certain communities may be the target of 'saturation' policing policies and may therefore have a high ratio of arrests to population. Consequently, general peer expectations may exist which encourage the youth to integrate their experiences of commonplace arrests – and perhaps resulting imprisonments – as 'normal' (Fanon 1968).

> Most of us have been picked up. I hate it, you never know when. If they [the police] know your family are inside, you never get no

peace. Last time they got me, I'd been in my mate's car. They had me on the van floor, kicking me and that. They had a good laugh, making me get up and lie down, over and over. If you say no, or get pissed off, they just threaten to take you in. It's no good thinking they can't get me this time, I'm clean, and anyway I haven't done nothing, because you know that's not how it works. They kept on like 'want to see Daddy?' – meaning if I didn't play their game, they'd have me too. My Dad's been inside a few times, so they know him. You just have to get on with it. As long as you don't lose your bottle, you know they'll let you go again, but only after kicking fuck out of you. What can you do? If I move away, there'll still be no work, and I won't have my family, and the mates I grew up with. You just have to put up with it, it's just how things are round here, and, anyway, it's not as if we don't get back at the bastards in other ways.

(Marvin, 14)

All of us knows they [the police] could kick the door in when they like. They really rip the place up. Like when our Carl was missing, they come here for him. They were really bad to me Mam, broke all the cupboards, smashed the place up. There's no respect, then they wonder why everyone's always trying to have a go at them. Now if me Mam's decorating she never finishes it, she always says what's the point, those bastards'll be round again anyway. If they know your family, they'll come round every time they want someone to fit up.

(Suhail, 15)

Such familiarity with police contact, arrest, and having a family member in prison can lead either to acceptance that this is an inescapable 'fate' or to a certain glamorization of crime and its consequences in order to assimilate the experience with some sort of rationale. This can, in turn, even create certain expectations of police harassment, involvement in illegal activities, and the expectation of probably 'doing some time'.

Sometimes it's good saying my Dad's in jail, the other kids think I'm hard, or if they skit me [tease me] I say watch out! when my Dad comes home, he'll sort you out.

(Nnuli, 7)

If I go to prison I'd start a riot. There's always loads of fellas on the roof, but you never see no girls. My Mum was always telling me girls are great, and they can do all what boys do, but I don't see them on the roof. I'd be the first girl to start a riot. I don't really want to go to prison, my Mum says she misses us and that, and she always has to do loads of work, and the food is horrible. But most of all because you can't do what you like, you can't watch the telly when you want, and they watch you on the toilet.

(Falisha, 10)

When you leave school, you need money for things. There's no jobs so you have to do what everyone else does. Some get caught and some don't. You have to be careful to get the right mates, the clever ones. If I did get caught, I'd be all right, I know plenty who've done time, so I know the score is keeping your head together; eat plenty, sleep properly and do loads of exercise, and avoid the nasty screws. It [imprisonment] is like the work for your wages. You can't get on no other way. If you can get a stash [savings] you can get a legit business going or something, otherwise you have to keep on trying till you get it right.

(Marvin, 14)

I don't want to do like the rest [be criminally active] but I know they'll [the police] keep on picking me up anyway, and they'll probably manage to hang some dodge on me anyway, so I may as well have a go. They always come round [this area] to get someone anyway.

(Suhail)

The young adults and children interviewed all seemed to feel they were at odds with a system designed for public protection, from the police, judiciary, and court processes, through to survival within the prison system itself. They all felt in some way that they had been greatly socially disadvantaged by a parent's criminality and/or imprisonment. Marvin further explained that, as they live within a small community used to continual police intrusion, if one had a family member in prison, everyone knew and, while this was no problem within the community, outside it was a different story (Balbus 1980).

They all expect us to carry on like him [father]. When there was a thing on *Crimewatch* about a woman robbing, they [school friends] said 'was that your Mum', and fell about laughing. The teachers think you're thick too, like your Dad must be to be inside. People joke and say only the stupid ones get caught, but they haven't got a clue what it's like. Everyone thinks you're all robbers from around here. I saw a thing about the police surveillance helicopters; they cost loads of money to run and all they do is fly round and round over our area. The women by us were complaining because they fly so low all night, waking the kids up. They [the residents] wouldn't put up with that in some posh area. The police say it's because we've got a high crime rate they have to keep their eye on us. So you see what I said, even though I'd rather go out and get a good job, when I went for a job the people will have read all that crap and no one'll want me.

(Marvin)

EDUCATION

Such an environmental context obviously extends its influence to education. In school, in addition to the possible racial prejudices a teacher may have regarding a child's achievement in direct relation to race/family background, the child may also be forced into an unconscious pattern of behavioural conformity, synonymous with being a 'problem child' from a 'problem family'. This may further be influenced by a child's low self-expectations. Real social unhappiness may be a barrier to learning, so how the school responds to a child's situation is crucial (Kozol 1968).

She [the teacher] gets all sorry for me. They sort of whisper to me when no one else is around 'Is she OK? Have you seen her?' [the imprisoned mother] like it's really wrong for her to be there. I say out loud that I don't care if she's inside, that doesn't mean she's no good. I can tell they think it does, though they never say it out loud, they try not to mention her, and if the word 'prison' comes up in anything they try not to let me hear and things.

(Falisha)

They seem to think you spend the whole time dodging the law. If you don't do homework, or are always off, they don't really say anything. They seem to expect it anyway. Sometimes for a buzz [joke] I do a really brilliant assignment after weeks of just messing about. They are always dead surprised, and usually think someone else did it.

(Michael, 12)

My friends know about my Dad. Sometimes they get told things by their Mums, like 'don't play with him', but they usually just do anyway. They ask you things about the jail, they think it's good.

(Nnuli)

We go to school from the foster home. There's two other kids there, but not because their Mum and Dad are away [in prison]. Julie's Mum is dead, and her Dad can't look after her, so I think I'm dead lucky. I see my Mum every few weeks. I could see her more but she's too far away. She writes me letters with smudges, where she cries over me, and when I feel sad that makes me feel better. She'll be home next year, and everything will be all right. I don't see my Dad so much. I don't think they want me to see him. He was doing this robbing with guns, but he's not bad, he's a nice Dad. Anyway, I hate school, you get picked on, they say I'm an orphan, and that I'm so ugly my Mum ran away so she wouldn't have to look at me, or they didn't like me and things like that. The teachers just leave you alone to get on with it. I like drawing and English. They say you better do your best, you don't want to end up like your parents. The kids call me a wimp because sometimes I cry in the toilets. Marie [foster mother] says they're silly, and it's good to get things out. When I'm in school I feel like a weirdo, but at the foster home, I feel like a normal kid again.

(Seun, 10)

'JUSTICE, IN PRACTICE'

The long process of injustice that black people experience begins with the harassment at street level, resulting in more frequently being stopped and searched, and continues throughout the social process of 'justice in practice'. Black people are more likely to be arrested, charged with an offence, remanded in custody by having bail refused, convicted and sentenced to a custodial sentence and such sentences may be disproportionately severe (Hall *et al.* 1986). Even after conviction and sentencing, the black prisoner is more likely to suffer higher prison security categorization and so be sent miles from their area of origin, to either one of the few and scattered women's prisons or a male dispersal prison – a high-security place, usually geographically isolated (McDermott 1990). This can cause great difficulties for families attempting to maintain close contact and some sort of family unity, as it is costly and time-consuming to reach such prisons.

The children really experienced it badly when he got shipped to all these places. Half the time they didn't know what black people were! In one place, it was three black inmates to every four hundred white, and those three were kept separated. The others used to call the screws 'boss', a sort of joke really, but can you imagine a black man saying that? Visits in those places were awful, just a strain. The kids would get called 'black bastards' by the other kids there. We never had a visit that was relaxed – the other parents seemed almost to encourage the kids, and were generally very hostile to us all. I used to have to keep my husband from beating up these other parents who wouldn't stop their kids racially abusing our kids, it was awful really, the whole visit was spent like that.

(Alia, 29)

If you drink out of a cup in the play area, they'd all go 'arrrghhh, don't touch that or you'll get rubber lips'. They pull your hair and say 'woolhead' and things like that.

(Nnuli)

Sometimes the tea ladies [WRVS] are dead nice, but sometimes they're a bit funny, like too nice. It's dead weird, I think it's because they don't want to act racist to a little kid.

(Falisha)

I don't like the long train journey. People just stare in funny country places. You feel like you're far, far away from home, and being safe.

(Marcus, 8)

Once allocated to a prison, the black prisoner also appears to be the subject of more disciplinary charges than their white counterparts (McDermott 1990). This may lead to a further internal isolation of the prisoner, making it even more difficult to function as an, albeit absent, parent. These 'operational' difficulties arise in situations of 'closed' (both parties behind separating glass) visits and loss of privileges such as letters and visits, and also, if 'wages' have been lost, having to ask the probably already financially struggling family to provide cash. There seems no doubt that as black prisoners are forced on to the sharper edge of the penal system, their children suffer accordingly.

For black women, there are further problems. They too are often sent very far away from their homes. In many cases it seems then that the remaining parent will have problems bringing the child/ren to visit regularly. In this area too, there are disproportionate numbers of black children with imprisoned parents being taken into the care of the local authorities and placed in fostering situations as a result of their only parent or sole 'carer' being imprisoned. These children have their lives radically altered, and it is not enough to trot out belaboured opinions that 'these parents should have thought about this beforehand' but it is necessary examine critically the social origins with regard to the processes of injustice, briefly explained by the sentencing policies of the Establishment's judiciary.

> We both got sentenced. It was from the beginning that the racism was apparent, from me being refused bail, even though the probation had produced a social inquiry report explaining how I had these twin babies to look after, to going through the system as black woman. For me then, the first question was who was going to look after the children; they were eighteen months old then and were still badly upset from the time of our arrest when the police had been very difficult about someone coming to pick them up from the station. We did get them well looked after, but I never got over badly worrying about them every second I was inside.
>
> (Alia)

> I hated it there [in the foster home], I never felt right and I hated shifting schools. I got so as I never used to unpack my bags as I was always being sent on somewhere else.
>
> (Kiya, 9)

> When Mum first went I used to cry all the time. I used to bite everyone, and smash their houses up [foster homes] so they'd put me with Mum. She is lovely, she's not bad or anything. I couldn't believe it when she was gone. I've got used to it now, but I still think a lot about how it'll be when we all go home.
>
> (Seun)

RACISM AND CRIME

Long-term consequences are far-reaching and possibly very damaging. If children suffer serious social and/or cultural dislocation, this can affect their whole self-perception in relation to being an integral part of the 'host' society. This is reinforced by the fact that those in authority and the general society never really see black citizens as a natural part of that society, whether or not they were born within it (Genovese 1969).

Within the criminal justice system, great injustices exist (Day, Hall, and Griffiths 1988). There appears almost an actual pressure to criminalize certain sections of society, via methods of policing and targeting crime, through the structural imbalances of the court processes, and so on. As black prisoners represent 14 per cent of the total prison population, but less than 5 per cent of the general population (McDermott 1990), this would seem to uphold the myth that black people are more criminally inclined – but in reality, an examination of how these statistics are constructed and of issues around police and judicial discretion would go a long way towards explaining and decoding the plethora of socially constructed assumptions that lead to black people being institutionalized, and kept there. These include the notion of the black family structure as 'subversive' (Davis 1990) and thus the black youth as being 'anti-authoritarian' and more 'violently' inclined. The inner-city unrests of the last few years now occur with regularity but are still interpreted as 'race riots'. However, these have far-reaching implications in reality (Gilroy 1987).

> It's not just mindless violence. It's like saying we've had enough. Our houses are falling down, there's no jobs and the schools are crap. You can try and protest any way you like, but if you write letters, no one answers them, and if you ask questions, no one hears them. So you make a racket loud enough for them to hear. Then they can't say they don't know what's going on.
>
> (Marvin)

> I like fighting now. When I was a kid I didn't, but it's all you can do. I like fighting white people; that's the only way you can get a fair go and can win them.
>
> (Michael)

> I know they think we're all bad. If you watch the telly and that the only black people you see are singers or footballers or Rastas and that. You don't see many women or families in adverts. My Mum told me that in America it's not so bad but I think they do it here because they're scared of us getting on in life, you know, getting some of what they have.
>
> (Falisha)

CULTURE

Cultural identity is of central importance to children who are constantly made to feel the outsiders. Their need to understand and assimilate their ancestral and cultural origins is integral to them not having their self-respect damaged by being in any way different either by skin colour, language, or custom. If they are to resist internalizing the pervasive negative stereotyping present at every level in a society such as Britain's, then it is essential they understand that being different should not be interpreted as thus being in any way inferior – they need to know why, and who they are, and to be proud of their heritage (Hansberry 1960).

Many children find that having a parent in prison can seriously limit their access to cultural identity and understanding. Furthermore, some seem to have found that they encounter concentrated racism upon visiting a prison, especially where the prison may be located in a primarily non-black area. I asked the children participating in this research to make a list of the most frequent racist abuse they encountered while visiting a prison, extended by other visiting children. I have omitted the more common and obvious terms such as 'paki' and 'nigger', preferring to use this shortened list to illustrate how the other *children* rationalized their racist abuse.

You eat goats, dirty bastards.

Your gums are all rotten.

Your lot brought AIDS over here.

Have too many babies, and don't look after them properly.

Have [indiscriminate] sex, all the time.

Can't think for yourselves, come from a backward country.

Have scabby skin.

Stink.

Had to have white people show you how to be civilized.

In Africa/Jamaica they don't have toilets.

Eat rubbish out of bins.

Have their tits hanging out.

Take drugs all day.

Eat worms and snakes.

Have disgusting hair, matted and filthy.

You all look like apes.

This frequently experienced abuse can be very damaging for black children if they are not able to contextualize the ignorance of the abuser with their own cultural/historical background, that is, talk it over with a trusted adult with whom they can identify and who has lived through such racism themselves. This is amplified where children have both parents in prison, or are 'in care', or have a mixed racial and/or cultural heritage and therefore have no access to a better understanding or way of living within their culture. This can be very destructive to self-image and may leave them defenceless to attacks as mentioned, especially if they have no access to an extended family who may have been able to impart cultural knowledge. This can make life even more difficult for these children and more stressful, as the lack of availability of a sympathetic parent strips them of an extra buffer between themselves and the every-day dealings within racist structures.

They need to understand their father's culture. Mine is totally different. He used to tell them things, make them Jamaica food, and tell them stories about Black history, and stuff.

(Alia)

The weirdest thing for me is trying to accept that because of my father's attitude to polygamy, I have four brothers and sisters (of these, I only know one sister well) who I am never likely to meet. The hardest thing, though, is not having known my Dad – because of the way he lives his life – my whole life, and now knowing that the only way I have of getting to know him is as a prisoner, if I want to at all.

(Krishna, 15)

A long time ago my Dad told my brother and me about when he was a little boy in Africa. He said when he came here he thought the people were disgusting and dirty because they used the same toothbrush every day. At home he used to get a new split-twig every morning to scrub his teeth with. When kids at school would skit us he used to tell us what to say and explain why they said what they said. Now I try to remember these things to tell him on a visit but I forget by the time I see him.

(Marcus)

POST-PRISON

Financial pressures also alter a child's experience of a parent's imprisonment. Once again black people are forcibly held at the edge of the economic power matrix by social processes such as sub-standard housing, poorer educational availability, employment opportunities, and health care (Davis 1990). Therefore, all these pressures considered, black families of prisoners may often be under more strain than their white counterparts.

This adds to the social and psychological pressures (Fanon 1985) on the remaining sole carer parent and may almost create a sub-class of prisoners' children within an environment. While some of these problems may be wholly or partially removed, or at least lessened upon release of the other parent, many issues accrue and are ongoing. Within the prison system, as in the social system, the black person will be less likely to have received extra education – penal policy's idea of rehabilitation – and so may have less than optimistic prospects for their resettlement post-prison (NACRO 1986).

When he gets out it'll be worse. At least now that I control our cash the bills get paid and that, but he can't live like that, he's never learnt how to. He always says 'why should we live like paupers', he was always making sure the kids had the best bikes, shoes. Well, you can't live like that on social security. Even now he's always on at me for this and that. He's always wanting cash sent in. Like when they collected for the Hillsborough fund. I felt like saying '*our* electric's been cut off again, you should be seeing to *us* first'. It's hard to keep him quiet, I mean it's bad enough getting the fares together, they [government] only pay us once a month, and when he gets out, he'll have to go 'on the rob' to get us out of debt. While he's away the kids get nothing, nothing. It all goes on him. You can only stand it for so long, then you have to say that's it and get a life for you.

(Carmella, 31)

He's all right in there; a big man. He can't cope out here where he's no one. In there he can work the system, do 'easy' time – we're the ones doing 'hard' time. I don't know what to think. He says he won't go in again but there's nothing out here for the black ex-con. He looks at what other men his age have and wants to catch up with them. He never can. He'll go down again.

(Ann, 24)

It's the kids that always suffer, they're the ones that get left out. I think it's hard for me to live in this all-black area, I feel like an outsider but I have to do it for their sake. They understand what it is to be black and glory in it. They very strongly identify with their Dad, they miss him so much and they are always talking about his release, but what if he goes in again? It'll break their hearts, they're older now. He's their hero but his periods of imprisonment are something I have no power to protect them against. They love him.

(Lisa, 26)

A particularly shattering experience for children in the aftermath of a parent's release is the threat of deportation. This is becoming increasingly common (Prison Reform Trust 1990). If the Home Office decides a particular ex-prisoner – who is not a British citizen – may constitute a threat to society they can post a deportation order on that person, regardless of their family circumstances. Even permanent residents may be ordered to return to their country of origin. Often they will have left that country as young people with their entire family and so have no contacts left there. In any case, if there is a partner and children who have been born in Britain and grown up as British, it will be particularly traumatic having to decide whether to stay in their country of origin or to accompany the deportee to an uncertain future with often no prospects for housing or employment (Anderson 1990).

This is where my kids are being penalized for something they've not done. As Black British, born here, they're being penalized because their father committed a crime. As far as the law goes he's paid for that and is rehabilitated, but it seems that's not enough. The racism of the Home Office is actively threatening everything my kids know. They have a basic human right to know who their father is and to be with him. If this means to survive as a family we will have to leave our relatives, friends, school, home, work, everything, then we will, but it's a disgrace. He's been the one closest to the boys, I feel boys need a father. He's the one who cuddles them most, who they run to. However, there's no question of him just taking them. It'd be so hard, we have no network of support there. He'd have to get work. We'd have no home or anything, just be dumped on the beach with all we own in bin-bags. Here they have a really settled home life and a new baby sister. It is essential to our total physical and mental well-being as a family that such racism is not implemented and we stay here together. Anything else would devastate the boys completely.

(Alia)

Given our societal structures and priorities, it would seem that black children of prisoners are in a no-win situation. However, it is extremely important to note that such children are not special cases but are part of a purposely oppressed section of society, within social power networks. To begin to deal with their needs would be to re-define power relationships and to begin to dismantle structurally perpetuated racism throughout society.

REFERENCES

Anderson, F. and Anderson, B. (1990) *A Long Sharp Shock*, Manchester: Free Press.

Balbus, I. D. (1980) *The Dialectics of Legal Repression*, New Brunswick, NJ: Transaction Books.

Buchan, H. A. (1985) *Frantz Fanon and the Psychology of Oppression*, New York: Plenum Press.

Catan, L. (1988) *The Development of Young Children in HMP Mother and Baby Units*, Occasional Papers in the Social Sciences, No. 1, University of Sussex.

Davis, A. (1982) *Women, Race and Class*, London: Women's Press.

Davis, A. (1990) *Women, Culture and Politics*, New York: Vintage Books.

Day, M., Hall. T., and Griffiths, C. (1988) *Black People and the Criminal Justice System*, Papers presented to the Howard League Conference on Minorities in Crime & Justice, Oxford.

Fanon, F. (1968) *Black Skin, White Masks: The Experience of a Black Man in a White World*, London: MacGibbon & Kee.

Gender, E. and Player, E. (1989) *Race Relations in Prisons*, Oxford: Clarendon Press.

Genovese, E. D. (1969) *The World the Slaveholders Made: Two Essays on Interpretation*, New York: Pantheon.

Gilroy, P. (1987) *Ain't No Black in the Union Jack*, London: Hutchinson.

Hall, S. *et al.* (1986) *Racism and Society*, paper prepared by Open University Press.

Hansberry, L. (1960) *Raisin in the Sun*, London: Methuen.

Kozol, V. (1968) *Death at an Early Age*, Harmondsworth: Penguin.

McDermott, K. (1990) 'We have no problem: the experience of racism in prison', *New Community* 16(2):213–28.

NACRO (1986) *Black People in the Criminal Justice System*, London: NACRO.

Prison Reform Trust (1990) *Report of the Immigration Prisoners' Project*, London: Prison Reform Trust.

Shaw, R. G. (1987) *Children of Imprisoned Fathers*, London: Hodder & Stoughton.

Part II
The response of society

8 The child, the imprisoned parent and the law

Richard Vogler

This chapter explores the apparent disparity between the approach adopted by courts in relation to the family life of children of parents who are at liberty and that adopted in relation to the children of imprisoned parents. The law in this area will then be set out briefly and consideration given to some comparable statutory regimes in other jurisdictions.

A child who is the subject of litigation in family proceedings is protected by a formidable array of statutory safeguards. According to s.1 of the Guardianship of Minors Act 1971 (GOM), the 'first and paramount interest' in cases involving the custody or upbringing of a minor is the welfare of the child. This so-called 'welfare principle' has now permeated throughout family law (Freeman 1983: 21; Bromley and Lowe 1987: 311–18) and in wardship proceedings, for example, it has become 'the golden thread which runs through this court's jurisdiction'. Moreover, in such proceedings 'the welfare of the child . . . is considered, first, last and all the time'.[1] By contrast, the rights and position of involved adults, the maintenance of marital relations, even the justice of the issue, all take a very subordinate position.

The recent Children Act 1989 reiterates the welfare principle in s.1(1), abandoning the word 'first' from the statutory formula as if to emphasize that all other considerations are marginal by comparison. Despite concern that this approach is merely a mask for adult-centred decision making (Maidment 1984: 150–1) and that it is fast losing ground to a 'family-orientated' perspective (Dewar 1989: 54–5), the principle nevertheless remains the judicial orthodoxy for English and Welsh courts dealing with the children of non-imprisoned parents.

In the international context, the welfare view is reinforced by Article 3(1) of the United Nations Convention on the Rights of the Child (UNCRC)[2] which states:

In all actions concerning children, whether undertaken by public or private social welfare institutions, courts of law, administrative authorities or legislative bodies, the best interests of the child shall be a primary consideration.

It is worth noting that Article 3 of the UNCRC refers to 'all actions concerning children' and not merely those proceedings which are focused on the children themselves.[3] Clearly, decisions in the penal process which primarily concern parents will have grave implications for the children of the parties involved and, it is submitted, are no less 'actions which concern children' than family law decisions.

Three areas of judicial and quasi-judicial decision making in the penal process will be discussed in terms of the 'welfare principle'. The first is the initial sentencing of defendants who are also parents, the second is the maintenance of family contact by imprisoned parents, and the third is the separation of imprisoned mothers from their newly-born children.

CHILDREN AND THE SENTENCING OF PARENTS

Historically, the parents of children have been given no special treatment by sentencing courts. Although a woman facing the death penalty could escape hanging if she could convince a panel of matrons that she was pregnant (Cockburn 1972: 129), the same privilege did not extend beyond the birth. The dangers of applying a double standard or of granting immunity to convicted parents have prevented the development of a coherent welfarist approach towards children whose lives are blighted by the sentencing of close family members. At best, the impact of a sentence on a child of the defendant is a peripheral consideration. It is a 'matter of mercy' (*Laurie*, [1980])[4] within the discretion of the court, but to be exercised only in extreme cases.

The 'normal' hardships occasioned to a child by the absence of a parent in prison are therefore irrelevant in sentencing. As Butler Sloss J put it in *Nihalani*,[5] where the children are not suffering 'other than any children suffer' when a parent commits offences and is sent to prison, their position may be disregarded.

Similarly, the provision of mother and baby units, the Home Office rules on separation, and the possibility of transfer to an open prison or remission are all equally irrelevant to sentencing. In *Ouless & Ouless* [1986],[6] a heavily pregnant woman was sentenced to five years' youth custody for a number of offences of robbery, committed jointly with her husband. It was argued on her behalf that a relatively short reduction in sentence would enable her (once remission had entered into the equation) to take advantage of the Home Office rules[7] which would permit her to keep her child with her in a mother and baby unit until her release. Continuity of relationship between mother and child could therefore be achieved by a fairly simple sentencing expedient. In the opinion of the court, however, these were matters for the Home Office, which alone could decide when the mother and child should be separated. The court therefore declined to intervene. Croom-Johnson LJ then went on to insist that the existence of a young dependent baby could, nevertheless, be considered in mitigation, but only as a 'fact that is personal to the defendant'.[8] The question of the best interests of the child and the importance to *him* of the relationship was not discussed by the court.

Again, in *Darby* [1986],[9] Lord Lane LCJ was prepared to admit consideration of the effect of the separation on only the mother:

> She is suffering under difficulties which many prisoners do not suffer, namely that she is not with her 12 month old child. The child has to be brought by relatives to visit her in prison, which is of course an added source of distress to her.[10]

This focus on the defendant may even imply that the suffering of the child is to be considered as merely a constituent of the deterrent effect of the sentence. As Lord Widgery LJ put it, in *Ingham* [1974]:[11]

> The crux of the matter is that part of the price to pay when committing a crime is that imprisonment does involve hardship on the . . . family, and it cannot be one of the factors which can affect what would otherwise be the right sentence.

The responsibility for the distress of the child therefore must be considered exclusively as a matter for the offending parent.

The harshness of this rule is mitigated, to some extent, in 'exceptional circumstances'. For example, in *Crompton* [1974],[12] where the support of a mother was denied to a disabled child because the former had also been seriously injured in an accident, the father was given a sentence which permitted his immediate release. A similar course was taken in the case of a man sentenced to twelve months for offences of violence where the wife had recently died of kidney disease, leaving a child suffering from the same ailment (*Haleth* [1982]).[13] In *Vaughan* [1982],[14] the Appeal Court substituted a sentence of twenty-eight days for one of nine months imposed for handling offences, on the mother of three unwell and mentally backward children whose husband was also in prison. All these circumstances, however, are unusual and distressing and do not affect the generality of the rule.

Predictably, the mercy of the court is more likely to be extended to defendant mothers who find themselves in this position, than to defendant fathers (Thomas 1979: 211–13) and the question of family repercussions is not usually considered at all when a deterrent sentence is called for. Moreover, even in 'exceptional' cases, the justification for a release from prison or reduction of sentence is rarely expressed in terms of the welfare of the child. In *Franklin* [1981],[15] Lord Lane argued that the sudden imprisonment of the sole surviving parent of four children would present the social services with a 'very great problem indeed' and the community might well be left with a delinquent family were he not released.

This reluctance to acknowledge the position of children is also a characteristic of both Canadian (Nadin-Davis 1982: 188–91) and Australian (Fox and Freiburg 1985: 488–9) sentencing practice. In the United States, the constitutional position of the child of an imprisoned mother was considered by the US Court of Appeal for the 5th Circuit in *Southerland v Thigpen*[16] and it was held that the right to be breast-fed by an incarcerated mother was outweighed by the 'compelling interests of the state'. This was the case even though the child in question had a high risk of diabetes which would possibly have been reduced by breast feeding. The Oregon Court of Appeals took a similar view in *Pendergrass v Toombs*,[17] and dismissed the idea that the child's right to associate with its mother could prevail over the state goals of deterrence, retribution, and the maintenance of security.[18] This, of course, begs the question of whether or not it is appropriate to extend deterrent or retributive penalties to innocent third parties.

In all these cases it is apparent that issues of deterrence and retribution outweigh all other considerations. Since the children are not party to the proceedings, may well not appear at court, and feature only in the small print of social enquiry reports, their future and welfare assume an insignificant role in sentencing policy.

THE CHILD'S COMMUNICATION WITH IMPRISONED PARENTS

The second area in which the welfare of prisoners' children is of relevance is in the provision of facilities for family contact. Article 8 of the European Convention on Human Rights (ECHR) holds that everyone has the right to respect for his or her private and family life and correspondence, except where interference is necessary in accordance with the law for the prevention of disorder or crime, etc. The European Court has consistently found that some interference with family life is an 'inherent feature' of custody,[19] but any unnecessary disruption would clearly constitute a breach.

This general approach is reflected in Prison Standing Order No. 5 which states unequivocally that:

> It is one of the roles of the Prison Service to ensure that the socially harmful effects of an inmate's removal from normal life are so far as possible minimised and that his contacts with the outside world are maintained. Outside contacts are therefore encouraged especially between an inmate and his family and friends.

Although this view is repeated in the Prison Rules 1964,[20] which call for 'special attention [to] be paid to the maintenance of such relations between a prisoner and his family as are desirable in the best interests of both' (Rule 31(1)), the detailed provisions are considerably more restrictive. By virtue of Rule 34(2)(b), the child of a convicted prisoner is entitled only to one 30-minute visit every twenty-eight days. The visit is arranged by the prisoner sending a visiting order (VO) to the prospective visitor and up to three adults and the prisoner's own children are allowed to come at one time. Although SO 5 (A5 & 24) requires prisons to provide 'the most humane conditions possible', facilities for children are often rudimentary or non-existent and the visit must take place within the sight, but usually not the hearing of a prison officer (Rule 33(4)).

However, the statutory 30 minutes is usually exceeded and visits of up to two hours are possible, depending on staff availability and conditions. In most prisons, parents are allowed to hold or embrace their children. Also, further visits are permitted at discretion, particularly where a family has come from far away. Prisoners (with an escort) may visit their children under 16 years of age in a children's home or foster home, once every three months, provided that there is no objection from the prison governor, foster parents, or local authority responsible for the home. Such visits may take place in private.

For the children of prisoners on remand and non-criminal prisoners (e.g. fine defaulters) the situation is considerably better. They are entitled to a daily 15-minute visit without a VO. The same distinction between convicted and unconvicted prisoners applies to written correspondence with the family. By Rule 34(1), an unconvicted prisoner may send and receive as many letters as he or she wishes, subject to conditions imposed by the Secretary of State. A convicted prisoner, on the other hand, is permitted to send a personal letter on reception into a prison and thereafter a further letter once a week (Rule 34(2)). The governor may allow a prisoner an additional letter or visit where necessary for his or her welfare or that of his or her family (Rule 34(1)).

The ominous reference above to conditions imposed by the Secretary of State is not directed primarily towards ordinary family correspondence. It is a residue of the previous much more extensive powers to censor and to interfere with mail for a variety of reasons. The restrictive regime of the period up to the early 1980s was the subject of severe criticism by the European Court of Human Rights in the cases of *Golder v UK* [1975][21] and *Silver v UK* [1983].[22] It was found to be inconsistent with Article 8 of the European Convention. Following these decisions, the Home Office decided to revise its standing orders and circular instructions to take account of the Commission's findings and the relevant regulations were published for the first time (Plotnikoff 1986: 67–8; Treverton-Jones 1989: 74–88).

The new Standing Orders provided for extra letters where possible (SO5, B7) and relaxed the censorship regime. The statutory weekly letter could now not be denied for disciplinary reasons (SO5 B21). Although, in theory, all letters may still be censored, outgoing family correspondence is not usually read and censorship at open prisons is cursory. 'Overlong' inward correspondence or an 'excessive' number of outgoing letters can, however, be returned under SO5 B14. The minimum one weekly letter regime envisaged by Rule 34(2) is also relaxed in practice and SO5 B7 specifies that further letters will be allowed subject to staff resources. A prisoner can also buy up to twelve cards with stamps from the canteen (SO5 B12). Moreover, governors have no power to forbid visits or correspondence from 'close relatives', such as the inmate's children.

Considerable disruption to the maintenance of family relations is always caused by the transfer of the prisoner to another part of the country. Indeed, the constant moving or 'ghosting' of a prisoner who presents a disciplinary problem can make visiting almost impossible. The situation is particularly acute for the children of women prisoners who, as a result of the limited accommodation available, are unlikely to find their mother located in a prison close to home.[23] In *R v Secretary of State for the Home Department ex parte McAvoy*

[1984][24] it was held that the decision to transfer could be reviewed by the courts and that prison authorities, when transferring, must take account of 'such rights as a prisoner has in relation to visits by his family . . . (etc.)'.[25] This is in accordance with successive judgements of the European Court of Human Rights to the effect that an unreasonable refusal to transfer could be an interference with the right to a family life established by Article 8 of the ECHR.[26] Unfortunately, the blanket justification of 'security' is almost certain to outweigh all other considerations (Treverton-Jones 1989: 140–2), including the welfare and rights of access of the prisoner's children.

The children of separated or divorced parents one of whom is in prison are in an even less advantaged position than those of parents whose relationship survives an imprisonment. Indeed, the imprisoned parent may have forfeited any chance of access as a result of his or her criminal convictions. Such a parent may not be deemed a 'fit and proper person' to have regular contact with a child in what is considered to be its own best interests. In *Sheppard v Miller* [1981][27] it was held that a father with a history of crime and imprisonment, who was awaiting a further lengthy sentence, would have little to contribute to the upbringing of a child who was reportedly unwilling to see him.

In *Watts v Watts* [1981][28] the Court of Appeal declined to intervene in the case of a divorced mother who refused to take her children to visit their father who was serving a life sentence in a semi-open prison. The court said that, where a mother was unwilling, in circumstances such as these, it would not be in the interests of the children to be taken to the prison. A similar concern at the effects of a visit to an imprisoned parent following divorce was expressed in *P v P* [1981],[29] and, in another case, 'an act of charity for a Christian family to preserve a link with a relative in prison' was not sufficient justification for a court to permit access.[30] In *Anon* [1963],[31] access was refused to a father imprisoned for seven years for manslaughter. There was a 'grave risk of possible harm' to the young child in seeing her father in prison conditions. She had witnessed the stabbing incident for which he had been imprisoned, and might be reminded of the traumatic event.

For a child to experience anxiety at the prospect of visiting a parent in prison conditions is natural enough. Sadly, the hostility of a separated or divorced spouse with day to day custody may convert this anxiety into a powerful weapon to deny access to an imprisoned parent. For such a parent, the likelihood of a successful access application is extremely remote. However, the existence of criminal convictions and the imprisonment of an estranged spouse is not an automatic bar to access. Indeed, in the case of *Re N (Minors)* [1975],[32] the view of the justices that visits to a divorced parent in prison would necessarily have an adverse effect on the children when they were old enough to understand the situation was rejected by the Court of Appeal. The appellant was in an open prison where facilities for children visiting were good and he was approaching the end of his sentence. Reasonable access was granted.

On the face of it, the general provisions for the maintenance of family relations by UK prisoners do seem to meet the relatively undemanding requirements of the European Standard Minimum Rules for the Treatment of Prisoners (ESMR). Rule 39 merely requires facilities for family communication 'subject only to such restrictions and supervision as are necessary in the interests of their treatment, and the security and good order of the institution'. However, Article 9(3) of the UNCRC goes much further by insisting on the right of a separated child to maintain personal relations and direct contact with both parents on a regular basis. Clearly a child would have difficulty in exercising such a right under the regime outlined above.

SEPARATING CHILDREN FROM THEIR IMPRISONED MOTHERS

This rather depressing outlook is mitigated, as far as newly-born and young children are concerned at least, by the provision in three UK women's prisons of mother and baby units. However, since places in these units are scarce, major problems have arisen with regard to eligibility.

Article 9(1) of the UNCRC requires that:

> States parties shall ensure that a child shall not be separated from his or her parents against their will, except where competent authorities, subject to judicial review determine, in accordance with the applicable law and procedure, that separation is necessary for the best interests of the child.

Unfortunately, the primary consideration in decisions concerning the separation of imprisoned mothers from their babies in UK penal institutions is not always the 'best interests of the child'. Rule 9(3) of the Prison Regulations states as follows:

The Secretary of State may, subject to any conditions he thinks fit, permit a woman prisoner to have her baby with her in prison, and everything necessary for the baby's maintenance and care may be provided there.[33]

This regulation was interpreted in instructions issued by way of circular by the Home Office Department P4 in 1983.[34] What is clear from these instructions is that the paramount consideration in the decision on separation is not the interests of the child but the length of the mother's sentence. Before 1983, children were allowed in mother and baby units up to the age of 3 years. Since that date, they have not normally been considered for admission unless they would attain the age of 9 months before the mother's date of release or by the date of her likely transfer to open conditions. They are not eligible for a unit in an open prison if they would attain the age of 18 months before the earliest date of release.

The assessment of eligibility is made usually by the governor of the holding prison and transmitted to the governor of a prison having a mother and baby unit (Black 1988: 143–4). Although it is good practice for the governor to seek the advice of medical, probation, or social service professionals, he or she is not obliged to do so.[35] The availability of places, length of sentence, state of physical and mental health of the mother, and her parenting capabilities are all crucial factors (ibid.: 143). However, it does seem extraordinary that, even bearing in mind the physical limitations under which the prison service labours, this decision should be made in such an apparently discretionary manner. The contrast with the careful consideration of a child's welfare by a case conference of professionals and the courts when a child is taken from a parent under normal circumstances is pronounced.

The question of decision making by prison governors in this area was raised in a particularly painful form in the case of *R v Secretary of State for the Home Department ex parte Hickling and JH (A minor)* [1986].[36] Dionne Hickling, the mother of a 4 month-old girl, was sentenced to twelve months' youth custody for fraud in April 1985, at the same time that the father of her child also received a custodial sentence. A month later, she was admitted to a mother and baby unit at Askham Grange where she was reunited with her child. The governor gave evidence that, after persistent disciplinary offences by Ms Hickling, he decided that her conduct was having a detrimental effect on the well-being and development of her baby and on that of others in the unit. She was therefore transferred to a stricter regime at Bullwood Hall where there was no mother and baby unit.[37] The child was received into the care of the local authority under s. 2(1)(b) of the Child Care Act 1980.

The baby herself was joined in proceedings for judicial review of the decision issued by her mother (thereby making the child the youngest applicant so far to challenge the prison rules). It was argued on behalf of the mother that the circular instructions were *ultra vires*, since the prison rules dealt only with admission and not separation and, in any event, the Secretary of State could not delegate his responsibility for such decisions, as he purported to do in the circular instruction.

The Divisional Court disagreed and found that, since the governor had given Ms Hickling the opportunity to put her case and to amend her ways and he had consulted a paediatrician, there was no possible breach of natural justice. The mother and child would not be reunited and no declaration would be granted. The decision, like that of the governor previously, seems to have been based on concern regarding the applicant's alleged parenting defects and the control problems she presented. It is difficult to escape the impression, however, that the latter predominated, particularly in view of the opinion of the paediatrician that 'ideally' the child should remain with the mother.[38]

The ESMR offer no guidance on the decision to separate a mother and child, merely asserting that, where mother and baby units have been provided, a qualified staff must be available (Art. 23(2)). The UNCRC, as we have seen, goes considerably further, calling for the child's interests to be the determining factor. Although this is clearly not the case in UK practice, nor are the facilities currently available to make it so, the *Hickling* case does establish that decisions under regulation 9(3) are subject to review by the courts. The governor must respect the rules of natural justice and consider (albeit among other factors) the welfare and interests of the child.

ALTERNATIVE STATUTORY APPROACHES

It is important that the British procedure is viewed in context. In almost all US states, imprisoned mothers are separated from their babies within forty-eight hours of birth. Only two states, New York and California,[39] have developed active programmes to allow newly-born children to remain with their imprisoned mothers (Schupak 1986; Deck 1988; Norz 1989).

S.611(2) of the New York Correctional Law allows a child to stay with his or her imprisoned mother in a prison nursery until the first birthday, subject to the discretion of the officer in charge of the institution (Deck 1988: 702). In 1973, in the case of *Apgar v Beauter*,[40] the New York Supreme Court held that the welfare of the child was paramount and that in general his interests were best served by his remaining with his mother.

A different view of the welfare of the child was expressed in the subsequent case of *Bailey v Lombard* (1979).[41] Here the court decided that the ultimate decision lay with the sheriff, whose reasonable exercise of discretion could not be challenged (Schupack 1986: 468–70; Deck 1988: 700–2; Norz 1989: 69–73).

California, on the other hand, has adopted a more innovative extramural approach. Under the *Community Prisoner Mother–Infant Care Program*, developed since 1978, a mother who is the primary caretaker of a child under 6, or an expectant mother, may qualify to serve her sentence in a halfway house, together with her children. The major requirement is that the mother should have a probable release date and a maximum sentence of six years.[42] Three such community houses have been established, but slow implementation, due to lack of funding, was challenged in the courts in *Rios v McCarthy* (1985).[43]

Other states have been prepared to develop less radical alternatives. North Carolina courts, for example, can defer sentence of pregnant women convicted of non-violent crime[44] and there are private task force programmes in Connecticut and Massachusetts (Deck 1988: 704–5). Australian solutions have involved the granting of permanent day leave to recently delivered mothers under s.29 of the New South Wales Prison Act (Hounslow 1984: 28). In Britain, James Anderton, the then governor of Styal prison, proposed immediate parole for mothers with new-born babies from the moment that they were fit to leave hospital.[45] Britten (1986) has suggested that children should be permitted to remain with their imprisoned mothers until school age and Black (1988) has urged the adoption of alternative forms of punishment, including daily prisons such as those in Sweden and Norway, extended use of community service orders under ss.14–17 of the Powers of Criminal Courts Act 1973, and the provision of further hostel accommodation. The extent to which these alternatives would meet the requirements of the UNCRC is of course open to question, but it is clear that the present UK statutory regime for the young children of imprisoned mothers and the procedure on separation fall very far short.

It is clear from this brief review that the interests of prisoners' children are relegated to a distinctly subordinate position, both in relation to judical decision making and in regard to the statutory regimes governing penal institutions. Moreover, it has been suggested above that there are strong grounds for asserting that this approach

does not conform either to the requirements of the UNCRC or to
the provisions relating to the maintenance of family life contained in
the ECHR. Of course the welfarist imperatives of the family courts
cannot be transposed without modification into tribunals and statutory
authorities operating within the penal area. However, that is not to say
that the the salutory influence of the family jurisdictions is entirely
irrelevant nor that a coherent judicial and statutory policy towards
unconvicted children based upon the precepts of the UNCRC is
beyond the realm of possibility.

NOTES

1. Per Dunn J in *Re D* [1977], 3 All E.R., 481 at 486. See also *Re KD*
   (A Minor), [1988] 1 All E.R., 577; *Re K* (A Minor), [1989] *Times*,
   4 December, C.A.
2. Adopted by the United Nations on 20 November 1989.
3. S.1 of the GOM refers, slightly more restrictively, to 'any proceedings
   before any court'.
4. Lexis Transcript No. 3599/A/80, 27 November 1980.
5. Lexis Transcript No. 5199/A/79, 31 October 1980.
6. 8 Cr.App.R. (S), 124.
7. See below.
8. *Op. cit.*, at 130.
9. 8 Cr.App.R. (S), 487.
10. Ibid. at 490.
11. 3 October 1974, unreported. Noted in Thomas, D.A. *Encyclopedia of
    Current Sentencing Practice*, c 4(2)a, p. 3021.
12. 22 July 1974, unreported. Ibid. c 4(2)b.
13. 4 Cr.App.R. (S), 178.
14. 4 Cr.App.R. (S), 83.
15. 3 Cr.App.R. (S), 65.
16. 784 F.2d. 713, (5th Circ. 1986).
17. 24 Or. App. 719, 546, p. 2d, 1103.
18. Ibid. at 717.
19. European Court of Human Rights, 4185/69, 13 July 1970.
20. SI 1964/388.
21. 1 EHRR, 524.
22. [1980] 3 EHRR, 475 (Euro. Comm.), [1983] 5 EHRR, 347 (Euro. Court).
23. *Childright* June 1990, 67, p. 14.
24. 3 All E.R. 417.
25. Ibid. at 423.
26. See European Court of Human Rights 7645/76, 2 May 1978; 8586/79, 10
    October 1980.
27. 3 FLR, 124, CA.
28. Lexis Transcript 21 October 1981, CA.
29. Lexis Transcript 24 July 1981, CA.
30. *Dean v Dean* [1982] 133 *New Law Journal*, 421.
31. *Times* 24 October 1963, p. 5.

32. 119, *Solicitors Journal* 423, DC.
33. Similar rules apply in Young Offender Institutions under s.22 of the Young Offender Institution Rules 1988, SI 1988/1422.
34. Circular Instruction No.51 of 1983, marked Standing Order Amendment No. 358 (1983).
35. Ibid., paras, 8–10 & 17.
36. FLR [1986], 543, DC.
37. See *Guardian* 10 August 1985, p. 2; 21 August 1985, p. 4.
38. *R* V Secretary of State for the Home Department ex parte Hickling, op. cit. at 556.
39. Kansas in 1973 and Florida in 1981 abandoned similar schemes.
40. 347 NYS, 2d 872, (1973).
41. 420 NYS, 2d 650, (1979).
42. Cal. Penal Code, ss. 3410–24.
43. No. 330211, Supreme Court, Sacramento (1985).
44. N.C. Gen. Stat. s.815A–1353 (1983).
45. *Childright*, October 1984, 11, 15.

REFERENCES

Black, D. (1988) 'Imprisoned children', *Medico-Legal Journal* 56: 139–49.
Britten, S. (1986) 'Children first', *Criminal Justice* September: 2–3.
Bromley, P. M. and Lowe, N. V. (1987) *Bromley's Family Law*, London: Butterworth.
Cockburn, J. S. (1972) *A History of English Assizes 1558–1714*, Cambridge: Cambridge University Press.
Deck, M. V. (1988) 'Incarcerated mothers and their infants: separation or legislation?' *Boston College Law Review* 29:689–713.
Dewar, J. (1989) *Law and the Family*, London: Butterworth.
Downing, D. S. (1989) 'The incarcerated mother's rights with respect to her children', *Columbia Human Rights Law Review* 20 (2):S.75–92.
Fox, R. and Freiburg, A. (1985) *Sentencing, State and Federal Law in Victoria*, Melbourne: Oxford University Press.
Freeman, M. D. A. (1983) *The Rights and Wrongs of Children*, London: Pinter.
Hounslow, B. (1984) 'Children and families of prisoners: convicted without a trial', *Legal Services Bulletin* 9(1):26–8.
Maidment, S. (1984) *Child Custody and Divorce*, London: Croom Helm.
Nadin-Davis, R. P. (1982) *Sentencing in Canada*, Ottawa: Caswell.
Norz, F. (1989) 'Prenatal and postnatal rights of incarcerated mothers', *Columbia Human Rights Law Review* 20(2):S.55–73.
Plotnikoff, J. (1986) *Prison Rules: A Working Guide*, London: Prison Reform Trust.
Schupak, T. L. (1986) 'Women and children first: an examination of the unique needs of women in prison', *Golden Gate University Law Review* 16:455–74.
Thomas, D. (1979) *Principles of Sentencing*, London: Heinemann.
Treverton-Jones, G. D. (1989) *Imprisonment: The Legal Status and Rights of Prisoners*, London: Sweet & Maxwell.

9 Prisoners' children

The role and responsibility of the prison service in England and Wales

Fiona Clarke, Tim Newell and Alan Rayfield

THE BACKGROUND

The task of the prison service as published by the Prisons Board in 1984 identified key areas for consideration in assessing responsibility for family ties.

> The task of the Prison Service is to use with maximum efficiency the resources of staff, money, building and plant made available to it by Parliament in order to fulfil, in accordance with the relevant provisions of the law, the following functions:
> - to keep in custody untried or unsentenced prisoners, and to present them to Court for trial or sentence
> - to keep in custody, with such degree of security as is appropriate, having regard to the nature of the individual prisoner and his offence, sentenced prisoners for the duration of their sentence or for such shorter time as the Secretary of State may determine in cases where he has discretion
> - to provide for prisoners as full a life as is consistent with the facts of custody, in particular making available the physical necessities of life; care for physical and mental health; advice and help with personal problems; work, education, training, physical exercise and recreation; and opportunity to practise their religion
> - to enable prisoners to retain links with the community and where possible assist them to prepare for their return to it.
>
> (Home Office 1989a)

This work is summarized in a purpose statement issued for the service in 1988 which states:

> Her Majesty's Prison Service serves the public by keeping in custody those committed by the Courts. Our duty is to look after them with

humanity and to help them lead law-abiding and useful lives in
custody and after release.

(Home Office 1989a)

Both pronouncements pay regard to the individual needs of prisoners in
a complex organization dominated by its duty to courts and the public.
Working with individuals and applying the rules to their needs is the key
component of prison staff's activity in achieving all the other functions.
Underlying our work is an awareness of the multi-faceted personality
of the prisoner and the consciousness that if this complexity of need
and expectation is ignored then the management of establishments will
soon become impossible.

The training of prison staff studies the motivation behind behaviour
and the relationship between the individual, his family, and his
environment. The actions of staff in the management of the prison
population are underpinned by an awareness of the family and group
relationships of an individual as central to his learning experience
over the years and critical in his approach towards his current
predicament.

The emphasis on the development of sound relationships between
staff and prisoners which has prevailed in prison life for many years
recognizes the importance of providing role models for prisoners
deprived of their autonomy by their detention. The significance
of Rule I of the Prison Rules – 'The purpose of the training and
treatment of convicted prisoners shall be to encourage and assist
them to lead a good and useful life' (Home Office 1964) – remains
a powerful influence on the work of staff.

Family contact is perceived by prisoners as being the most important
right they have in prison. A survey of remand prisoners' perceptions
showed that visits were consistently seen as the most significant
experience during their custody (Williams and Matthews 1983).

This dominance of importance is reflected in the priority prison
management places on maintaining visiting facilities, on ensuring mail
is processed as quickly as possible, on enabling telephone contact to
be developed, on arranging home leaves whenever possible, and on
preparing prisoners for their eventual return to their community on
release. The resolution of crises related to the above issues dominates
much of the day to day work of prison and probation staff working with
prisoners.

Some caution must be introduced into this consideration of family
contact. Many prisoners, perhaps the less adequate ones, need to
put across the idea that their children are the be all and end all

of their existence. Part of this is emotional over-investment and part of it represents on occasion an attempt to whitewash what is often a poor record of family relationships. The assessment of particular children's needs in relation to fathers or mothers who are in custody is often a matter about which prison staff need to be guided by outside information – from social services or the probation service. The increasing emphasis on throughcare in prisons will lead to clarification and identify areas for appropriate intervention and action. The White Paper *Crime, Justice and Protecting the Public* (Home Office 1989b) provides the stimulus for such work, given the automatic supervision for larger numbers of prisoners in the future and the additional emphasis on preparation for release this will entail.

The problem of separation from society for a prisoner is met by an effort from the prison service to minimize the damage such separation can bring about. Much of this approach concerns the development of opportunities provided for the prisoner to use time constructively and purposefully and includes encouraging the motivation of the individual to make use of such opportunities.

A different aspect of the problem of separation from society is the welfare of those who are left behind: family, lovers, friends. Something can be done to maintain ties through letters and visits, but these are limited and best concentrated where priorities are highest. Those prisoners with family responsibilities face these questions in their most acute form – how to go on being a mother or a father to children you see only once a month, or even less often. It is not a problem unique to someone in prison, but the additional and complicating stigma of conviction may rub off on immediate kin, and children may be labelled at school by staff or other children. There are inevitably financial problems, and the corroding anxiety about sexual fidelity that can burn through the strongest links in relationships.

There are no ready answers to any of these difficulties. They need to be thought through in each case, discussed with involved parties, and plans drawn up to face the issues.

One way of tackling these issues is through an institutional career plan, particularly concentrated on the prospect of release. Taking action in preparation for release is an important part of tackling the problem of separation. Part of that involves maintaining family relationships and commitments which undoubtedly feature high in an individual's priorities but not substantially in the provisions made by the prison service.

THE CURRENT POSITION

The current practice of the prison service in its management of the population recognizes the significance of the prisoner's family in a variety of ways. Because of the pressure of numbers and a historical legacy of establishments developed in locations which do not always reflect the importance of proximity to home, there is a tension between the recognition of maintaining such ties as easily as possible and the need to make satisfactory arrangements for the custody of large numbers of prisoners.

The local prison exemplifies best the significance of prisoners being located near home. The position of those remanded in custody for court appearances is often stressful and the importance of family contact cannot be exaggerated in the welfare of the individual. The right of unconvicted prisoners to daily visits reflects this emphasis. The majority of prisoners serve their sentence in the local prison when convicted and the atmosphere of such establishments, in spite of the worst physical conditions, the most overcrowding, and the least developed regime activities, reflects the investment such men have in staying near home and loved ones.

Training prisons and their resources

Once a prisoner has been allocated and transferred from his local prison, he is expected to take part in the training on offer at his new establishment. The prison service quite rightly places great importance upon each training prison making best use of its resources so as to provide a full and purposeful regime for its inmates. In the long run, such a regime will probably help the majority of inmates to make best use of their prison sentence. The hope is that they will return to society better equipped to face the problems of freedom and the pressures of normal life.

Unfortunately, there is little provision made for families. Training prisons are usually built on open sites, well away from centres of population, with poor means of communication other than by private car. There are good historical reasons for building prisons in these places, not least of which is cost. Attempts to build them in more convenient places usually meet with considerable public opposition which leads the prison service to deploy its limited resources in less hostile territory.

Under these conditions, it is difficult for families to maintain their relationships, let alone strengthen them. It is true that their visits are more relaxed and can last for longer than those conducted in local prisons or remand centres but the sense of psychological remoteness is too often reinforced by the isolation of the prison itself. It does not require much imagination to visualize the effect this must have upon young children.

Family relationships and the long-term prisoner

Most inmates serve sentences of less than four years. In 1987, out of 28,587 adult males in prison on 30 June, only 8,731 were serving over four years, of whom 2,159 were lifer prisoners. (Home Office 1988). It is no surprise to learn that the vast majority of prisoners return to their families within a matter of months. This does not diminish the trauma but it does mean that the term of imprisonment can be comprehended and realistic plans for the future made for the reintegration of the absent member within the family unit.

With long-term prisoners in general, and lifers in particular, this is difficult, if not impossible. Most relationships survive the shock of remand, trial, and sentence, but after that the future disappears into the darkness and hope struggles to stay alive. There is plenty of evidence collected after the Second World War to show how difficult it was for families to keep alive their hopes for each other when separated by war or capture by the enemy. The return of the soldier or prisoner of war was even more traumatic but at least he was regarded as a hero by society and those who received him back. He did not bear the stigma of imprisonment.

The problem for the long-termer and his family is how to be *realistic* about their relationships. Years pass and the family is subjected to all the strain of normal life with its gradual changes. People grow older, children grow up and go through the usual adolescent stages, they marry or get into trouble, but the prisoner sees only a partial view of things. Letters and visits, even telephone calls, can project a two-dimensional image of reality. Time in effect has stood still for the long-term prisoner. Within his own world, the trivial becomes important and the problems faced by his family are seldom properly understood by him. It is not surprising that in many instances marriages and relationships do not survive. Where they do there is a real danger that the prisoner is not treated as a full member of that family because he has not shared in the life and experiences that that family unit has experienced. Children and wives can be resentful and the man himself will be hurt and angry at the unconscious rejection that may accompany these feelings.

Visits

For the majority of prisoners, the most important events in their sentences surround the visits they receive from their families and friends from the world outside. The visits room is one of the most important places within any prison and considerable skill and tact needs to be used by all prison staff connected with it. In training prisons, visits can sometimes take place twice a month and last for up to two hours. Measured against a sentence of many years or life, it is not much.

Facilities vary greatly within the system. In modern prisons built within this decade, these are well-designed, comfortable rooms with crèche facilities and refreshment bars. Unfortunately, these are an exception. Most visits take place in overcrowded, smoky, noisy rooms with little space for children to play and almost no privacy. Until recently prison architects did not provide the kind of accommodation we now know to be necessary. It was not their fault; they merely reflected the priorities of those who commissioned the buildings who, in turn, reflected the views of the society which they served.

Visits in prison are inevitably surrounded with tension for both sides of the family. Those outside often have to travel distances to reach the prisons. The Assisted Prison Visits Unit in Birmingham co-ordinates the provision of financial assistance to families visiting prisoners. The scheme recognizes the prison service's responsibility towards prisoners' visitors. More prisons are developing, with grants from the Prison Service for running costs, visitors' centres where families can refresh themselves after the journey – but for many there are no such facilities and the waiting outside the prison is often uncomfortable, public, and demoralizing. Facilities in the visits room are sometimes limited and not conducive to privacy. The development of crèche facilities enables families to have better visits and for children to experience the time in the prison as not too stressful. For the children a visit to prison can be a frightening experience. Locked doors along the route to the visits room, mothers being searched, and the endless waiting, often after a long and tiring journey on public transport, all add to the sense of bewilderment that many children feel about the visit.

A crèche in a visits room is a way of enabling the mother to have a quiet conversation with her partner without constant interruptions from children, and of giving the children some fun. Mothers sometimes have to break bad news to prisoners or discuss marriage problems and it is easier to do this without children present. It is important for children to see their fathers during the sentence to keep up the relationship until the eventual release of the prisoner. Without toys to occupy them children tend to rush up and down the visits room between the tables disrupting visits for their parents and other prisoners who do not have children present. Prison officers generally agree that a crèche gives the visits room a quieter and calmer atmosphere.

The crèche should be a bright 'inviting' space, perhaps with pictures on the wall. It does not have to be big. Most of the children enjoy being able to draw, do puzzles, or construct lego with some help. Dolls, tea-sets, toy cars, and a garage are all well used. The children are able to wander in and out at will, and can show their parents a picture they have drawn or a lego model. On arrival they tend to sit and talk and then wander over to the crèche. It is important to have a volunteer in the crèche to look after the children and help them to play happily with the toys. There will always be the over-enthusiastic toddler creating chaos for the other children! There is a wide age range of children and many miss school for the visit. Older children are quite happy to relax on a bean bag and read books or comics. Many of them enjoy helping with the toddlers.

Crèches are not expensive to start or run. The success of a crèche depends on the enthusiasm and commitment of the volunteers, with the positive backing of the prison staff. The Butler Trust has recently done a survey of all prisons, asking them what facilities they have for children during visits and whether they need help or advice. The response to the survey has been very positive and a number of crèches will be starting in the near future.

Adults make a choice about visiting prisons, children do not; anything that makes the visit easier and happier for them in the way of a crèche should be done.

Isolated prisons arrange transport to and from the nearest railway station and there are a few overnight stay houses in some locations. In spite of these difficulties, most men receive their family visitors and regular contact is maintained but the odds are heavy and the pressure to keep the visit 'nice and bright' is felt by both. This inhibits communication and, unless it is addressed with the help of skilled counselling, families will inevitably drift apart as men and women become unable to express their true feelings.

Communications

Apart from visits, the main vehicle of communication for most prisoners is letters. In our society, the art of letter writing is declining, even among those who are used to expressing themselves on paper. Suddenly, prisoners and their families find themselves trying to use letters to express what they would like to say in person or what they cannot say on visits. Even with the abolition or reduction of censorship, there are inhibitions over expressing oneself on paper. The written word is a clumsy instrument in the hands of all but a few and once put down on paper it remains to console, baffle, or taunt the recipient without explanation. Much correspondence is wasted in an attempt to get at the 'true' meaning expressed in a letter. Many a visit is flawed as explanations are demanded and resentfully given. Distrust can be created simply by lack of writing skills in the sender and an overheated imagination in the mind of the recipient. It is difficult in these circumstances for prisoners and their children to communicate at all, let alone with meaning and truth.

In order to make contact with children less stark, permission is given to use unheaded paper in order to disguise the location of the writer. A key issue for families is how open to be about the custody of the parent. Some help can be offered to maintain secrecy of location if required. The issue of censorship remains a constraint for prisoners and families. Relaxation in lower security category establishments and now in some Category B prisons should lead to a reduction in inhibitions.

More readily used by families to communicate with each other is the telephone. The use of payphones in Category C and D prisons has now made considerable progress in aiding good contact. Access and finance arrangements are eased to recognize the importance of the medium. The development of phone use for remand prisoners has begun with an experimental scheme at Winchester prison and once that has been tested it is hoped to extend it to other locations. The needs of this group for ready, immediate contact are vital and already staff exercise discretion in the use of the phone for personal contact. Access to legal representatives over the phone has been available for some time.

This is one of the most important advances in recent years. Not only is communication made easier but in one small area at least the prisoner can be in control of his environment. Contact with home can be normalized in this respect at least. Without pay telephones, conversations can take place on the telephone in exceptional circumstances but they are initiated and monitored by staff. They usually occur during periods of crisis or turbulence and no matter how caring or sensitive the staff are, it is one more thing over which the prisoner has no control. Certainly, the telephone cannot be used as a 'normal' channel of communication. It cannot be used to convey the minutiae of family life, gossip, or affection which cements most family relationships.

There are opportunities for special visits for family purposes in prison, often assisted by social workers or probation officers. Such planned events can be very productive with support. There have been examples of imaginative occasions when this facility has helped prisoner and child. One tragic domestic murder in the setting of depressive illness left a one-year-old and a 6-year-old. A psychiatric social worker, a nurse, the inmate, and the 6-year-old met with a Senior Medical Officer in his office in order to enable the child to say to her father 'Daddy why did you kill Mummy?' Most experts in child care would agree that it is better for children to be able to formulate painful questions and exteriorize them in such a fashion. In cases less extreme than this such a process looks towards the day when there can be a resumption of family communication on a realistic and healthy basis.

Home leave provides the best opportunity for restoration of family relationships. Preparation for such an event can be crucial in ensuring a successful experience because often the tensions developed during the period of separation are exposed during the brief period of restored full contact. The expectations of both sides, prisoner and family, are high and rarely realized. The experience can lead to further anxiety and often to a breakdown in the commitment to return to prison with consequent penalties and recriminations. A more regular experience of home leave would ease this heightened expectation and contact would become more realistic, and contribute positively towards eventual release.

FUTURE DEVELOPMENTS

Regime development

Regime activities in prisons are developing in variety and in specialization in throughcare matters. The concentration on social skills and pre-release courses involves working with the prisoners in addressing the issues they will face on release, including those involving family commitments. More work is being done to address the issue of criminality with prisoners – drug offenders, sex offenders, violent offenders, and those committing driving offences. The effects of criminal behaviour, on the victim, the offender, and their family, are explored to face prisoners with something of the reality following their actions.

Future

One advantage that training prisons have is that the size of their populations is fixed and they move slowly through the establishment. Thus it should be possible to tailor individual training plans to suit individual needs. This already exists in part for lifer prisoners and there are plans to extend the principle to all long-term prisoners. The key to progress must be the ability to treat prisoners as individuals and thus begin to provide them with the training they will need in order to cope on release. We must help them to address their criminality and to examine the reasons why they offend. Such an approach will inevitably include a close examination of their relationship with their families and the effect of their criminality upon those relationships.

To develop in this way has major implications for the staffing of prisons and the training of those staff. It will require a reappraisal of traditional routines and activities which will be painful but necessary if the individual prisoner and his needs are to take centre stage in regime development.

Visits

More resources need to be invested in visiting facilities so that prisoners and their families can spend more time together working through their problems and strengthening their relationships. Even in training prisons, the visits room is poorly equipped and ill-designed with most of the unlovable characteristics of a mainline railway buffet. Most of them do not have the facility of a private area where husband and wife can come together to work out the problems of their marriage, if necessary with the aid of a skilled counsellor or welfare worker.

As well as providing better facilities for the adults, we must not ignore the children's needs. Separate play areas with qualified supervision are necessary to give the parents some peace but they must be close enough to the visit for the child to return to its parents for reassurance every now and then. Imprisoned parents may need help in learning how to play with their children and the provision of proper visiting facilities will play a major part in this objective. The visits room will thus form an integral part in the training plan of each prisoner where he or she can learn to put into practice some of their new skills.

Overnight stay

The need for overnight accommodation for families that have travelled long distances to visit is clearly established. The experience of such a stay can be supportive to the visitors. The Woolpack in Evesham provides the sort of facility that enables families to prepare for a visit to Long Lartin or relax after it. Families can use the centre as a home: cooking when they need to, relaxing in the lounge, watching TV, and the children playing in the well-equipped play area. Practical needs are only a part of the torment endured by prisoners' families. The opportunity to talk to someone who understands is often a rarity in a society which shuns not only the offenders but also their families. Administrators provide information about the prison but also about support in the families' own areas.

The administrators visit the wings of the prison in order to maintain contact with prisoners and promote the centre. After a visit to the wing by one, a prisoner commented on her warm nature and very soon his family were using the Woolpack. Seeing her later in the prison, he thanked her for taking care of his family – a relief he obviously felt, knowing the limitations of his own ability to support them, as he is serving a life sentence.

The Woolpack is thus now more than a roof for the night. The welfare of families is sensitively considered and provision is made for their many needs to help them survive.

The prospect of family visiting centres to enable families to be together for a weekend within the perimeter of the prison was raised several years ago. The practical and emotional difficulties of such a facility were such that the proposal was not pursued but, as the prison population gets smaller and longer serving, this plan should not be discarded. In the absence of the prisoner going home the arrangement of the family coming into the prison for a longer period would be the next best option, given sensitive handling and good preparation.

Telephone

The prospect of more ready access to telephones will ensure an easing of the dependency prisoners have on staff to resolve their problems. The ability to take responsibility for decision making and exercising choice are vital aspects of reducing institutionalization and maintaining and improving skills for use when eventually released.

Censorship

The relaxation of censorship in the future will add to the regular communication channels being more easily used. The crises arising from critical communications, news of breakdowns, deaths, illness, will have to be handled by the prisoner using appropriate staff resources. The prisoner will make the choice and thus have more responsibility. There will be a need for staff to ensure there is an environment of trust in order to be in a position to be approached by prisoners with such issues.

Home leave

Together with an improvement in the quality of visits must go a positive development in the use of home leave, especially in the final year of imprisonment. The present rules allow for short leave (three days) within nine months of release and terminal home leave (six days) within the last four months. (Pre-parole leave is also granted for those who are to be released under licence but one cannot legislate for that in any training plan.)

There are a number of suggestions for improvements. However, home leave must not be thought of as just a chance to be reunited with one's family. It must also be seen to be preparation for release in the widest sense. This argues for more periods of leave from Monday to Friday so that the inmate can meet with probation staff, potential employers, skilled counsellors, or local authorities, in fact any of the myriad agencies with which he/she will be dealing with on release.

Throughcare

The involvement of the probation service in supporting prison officers in addressing throughcare concerns is the developing relationship in many establishments. With more prisoners having supervision as an integrated part of the sentence this work will be more critical. More agencies from the voluntary sector could be involved in this work, addressing particular issues of prisoner need and working with families as well. The Citizens Advice Bureau can span the family members by working inside prison and outside. Relate also works across the boundaries.

Information

There will be an increasing need for the sort of publication developed by the Prison Reform Trust (1990) in its Information Pack for prisoners and their families. More material could be directly produced by prisons to describe their own operations and opportunities during the sentence for the family use.

CONCLUSION

The responsibility of the prison service towards prisoners' children is directly relevant to the task of looking after prisoners with humanity and helping them lead law-abiding and useful lives in custody and after release. There is a longer-term responsibility involved in ensuring that the deprivation of the prison experience does not damage unduly the children of those in custody.

There is an awareness of the importance of family ties in many of the developments taking place in prison regimes. There remains much to do to minimize the harmful effects of custody. More information is needed about the prison dimension and how that experience affects relationships between parents and children. The Home Office study recently commissioned in this area should provide more information upon which to construct further action in order to ensure relationships are maintained and to improve resettlement on the prisoner's return to the family.

We should look again at the concept of the local prison. If numbers in prison fall, either as a result of legislation or through demographic causes, then it should be possible for some prisoners to serve all or part of their sentences near to home. Priority should be given to those with family commitments. By investing our social resources in those in greatest need we can begin to break the circle of deprivation and prevent other generations from following the same path as their parents.

REFERENCES

Home Office (1964) *The Prison Rules*, London: HMSO.
Home Office (1988) *Prison Statistics England & Wales 1987*, London: HMSO.
Home Office (1989a) *Report on the Work of the Prison Service*, April 1988/89, London: HMSO.
Home Office (1989b) *Crime, Justice and Protecting the Public*, London: HMSO.
Prison Reform Trust (1990) *Prisoners' Information Pack*, London: Prison Reform Trust.
Williams, M. and Matthews, R. (1983) *Relative Preferences for Privileges Available to Prisoners on Remand*, London: Director of Psychological Services, Prison Dept.

10 Health, social, and educational needs of parents and children affected by imprisonment in Scotland

Dan Anderson, John Basson, Kay Blackstock, Tom Buyers, Angus Creighton, Kate Gill, Roisin Hall, Moira Maclean, Margaret McTaggart and John Pearce

Edited with an introduction by Ian Thompson

INTRODUCTION AND BACKGOUND TO CURRENT WORK IN SCOTLAND

For the past decade, a number of individuals and small groups have been concerned to find imaginative ways to work with and within the prison service in Scotland to address the needs of parents and children affected by imprisonment. Some of the initiatives reported in this chapter have paved the way for the setting up of a Scottish Consultative Group (SCG) which is seeking to co-ordinate these initiatives and to develop an approach to working with and within the Scottish prison service to address these concerns. The Scottish Consultative Group combines membership from SACRO and various voluntary groups, the Health Education Board for Scotland, the Open University, the Scottish Office, and professionals working in the Scottish prison service.

Two initiatives led to the formation of the Scottish Consultative Group:

i) The first was a scheme to provide toys and play facilities for children visiting a parent in prison and to humanize the reception areas in which children and parents meet within the prison. Diplomatic work with governors and the prison authorities, as well as the commitment to do something for children, opened doors to a number of far-reaching developments concerned with the well-being of parents and children affected by imprisonment. In this connection it is perhaps appropriate to mention in particular the work of the dedicated women, led by Moira Maclean, who started the TOYBOX scheme (see Section 1 of this chapter).

ii) The second initiative was that led by the Open University in piloting the use and adaptation of a number of their community education materials for parent education work with pre-release prisoners and their partners, in collaboration with staff at HMP Barlinnie and HMP Staughton in 1984. The success of this project in opening up new approaches to working both with prisoners and with prison officers indicated that opportunities existed and that new possibilities for work in Scottish prisons should be followed up. The SCG came into being in an attempt to meet a number of the needs which had been uncovered by both these pilot projects.

The remit of the SCG was defined by its members, drawn from the groups mentioned above, and was approved by the Scottish Office. This has meant both 'political' support and active participation on the SCG from the Prisons Division. The remit and agreed initial objectives of the SCG are as follows:

Remit of the Scottish Consultative Group

a To seek ways of building on the OU Report *Prisons, Parents and Children*, and to develop appropriate methods and educational resources to facilitate family relationships groups 'to ease prisoners back into their families'.

b To explore appropriate structures for the formation of family groups inside and outside prison.

c To establish the appropriate channels for communication within the Scottish Prisons Service about education and training relevant to promoting better relationships between prisoners and their families

Initial objectives of the Scottish Consultative Group

i To get the OU Report *Prisons, Parents and Children* better known. To seek permission to circulate it to all prison governors for comment, and to elicit information about what is already being done. To ensure that what was learned in the pilot use of the Open University materials in prisons is not lost, and to avoid 'reinventing the wheel'.

ii To seek ways to get acceptance of outsider involvement in the provision of support to prisoners and their families, in co-operation with prisons staff in such educational initiatives.

iii To review the suitability of available educational materials, for example, from the Open University, Scottish Health Education Group, and other sources, both for prisoner education and for the professional development of prisons staff.

iv To explore avenues for doing 'consumer' research on available educational materials and needs of prisoners and their families, (for example, by monitoring the Barlinnie pilot scheme).

v To provide a focus for enquiries related to educational resources available: training, health information, family well-being, etc., thus providing support for those working with prisoners and their families.

vi To explore with the Scottish prison service whether the SCG could provide support for professional development for staff, for example training for trainers and training for those working with prisoners and their families in a range of skills and expertise.

A great deal has happened in Scottish prisons since 1985, and there have been most encouraging developments in the area of policy, service provision, and training. The SCG has perhaps contributed in part to some of these changes, by exerting some influence on the thinking of policy makers in the Scottish Office, by the training programmes which have been run for a wide range of staff in the prison service (for example, on drugs, AIDS and sexuality, counselling and helping skills and groupwork skills), and by specific initiatives of the kind discussed in this chapter, namely:

1 The TOYBOX scheme
2 The Open University parent education initiative
3 Staff participation and training
4 Training video and training notes: *'Do they forget?'*
5 Barlinnie: family relationships groups and families days
6 Information directory: *Families Visiting Scottish Prisons*
7 Edinburgh: information services to prisoners and their families
8 *Custody and Care* – possibilities for the future

1 TOYBOX SCHEME

The provision for play in prisons in Scotland began when Moira Maclean, a voluntary prison visitor, saw how effectively a few toys and a friendly presence could help reduce the anxiety of the children in a prison setting – usually when visiting fathers. Their visits became, through the children's play, a more relaxed and positive time for all the family. The benefits also extended to the prison officers, their responsibilities for discipline and security being more easily carried out without the children running up and down and generally behaving in a disruptive fashion.

The Saughton prison initiative began in 1976. It attracted attention from the authorities and paved the way for a similar endeavour in Barlinnie. The two projects ran on similar lines – Saughton operating for an hour each Saturday and Sunday throughout the year for the children of sentenced prisoners, and Barlinnie operating on the weekdays in the waiting-room. Sadly in 1984 the Barlinnie project had to be temporarily disbanded. The Saughton project continued to run in its original form as a toy library. A walk-in cupboard was provided from which the children borrowed toys, returned to the tables where they were visiting their fathers and played there. In 1988 the prison authorities in Saughton set aside an area outside the cupboard as a play area. This marked a significant change in the project. TOYBOX was adopted as the name. In Barlinnie the facility was reintroduced with much co-operation from the prison authorities and several volunteers. Both projects continue to be serviced by women volunteers only.

At Saughton the activities of TOYBOX are steadily expanding. There are now twenty volunteers actively providing play in four-hour sessions on three days a week. An average of twenty children use the facility. Further sessions are planned. Children may take the toys to their parents, stay in the play area, or do both. Volunteers encourage children to involve parents with the toys, for example: 'Go and show your Dad the car/jigsaw/dolly.'

At Barlinnie the scope for expansion will continue to be limited until the new accommodation is ready. Tentative talks with TOYBOX have begun in other prisons, while other agencies (WRVS) provide opportunities for play in prisons elsewhere.

In 1988 TOYBOX gained first prize in the Post Office Carnegie Scheme. Since then, further funds have followed from the BBC 'Children in Need' and the Mugdock Trust. Needless to say, these developments in Saughton and Barlinnie would not have been possible without the full co-operation of the prison authorities there. There is hope that with the new dispensation further opportunities will open up in the coming year at other Scottish prisons.

2 OPEN UNIVERSITY PARENT EDUCATION INITIATIVE

The original focus of this Open University project was rather more on the needs of parents in prison than on the children affected by their imprisonment. The Prisons Department and governors concerned were convinced by a number of prison teachers and voluntary workers of the value of parent education as an important component of preparation for release into the community. The eventual wider focus of the SCG to include work aimed at the parents outside (e.g. support groups for wives of prisoners) and at the children themselves (e.g. the improvement of visiting and play facilities) was a natural development of this project.

The formation of the SCG was inspired in part at least by the success of the first projects as evidence of what could be achieved by a type of collaboration between prison officers, teachers and other professionals, voluntary workers, and an external educational institution (the Open University). Publication of the OU report *Prisons, Parents and Children* in 1985 attracted attention to these successful projects, including funding support from the Scottish Health Education Group for the SCG.

The use of the OU materials in Barlinnie and Saughton prisons proved to be a most instructive means for promoting a new type of collaborative activity in prisons. The overwhelming impression from the report is of the importance of participation and sharing in the activities for every one of the collaborators involved, not least the prisoners themselves. While the Open University materials used (*The Pre-School Child* and *Family Relationships*) were not ideal for the purpose, being designed around the day-to-day presence of children to observe and interact with, they had one great advantage as compared with other possible learning materials. OU community education packs and courses are all designed to provide a framework for group learning and support rather than as sources of authoritative information designed to tell individuals how to be healthy, how to have a balanced diet, or – as in this case – how to raise their children properly. This approach worked well from the point of view of bringing the prisoners themselves fully into the collaboration. As one of the external evaluators of the first projects commented:

> what really attracted the men to the course was not its content, but the opportunity it provided to express themselves. It gave them an opportunity to articulate their own thoughts, feelings, problems and ideas. The expressive benefits were more important than the content benefits: (as one prisoner said) 'the group represents a family situation for me – warmth, acceptance, support and an opportunity to be myself'.
>
> (Open University 1985: 34)

It would be difficult to articulate the aims of these OU materials better and this approach undoubtedly helped to overcome their more obvious disadvantages – a possible middle-class 'up-market' bias and above all their dependence on regular contact with children in order to obtain full benefit from the kind of reflection and discussion they seek to promote.

The enthusiasm and ingenuity of the first tutors in overcoming these problems was an essential key element in the partnership. The fruitful use made of such contacts as were available during visits led to much encouraging growth in awareness and sensitivity on the part of the fathers involved. One father showed an external evaluator a drawing by his son and proceeded to offer a sensitive interpretation of the insight it had given him into the child's feelings about his need for 'a secure and loving family. . . . The prisoner . . . would not previously have given thought to a child's drawing. His sensitivity is revealed in his interpretation. He views himself as having reached an understanding of this child's feelings and needs' (Open University 1985: 31).

Apart from the benefits of this pilot project for the principal clients, the prisoners, an extremely interesting and valuable spin-off was the involvement of prison officers. In spite of the many disruptive events of the intervening years, enthusiasm for this quite new area of staff development has been maintained. The foundation of trust and collaboration involved and developed in this project has undoubtedly been a major feature in facilitating the on-going work of the Scottish Consultative Group.

3 STAFF PARTICIPATION AND TRAINING

The family relations groups at HMP Barlinnie, as described elsewhere in this chapter, provided a stimulus for the development of the Consultative Committee and its work. Run by a tutor in the prison's education department, the success of these groups raised several issues about the participation and training of prison officers in these and other groups.

The first issue concerned the role of the prison officer. The May Committee (Home Office 1979) defined this role in the context of 'positive custody' and gave support to the idea of officers working with inmates on their problems. However, until the late 1980s the training of prison officers in Scotland had more to do with issues of discipline and security than with the interpersonal and group skills necccessary for casework or groupwork. In this context there had been initial unease when management suggested that a prison officer should be present at the family relations groups to provide security cover and to gather experience. As inmates often revealed quite personal problems in group sessions, sometimes with considerable emotion, it was felt by those leading the groups that the presence of an untrained officer in a group could be counterproductive. This viewpoint was reinforced when a pilot group run under these conditions was disadvantaged by the highly directive manner of the prison officer. The experience of the group programmes run by two officers in HMP Cornton Vale, the Scottish women's prison, however, demonstrated that, under the right conditions, discipline staff could become highly effective group leaders.

The second issue was to identify the components of such success. The Cornton Vale programmes for women prisoners had been developing in their current form since 1986 and several important factors had emerged. These included the necessity for the selection of appropriate volunteers from staff, the provision of theoretical and practical training in groupwork skills, group dynamics, and ongoing support; and input from other professionals, such as psychologists and social workers. Finally, the active interest and support of all levels of management had been seen in a number of settings to be of fundamental importance to both officers and the group. It was observed, for example, that no amount of knowledge of group dynamics could overcome the problems of a group whose leaders varied according to the vagaries of an external shift system.

The third issue concerned the development of training initiatives. The revised training for new recruits to the Scottish prison service in 1988 gave, for the first time, a high priority to the need for the acquisition of interpersonal skills. This enabled new officers to receive both practical and theoretical training in skills such as listening, assertion, defusing aggression, and other relevant communication skills for the prison setting. This training has been well received, but it is not designed to equip officers for leading groups, nor is it available for officers already in the service. Meanwhile the need for training in handling group situations has been noted in a number of initiatives in Scottish prisons. Some of these concern the management of small units to deal with particular inmate problems, for example those returning to circulation after a long period in solitary confinement, or those whose behaviour cannot be managed within the mainstream. Others concern the use of groups in the everyday running of the prison or groups for specific purposes such as the family relations groups, alcohol and drugs counselling, or preparation for release. Some officers have been seconded on to courses run by outside agencies, but the wholesale use of this practice can have disadvantages in terms of cost and availability of places or in terms of a limited appreciation of the particular problems created by the prison environment. Clinical psychologists providing services to the Scottish prisons on a sessional basis are increasingly being asked for assistance in the design, training, support, and evaluation of local group programmes. To date, however, such work is being done on the basis of local initiatives and lacks the central co-ordination which could develop the training more effectively.

4 TRAINING VIDEO AND TRAINING NOTES: 'DO THEY FORGET?'

Two branches of work led to the making of a training video in which the partners of prisoners discussed their feelings and the problems they encountered as prisoners' families. The first was Margaret McTaggart's work with prisoners' wives and families, originally with the Families Outside group which later became integrated with SACRO Strathclyde. The second was the work being done in the education unit at HMP Barlinnie in Glasgow, where Kay Blackstock had for some years been organizing courses for the men in 'Family Relationships'.

Members of the SCG were invited to attend the prison course in order to highlight the families' own perspective. It was felt that the men did not want to face realistically the problems the women were having and through this the idea of making a video of the women's views emerged. Three of the women, who were receiving support from SACRO Family Services, agreed to be filmed and talk of their experience of 'dismemberment'. (The statements included in the video script were very low-key compared to some of the horrendous acts of harassment that the women actually described, but which they were reluctant to relate direct to camera.)

The video was made on a shoe-string budget, in one take with no rehearsals. This accounts for the spontaneity and genuine feeling that the women put across. An officer from Barlinnie supplied the equipment and shot the video in his own time. Although it had originally been intended that the video be used in the family relationships courses, this officer maintained that listening to the women had been a learning experience for him and suggested that the film could also be used in officer training. To date it has been used in five prisons, at the prison service training college, by social work departments and family support groups.

To allow for free flow of conversation, the women were not confined to speaking about specific subject matter. As a result each individual interview could stand on its own for training purposes. However, several important issues emerged as each woman spoke, common to all three of them:

- the shock of being left alone or at the nature of the crime;
- the resentment and isolation they felt;
- the anger and bitterness towards the men: 'I could have killed him'.

One woman blamed 'the system'.

Financial problems were high on the list. The immediate drop in income was difficult to cope with. They felt the men were selfish, making demands for money, sports gear, etc. As women became the breadwinners and more independent this was seen as a potential problem when the men were released.

What emerged from the interviews with the women was a consistent story of how the problems they faced, particularly trying to cope with supporting the children without the support of their fathers, had disturbing effects on the children. Often children, especially boys, were undisciplined. This caused problems at school. There was worry over what to tell the children and sometimes the children had enormous responsibilities placed upon them: 'You're the man of the house now.'

The women expressed feelings of depression and loneliness in the film but said that they hid these feelings from the men and their families. They were unwilling to discuss these feelings with others because they feared the loss of approval of friends and neighbours. The general impression they received from all sides was that they 'should' be able to cope.

The end of the sentence and the man's release was viewed with mixed feelings. In spite of long periods of anticipation, the women were worried about how the partners would adjust to the situation. The women recognized that they would have to rearrange their lives once more. Having developed coping mechanisms, they realized that they might be unwilling to relinquish them. They needed time and space to get to know one another again. One woman said that home leave should take place much earlier and throughout the sentence to enable the men to take part in decision making within the family. This would alleviate many of the problems the family have at present when the man re-enters the household.

There were difficulties for the fathers, adjusting to living with the demands of children. Children too had to adjust to having a strange man in the home, making demands of them and expecting obedience. These issues were frequent sources of difficulties and conflict. The women often felt torn between their loyalty to their menfolk and the need to protect the children from unreasonable demands.

The men's reaction to the film was mixed: initially stunned or on the defensive, but after some discussion the response was often very positive. There were comments such as 'If I had known my wife felt like that maybe we would still be together'. One prisoner said that if the video was shown early in the sentence it would help relationships.

People working in the offender field agree that reinforcing ties with the family, which provides a support network, will aid the successful integration back into society. The value of good parenting should not be underestimated, as Mario Cuomo says: 'Ex-offenders who become good fathers may well be the most significant deterrent to the next generation's involvement in crime' (Mario Cuomo, New York State Governor).

There is a need to extend family relationships and parenting courses throughout the prison system. The initiative of Barlinnie, allowing the women and children to participate in the family relationships course within the prison, should be more publicly welcomed in the hope that other establishments may be encouraged to follow suit.

5 BARLINNIE: FAMILY RELATIONSHIPS GROUPS AND FAMILIES DAYS

In HM Prison Barlinnie, members of the education staff have been running a group called 'Family Relationships' since 1983. The following is a brief account of this iniative.

Initially, as described in Section 2, the Open University courses were used to help the men become more aware of appropriate parenting, but, as time went on and the families were being discussed at length, it was realized that women and children should have a part too – the women in order to look at the issues of relationships along with their partners and the children to have a chance of 'bonding' more with their fathers. Various suggestions were made and finally in 1988 the staff were allowed to initiate Families Days. So far, five have been held:

March 1988	Afternoon only	(No officer)
November 1988	Afternoon only	(No officer)
June 1989	Lunch and afternoon	(Officer present who had participated in group)
December 1989	Whole day	(Officer present who had participated in group)
February 1990	Whole day	(Officer from group plus case worker)

The families' expenses were paid, no matter how far they travelled and latterly lunch was provided.

The day (or half day at the beginning) was never intended to be simply another visit. Initially, it was held in the rather cramped quarters of the education unit. Toy library ladies looked after the children while the partners were given questionnaires (mostly from the Open University family relationships pack) to help them focus on their feelings, to be straight with one another, and to feel totally safe about anything they said. Education staff, a prison psychologist, and either a social worker or officer worked with the groups, circulating and facilitating the inevitable discussions. Each family had their own little table and until the last meeting there were no security staff present. Even in the last group, when this was requested, the case-worker acting as observer (a senior officer appointed in each hall to look after the social problems of prisoners) was allowed to wear civilian clothes. The children could come and go as they pleased, checking out both parents as they felt the need, and in every group so far there has been such a harmonious atmosphere that the children have felt completely comfortable and at ease in spite of the strange surroundings.

In the meetings with the men beforehand (usually eight sessions of two hours each) stress was laid on the need to show feelings and how important touch is in all relationships. So on the day there is a lot of contact – hugging and touching and the children feel very secure.

The most successful meeting was the first whole day in December 1989, when, with nine families to cope with, the staff were allowed the use of the prison chapel. Some good quality toys were acquired and staff were hired from the Centre for Under Fives in Glasgow to help with the children, especially during the sessions when the partners worked together (in the morning). In the afternoon play workshops were held, teaching both parents the endless possibilities of play – and how, with a little bit of imagination, this need not be a costly exercise. It was most gratifying to watch how wholeheartedly this game was taken on – especially since little Christmas presents had been provided for the children and the week before it had been discovered that *none* of the men had ever before wrapped a present! Both parents and children learned to make all sorts of interesting things out of junk, but it was felt that the main gain from the day was the families' constant access to partner/father – being given his undivided attention – which most of them would not even have at home, never mind in a prison. In a questionnaire completed by both partners after the day, 100 per cent claimed that from 10 a.m. to 3.30 p.m. was certainly *not* too long and that they would have loved more time.

The staff realize that one such day is not going to totally reform most inmates' attitudes to their families. However, the initiative had at least shown prisoners and their families the possibility of being able to confront issues in an amicable way, had made them aware that their own attitudes can create positive responses in the children. On one of the Families Days, the opportunity was created for the first real bonding between a father and his first, newborn child – but he had to be taught how to hold the baby!

The one hurdle to be overcome is that of security. Until the last Families Day the staff had resisted the presence of uniformed staff because it was felt that it would alienate the children. However, there is increasing pressure to be more vigilant, even though there have been no 'incidents' so far. While staff would prefer to create the most natural environment possible, they need the co-operation of everyone in the prison and do not wish to antagonize other staff by their very success. They are now negotiating for the presence of a case-worker who would hopefully work on the group sessions with them, and then attend the Families Day in civilian clothing.

The one aim for the men both inside and outside the prison is 'presence, not presents'. If the staff can give them just one relaxed day when they see how good their families feel being around them it will perhaps help in the period of adjustment on liberation. For instance, in the partners' questionnaires the attempt was made to address many of the underlying issues that cause anxiety, such as the woman's growing confidence and ability to cope on her own.

Ideally the staff involved would also like to have a twelve-week programme in which the women could attend the group sessions more regularly. In the meantime, they intend to continue with at least four groups per year and at least one Families Day for each group.

6 INFORMATION DIRECTORY: FAMILIES VISITING SCOTTISH PRISONS

'Ignorance doesn't kill you but it makes you sweat a lot'
Haitian proverb

During 1988 the Scottish Consultative Group became aware of an information booklet which the Prison Reform Trust produced covering English prisons, entitled *Visiting Prisons*. This booklet provided useful information for families covering access, visiting regulations, and various services provided locally, either by the prisons or by various voluntary organizations, to ease the stress on the families during visits.

On looking at the situation in Scotland it was discovered that some prisons already sent out information to families following admission. Social Work Services Group and the social work unit at Staughton prison also had produced useful directories aimed at social workers, and a number of organizations such as SACRO Strathclyde and the Sunnyside Ex-Offenders Centre Coatbridge, had useful information leaflets and booklets.

It seemed clear to the Scottish Consultative Group, however, that there was a need to provide information aimed *specifically* at the families of prisoners covering *all* the Scottish prisons, and made available where the families were most likely to need this information, such as in social work local area offices, the courts, DSS offices, lawyers' offices, as well as in the prison visiting areas.

Rather than having a national booklet as in England, the Scottish Consultative Group came up with the idea of individual leaflets for each prison produced to a standard A size, which would both provide for the needs of the families visiting individual prisons and also be useful as a kind of directory when provided as complete sets to various organizations with regional or national interests. The Scottish Health Education Group was able to offer to cover the cost of producing the leaflets, and also suggested (albeit without a prize!) a 'competition' for the best cover illustration for the leaflets. Over the past year members of the Scottish Consultative Group have been in touch with each of the social work units in the Scottish prisons, who have almost all responded by producing information for individual leaflets, with the approval of their respective prison governors. (Sadly, no one in the prisons was inspired to produce a suitable cover illustration.)

There were felt to be various advantages to the Scottish version of this information for the families. Leaflets can easily be adapted to meet local changes, and the provision of high quality 'originals' on up-to-date equipment by SHEG allows individual prisons to 'top up' the amounts of their leaflets. Also important is the fact that SHEG's backing of the Scottish Consultative Group over these leaflets makes the leaflets more acceptable to organizations which might otherwise be reluctant to provide space for them.

The Scottish Consultative Group with its remit to help families of prisoners is delighted to be able to 'plug a gap' where ignorance of some basic information at a crisis point for Scottish families could lead to tears as well as sweat.

7 EDINBURGH: INFORMATION SERVICES TO PRISONERS AND THEIR FAMILIES

There are several initiatives at HM Prison Edinburgh, Staughton, which have a bearing on family relationships, and are intended to improve communications between inmates and their families, and ease access for families to prisons for visiting.

Payphones

i) Conditions of access: all prisoners are permitted access apart from prisoners in special security categories, and the untried.

The telephone is switched on in halls at specified times during the morning, afternoon, and evening sessions. Prisoners are permitted to withdraw up to £4 per week from the canteen in tenpence pieces for telephone, and permitted a maximum of £5 in their personal possession at any one time. Telephones have been in use in Edinburgh prison for the past three years.

ii) Problems: making of threatening or abusive phone calls; ability to charge calls to private numbers; direct access to Prisons Department, ministers, media; ability to organize criminal deals or drugs infiltration into prison; and security implications. All have to be recognized and dealt with as far as possible.

iii) Advantages: prisoners are able to exercise personal responsibility and influence over relationships; maintenance of family network; immediacy of information; lessening of areas of possible contention or confrontation with staff; freeing of discipline and social work staff to develop other areas of work which are more effective and meaningful.

Special Escorted Leave scheme (SEL)

i) History: the SEL scheme evolved in the early 1970s from initial requests by works staff to take their long-term prisoner passmen to football matches or events of special interest in the city. These outside visits were extended, due to the success of the initial experiment, to permit staff on a voluntary basis to escort long-term prisoners serving over five years and situated in Forth and Pentland Halls on visits to home/family addresses. At present there are ninety prisoners who actively participate in the scheme, and escorts are drawn from a range of prison staff including chaplains, teachers, nursing, clerical, and works officers as well as prison visitors. It was recognized from the outset that these visits afforded long-term prisoners the ability to maintain family relationships more realistically. The SEL scheme is now resourced for all prisoners qualifying for inclusion to be escorted to their homes once per quarter by prison officers as official paid duty.

ii) Future plans: it is intended to introduce a rostered SEL scheme shortly which more appropriately recognizes the primary role of this prison. The new scheme will be a more equitable one, guaranteeing SELs for those who qualify, extending the geographical range of addresses to which SELs can be taken, and further fostering or enhancing relationships between staff and long-term prisoners.

Christmas gift scheme

The Christmas gift scheme has been up and running now for ten years or so. From the original dozen contacts in churches and schools, there are now forty-seven resource agencies and individuals, who contribute gifts each year.

Staff at the library receive details from halls of families who have requested a Christmas parcel and thereafter, as gifts come in, they are sorted out according to the requirements of age and sex. The gifts are either collected by the staff from the churches and schools, or are delivered to the prison. Once the parcels have been made up, they are handed over at visits, posted, or delivered locally by hand. Normally there is a fairly large surplus of gifts left over each year, so that the staff can make a 'flying start' on the following Christmas.

The quality of the gifts received is very good indeed, and the donors have maintained their interest over the years, which is very encouraging. Over 200 parcels are dispatched per year.

Prison visitors scheme

Originally known as Church Visitors, the scheme goes back to 1947 when the Reverend David Read back at his church at Greenbank, Edinburgh, after four years as a German POW, managed to persuade members of his Kirk Session to volunteer as visitors at Staughton prison, and it was one of those flashes of 'vision' which has borne fruit over the years.

These, of course, were the days when a prisoner, once convicted, was immediately 'disowned' by the family, and without newspapers, radio, and TV, lived a very lonely and isolated life. In these circumstances, the church visitor acted as a counsellor and friend and provided a ready made 'window' to the outer world during the period of incarceration and this relationship was valued by both the prisoner and visitor. Many of the relationships survived the sentence, and life-time friendships were established. Over the years, visitors were recruited from a wider spectrum of society, and, although they still mainly come from churches, the scheme is now referred to as the prison visitors' scheme.

From the original dozen or so, the number of visitors in the scheme is now nearly fifty, and again, over the years, the scheme has led to the establishment of family friendships and exchange visits to the homes. With the recent addition of a governor to help the chaplain in the co-ordinating of the scheme, there has been a greater efficiency in the administration and the general running of the scheme.

HIV/AIDS information and education

It might not be obvious that health education about HIV disease and AIDS is relevant to family relationships, but anxiety about infection and sexual contacts in or out of prison has to be allayed if these anxieties are not to affect family relationships, as well as to contain the spread of infection when prisoners return to their families.

a) Problem areas: concern or fear that their men will catch HIV while in prison; concern or fear that their men who are sero-positive may not receive similar treatment to that in the community or may die in prison.

b) Communication: targeting the audience; difficulty in gaining access to those who most need help; effective communication strategies on a number of issues – for example, not to bring needles or drugs into prison.

c) Strategies under development/consideration:

i) The use of video and static display located in visitors' reception area – a joint venture with Lothian Health Board HIV/AIDS team. The video will incorporate strategies in both prison and community. Technical assistance on video will be given by Media Studies at Stevenson College.

ii) Talks to prisoners' families prior to the start of specific main visits – also joint venture with Lothian Health Board HIV/AIDS team. A standard letter would be available in advance to prisoners which they would then send out to their families.

iii) The appointment of a new drugs/AIDS worker in the social work department. The job description will include the provision of an information service on HIV/AIDS and support services available during visiting times. There is at present no suitable accommodation within the present visits area, but it is possible that a mobile office may be situated in the prison forecourt.

iv) Training of prison officers in generic counselling and helping skills and HIV/AIDS counselling – a joint initiative with the Scottish Health Education Group.

8 *CUSTODY AND CARE* – POSSIBILITIES FOR THE FUTURE

The paper *Custody and Care* was issued in March 1988 by the Minister for Home Affairs and the Environment at the Scottish Office. This detailed statement of the corporate policy and plans for the Scottish Prison Service (SPS) was described as a starting point, which would initiate a period of sustained and intensive development. The paper is presented under four main headings.

Task and Responsibilities of the SPS
Policy and Priorities for Inmates
Planning for Individual Establishments
Training and Development of Staff

In the first main section there is a six-point definition of the task. Two of these points are of particular interest in the context of the families of prisoners, viz:

To enable prisoners to retain links with family and the community and . . .

To encourage them to respond and contribute positively to society on discharge.

Within the main body of the paper, these aspects are considered in more detail. Means of maintaining family contacts are described and it is emphasized that as far as practicable prisoners should have the opportunity to meet their families under the informal conditions provided by 'open visits'. The norm envisaged (and currently practised in many establishments) is that a prisoner sits at a small individual table with his family in a relaxed atmosphere, with availability of light refreshments; such visits can take place at least twice a month. To facilitate family visits, the paper indicates that as far as possible prisoners should be located in an establishment within easy travelling distance of their home area and that this factor should be taken into account in the proposed development of sentence planning. A further means of maintaining family contact is the provision of pay-phones for prisoners and *Custody and Care* indicates continuing support and possible extension of existing provisions (currently almost all prisoners in Scotland have access to telephones located in their accommodation areas – the main exceptions are those subject to high security Category A restrictions).

In developing these concepts, it is stressed that 'open' visits and use of telephones are privileges which can be withdrawn if abuse occurs. It is also pointed out that improvements in contact between prisoners and their families, while beneficial to most, can in some cases raise serious personal problems for the parties involved. Such difficulties may require counselling, or the encouragement of improved social skills; it is stressed that counselling must be positive, realistic, and sustained if there is to be real progress in the prison environment, where peer group pressures and cynicism can be pervasive. In this context, reference is made to the social work units located in each establishment. Carrying out many of the functions performed by the probation service in England and Wales, prison social workers can form a bridge between the prison and the community outside. Recent developments in the organization and objectives of the social work units are mentioned and hope is expressed that these will lead to a more effective service, geared mainly to the needs of prisoners and their families.

Preparation for release is also reviewed in *Custody and Care*. It is stated that inmates should be encouraged to draw up their own plans for accommodation, employment, etc., after release, with appropriate support from prison staff. Pre-release courses are available in most establishments, with many of the prison support services involved and can be of considerable practical help to the prisoner. Mention is also made of the support available from SACRO and the Apex Trust, which helps prisoners find employment on release. Another aspect of preparation for return to society is the provision of places outside the prison, for example, in community care units, for prisoners approaching release. Home leave periods are also made available, either escorted or unescorted, and recently the SPS has issued new guidelines on this matter.

In the final section of *Custody and Care* staff training is reviewed and new initiatives are described. Since the issue of the paper in 1988 major steps have been taken towards provision of improved training for all staff with extension and development of the existing scheme for new recruits. As in the training programmes in England and Wales, much greater emphasis is being placed on interpersonal skills, encouraging staff to form firmer relationships with prisoners. In this way, staff can gain a better appreciation of the family problems faced by many inmates, can offer some counselling in liaison with the social workers, and can become more caring during their supervision of family visits.

The Consultative Group, with its broadly based membership, has been able to keep in close touch with various developments regarding the wives and children of prisoners which are described in *Custody and Care* and has sought to provide additional practical support. Several of these initiatives have been described above. They include help in the provision of simple information sheets for prisoners' visitors, encouragement of the development of counselling for prisoners and their wives, creating awareness among prisoners of the very real problems faced by their wives; there is also the provision of play areas/facilities for children of prisoners at visiting times, with supervision by voluntary helpers – the 'Toy Box Volunteers'.

However, it has to be recognized that maintaining good family relationships within a prison environment is no easy task. By its very nature, incarceration is a major disruption to the family, isolating the prisoner and forcing the family members to become more self-supportive and independent. Yet it is widely accepted that the probability of a prisoner turning away from crime on release can be influenced to a considerable extent by the support and attitude of the family. Prisoners with children often express deep concern about their welfare and seek to maintain contacts and influence as far as practical.

There are no easy solutions to this important yet seemingly intractable problem, but the Consultative Group is continuing to seek new initiatives to provide at least an increased element of amelioration. In addition to regular meetings of members, it promotes seminars where a broader body of opinion can be tapped and new ideas discussed. Areas which are being kept under review and where further development can be envisaged include the provision of visitor centres (or improvement of waiting facilities) where prisoners' families, often under stress, can relax and receive some counselling. This can be linked with counselling for prisoners and the Consultative Group has supported the joint counselling (husbands and wives) which has been made available at one establishment.

An important aspect of counselling is the provision of advice to prisoners on all aspects of parenting and this is an area deserving further effort. Extension of the system of home leaves prior to release is another area for development, allowing the prisoner to re-establish family life in a series of steps; provision of counselling before and after such home leaves is seen as an essential feature of that development. Other possible initiatives include the promotion of 'family days' within prisons, where families can spend a longer period in relaxed conditions with prisoners and the provision of extended family visits in special facilities under careful control, as has been practised successfully in Canada in recent years. It is encouraging that many of these aspects are described in the very recent follow-up to *Custody and Care*, entitled *Opportunity and Responsibility*.

REFERENCES

Home Office (1979) *May Committee of Enquiry into the United Kingdom Prison Services Report*, Command 7673, London: HMSO.
Open University (1985) *Prisons, Parents and Children*, Scotland: Open University.
Open University (undated) *The Pre-school Child*, Milton Keynes: Open University.
Open University (undated) *Family Relationships*, Milton Keynes: Open University.
Prison Reform Trust (1988) *Visiting Prisons*, London: Prison Reform Trust.
Scottish Office (1989) *Custody and Care*, Edinburgh: HMSO.
Scottish Office (1990) *Opportunity and Responsibility*, Edinburgh: HMSO.

11 The Northern Ireland troubles

Long-term prisoners and their children

W. James Hughes

This chapter is an abridged extract from an unpublished thesis submitted to the University of Ulster by the late Reverend Jimmie Hughes, chaplain of Maze prison, shortly before his sudden and tragic death. The editor is most grateful to the family of Jimmie Hughes and to the University of Ulster for permission to use part of his work in this book.

LIFE SENTENCES AND WHY THERE ARE SO MANY IN NORTHERN IRELAND

Her Majesty's Prison Maze has, as Cohen and Taylor (1972) wrote of the top security 'E' wing of Durham Prison, 'its own history, with a distinctive cultural tradition, a tradition which informs present attitudes and behaviour'. That history has been turbulent, with internment in the early 1970s as the government struggled to contain escalating violence, the burning of part of the prison, the 'dirty' protest, the deaths from hunger strikes, and a mass escape in 1983 when republican prisoners took over a wing of their H block and succeeded in breaking out of prison. Nineteen escaped, most of whom have been recaptured during the years since 1983. After twenty years and almost 3,000 deaths, and countless injuries, not only does the prison hold a disproportionate number of 'lifers' but also a steady stream of offenders continues to replace them as they are released. Seen in prison they remind one of Jemmy Hope's words in a letter from Kilmainham Jail in 1798:

> they were men who unthinkingly staked more than was really in them, they were like paper money, current for the time, keeping business afloat, without any intrinsic value.

Beyond them is the correspondingly high number of families, parents, wives and children especially, whose lives have been devastated with an on-going suffering, worse in some ways than bereavement, and for whom in many cases the only solution is to divorce themselves from the prisoner and sever all links with him.

Many in Northern Ireland society are not caught up directly in the tragedy, except perhaps peripherally, until someone dear to them or known to them is killed or injured. There may then be a surge of sympathy or revulsion, but for many this passes. In briefly examining some of the factors affecting the Northern Ireland situation it is clear that, while many people remain on the periphery of the tragedy, great attention must be paid to the fact that elsewhere in the province whole urban areas are under the control of paramilitary organizations. Such areas are generally working class. It is mostly from these areas that 'lifers' come, but not exclusively so. But despite the generally similar backgrounds shared by 'lifers', there has been observed a subtle change in the 'types' over the years. Men who came into prison ten plus years ago appear to be somewhat different from those coming in now. Men who entered prison in the 1970s have a perception of having *had* to do what they did. One of them explained it in this way:

> Our area was under attack, houses were strafed with bullets, and the army and police were struggling and sustaining many casualties. They appeared to be unable to defend us so we had to defend ourselves.

They are ordinary men who were drawn into violence, first as vigilantes and then as active paramilitaries. They nearly always responded to violence rather than initiated it. That is their perception and wives agreed with it in interviews in their homes. One said: 'If I had been a man in the same circumstances I'd be in jail too.' Most of them claim that they would never have been in prison if the government had effectively defended their areas. They are mostly deeply regretful about the past, and accept that they deserve imprisonment for taking life.

On the other hand, those coming into prison today can claim no such justification but are the children of violence. In prison in the early stages of their sentences, reacting to their loss of freedom and determined to limit damage to themselves, they assume a tough 'macho' image – truculent, aggressive, cynical, and at times exceedingly hostile, all of which appears to be a defensive posture. A posture it may be but there does seem to be a greater criminal element involved nowadays, and sociologists may well wonder why. If crime is increasing then this is only a symbol of a more profound problem. Shaw (1987) quotes Lea and Young:

> Crime is the end point in a continuum of disorder. It is not separate from other forms of aggravation and breakdown. . . . It is graffiti on the walls . . . it is streets you dare not walk down at night, it is always being careful, it is a symbol of a world falling apart. It is a lack of respect for humanity and for fundamental human decency. Crime is the tip of the iceberg. It is a real problem in itself, but it is also a symbol of a far greater problem, and the weak suffer most.

adding:

> and the weakest of the weak are the children of imprisoned criminals.

This description of disorder is appropriate and the hapless citizens of Northern Ireland will recognize how accurately it portrays those large areas where the troubles are concentrated. In such places there is a lot of the iceberg visible. Part of the ethos of such environs is an obsession with armed conflict and delusions of the glory of the 'struggle'. The onward progress of time has not been permitted to dim this vision. The crown of life is to die for the 'cause'. Resentment over injustices long since resolved and hostilities no longer relevant in the modern world are kept aflame, and every opportunity is seized to fan the fires of hatred. The 'godfathers', the informed, are obviously not so simplistic in their aims and they will use the idealist who imagines he is waging a just war until he is either killed or imprisoned for life. It is significant that neither the manipulators nor their families suffer as the exploited do. This short discussion of some of the background to the Northern Ireland situation is given in order to elucidate some of its especially difficult problems.

In Northern Ireland the prison population is significantly different from elsewhere in the United Kingdom because of the very high proportion of prisoners serving indeterminate sentences (Northern Ireland Office 1989). At the end of March 1988 there were 444 prisoners, or 26 per cent of the entire prison population, serving indeterminate sentences, and 92 per cent of these prisoners had committed a terrorist-related offence.

Why are there so many 'lifers' in Northern Ireland's jails? Northern Ireland has had its problems in the past, with oppression of the minority, discrimination in jobs and housing, and high levels of intolerance, but it is undeniable that government action leading to reforming legislation has been changing that. These grievances from the past cannot justify the murders and destruction which are a feature of life in the province.

Yet rank and file members of paramilitary organizations, whatever the aims of the leadership may be, perceive the problems as belonging to a struggle for domination and power. How do these organizations recruit, control, and manipulate such numbers of people to support them in various ways, or actively engage in paramilitary operations on their behalf?

Some of the answer may be found by examining the degree of choice the exploited may in fact have. Berger (1985) refers to Arnold Gehlan, a contemporary German social scientist, and quotes his description of an institution:

> as a regulatory agency, channelling human actions in much the same way as instincts channel animal behaviour. In other words, institutions provide procedures through which human conduct is patterned, compelled to go, in grooves deemed desirable by society. And the trick is performed by making these grooves appear to the individual as the only possible ones.

Berger makes the obvious criticism that 'the animal following instinct does not have choice, while the human being can say "No" to society, and often does. To say "I must" is a deceptive statement in almost every social situation.' Some years ago I would have agreed with Berger, but since coming to work as chaplain in Maze prison I am no longer sure that he is correct.

In Northern Ireland there may be found what are best described as 'subcultures' in which exist institutional imperatives alien from those in normal society. Most life sentence prisoners, and often their families, are products of this kind of society. They are not normally aware of choice. There have developed in Northern Ireland over twenty years of violence large areas where the norms of society do not hold. It has to be recognized, and thus far does not seem to have been recognized, that this is not merely a problem of deviance but a social phenomenon which has powerful implications. Here education and upbringing have difficulty in effecting the normal socialization of people. Violence, wild lawlessness, children running out of control at all hours, unloved, uncared for, and undisciplined, with many parents most of the time in drinking clubs, are reported by many caring agencies at work in these areas. A whole generation of these children has been lost to normal life in such areas, yet another is growing up which may well exceed the excesses of the previous one. The roots are to be seen, however unpopular it may be to say so, in our high levels of social deprivation, in which the gap between what might be seen as normal and abnormal society is ever widening. This creates conditions in which vulnerable people can be exploited by criminal elements. Children of fathers imprisoned for life who are being reared in such an environment, where already high levels of social deprivation are exacerbated by the fact of the father's imprisonment, are much more likely than children from 'normal' society to become involved in violent crime and follow their fathers to prison. It is a sad commentary that 'lifers' are still coming into prison today from these same areas. After years in prison, when they are prepared to discuss the past, most older prisoners, who incidentally were young when they came to prison, will echo a recurring theme of being 'led into violence'. There is no self-pity in that. It is disillusionment, and any resentment is usually directed at politicians, who are perceived as being the leaders. Conditioned to think and react in prescribed ways, and to feel part of a particular ethos, many of these men blindly followed their community's institutional imperatives. They appear not to have seen or understood the issues involved and the choices to be made. After years in prison, reading, studying, and so on, all this may have changed, but at the time of the offence they did not perceive any choice. As one of them recalled: 'In the seventies (1970s) I saw police and army being killed and I decided their hands were tied and mine were not. Where I lived we were under attack.' This man's family did not in any way approve of what he was doing. His youthful perception was that they were wrong, and he was doing what had to be done – responding to attack.

The republican who, all his life, has been conditioned to see one imperative, who believes that the crown of his life is to die for 'the glorious cause', who sees the need for armed struggle against 'the forces of occupation', to free and unite the Irish nation, is unlikely to be amenable to reasoning as to alternatives to violence however admissible. The fact that the majority of people do not want bloodshed, whatever their political aspirations, does not come into his reckoning. Similarly, the loyalist may know only one option, 'No Surrender', and a fight to the deaths of as many as it takes, or his own death if that becomes necessary. Neither contemplates any other choice. Their communities' institutional imperatives have determined the choice!

The norms of the wider society are alien to such groups. The upper strata of society are perceived as not having their problems and as riding on their backs. The fact that in unbroken sequence for twenty years well over 2,700 often inoffensive, harmless people have lost their lives in savagery and brutal atrocity does not seem to have been considered by them. They profess to regret the bloodshed but on both sides they admit no other course of action. Nor do they seem able to comprehend that they themselves are being used and manipulated by those whose motivation is different, and whose goals are different, from their own. For 'lifers' liberation from all this begins, not so much by their overdue perception of the moral issues, as by a process of disillusionment. That is why there has to be a constant recruitment of new men by the 'godfathers', and why no Northern Ireland paramilitary 'lifer' yet has become re-involved after release from prison.

Asked after thirteen years if it had all been worth it, one 'lifer' replied:

> My wife has lived her young life without me. My children have grown up without me. My best years have gone, wasted in this place. I had a skilled, well-paid job when I came here, and if I do get out who will want me now?

Disillusionment indeed.

Northern Ireland's society created the conditions in which these problems cankered, and it allowed them to canker worse. The separate development mentality regarding schools, sports, music, culture, and even language, created ghettos, and today's children in these areas are being conditioned to carry it all on for more years to come. In some areas, not only has law and order broken down, but family life as well. In twenty years of incredible viciousness and violence, displaying hellish sadism at times, a whole generation has grown up who have no concept of a normal, peaceful society. They know nothing but violence. Children too, at times, are involved in minor roles in acts of such violence. The violence is sustained by an ever increasing brutalization and deprivation, which in turn is maintaining the life sentence population, and which again in turn means families still caught up in the 'web of punishment'. Children are growing up with bitterness and hatred, without respect for law, without discipline and control, and they are candidates for murder and life imprisonment. As another 'lifer' said:

> I grew up in a prison, my heart and mind in bondage from my earliest days and neither the churches nor the state did anything to help me find liberation.

Berger is right when he dismisses Gehlan's submission by pointing out that people have choice – but only if he is referring to a normal society. What would Berger say of areas and populations controlled by gangsters and of children who have known nothing else? One wonders if perhaps Gehlan, writing in the immediate aftermath of World War Two, was thinking of the plight of the German nation under the Nazis? As one German churchman told me:

We were taught and trained by, in, and for the Hitler Youth Movement from when we were very small; we did not understand what was happening. It all looked so good that it never occurred to us to question Nazism.

These people were not aware of the choice that Berger suggests. Only the dissolution of the Nazis made them aware of this freedom to choose. In a similar way only a change towards the elimination of the social conditions on which discontent and ultimately rebellion thrive, and only the dissolution of the whole structure and machinery of terrorism, will emancipate those under domination. No change is possible while terrorism controls the institutional imperatives which govern people's lives. There has been a preoccupation with quantitative considerations as to how many people vote for this group or that, but the qualitative element is the more important. People adopt the attitudes they do for what they conceive to be very good reasons, and politicians may well need to give these more careful consideration.

LIFE IMPRISONMENT AND THE FAMILIES: THE RESEARCH FINDINGS AND THE ISSUES

The research findings described are based on interviews with both prisoners and their families and an analysis of their perception of their situations.

At the time of the study it was found that the numbers of children of life sentence prisoners in Maze prison were as follows:

Children under 5 years – 35 (of whom 32 are in regular contact with the father)

Children over 5 and under 21 years – 91 (of whom 70 are in regular contact with the father)

What emerges very clearly from the discussions with the families of long-term prisoners is an awareness of neglect, and this is in accordance with the findings of Morris (1965) and Shaw (1987).

In the interviews women spoke of the seriousness of the father's enforced absence for such a long period of time. The most damaging deprivation is one which affects the children most directly, and that is the absence of the father's contribution to his children's development. The fathers are, to all intents and purposes, removed from their children. They see them only occasionally, and then for short periods, and in extremely limited conditions. The child whose father dies, or disappears permanently through desertion, will grieve, but will recover and adjust in time to his loss. Bereavement will pass for such children, but the life-sentenced prisoner's child never comes to that state. The father is not there, but neither is he completely absent, so the hurt of the child never heals. It is small wonder that many of them have and create problems. Society would do well to look to its priorities and place the rights, problems, concerns, and needs of its children rather closer to the top. And the needs of prisoners' children must be included in the equation.

Clearly the extent of that deprivation will depend upon the character of the father and his perception of his parental responsibilities. If his character is weak and his presence is harmful to the children then his imprisonment will come as a relief to them, but it would be quite wrong to assume that because he is in prison he is unlikely to have been, or to continue to be, a good father. Women on their own, distressed by emotional and economic problems, find it extremely difficult to help their children. It is an unwise policy to neglect such problems when the result could well be a worsening continuation of them in the future as the children grow up to disadvantaged adulthood. There is found in these families what Shaw calls 'the Cinderella of penology, unrecognized, abused by the system, and neglected by those with power and influence'. Families of life sentence prisoners may become single-parent families for up to twenty years and therefore face acute problems for the whole time the children are growing up. Some of the wives made the point very strongly that they had committed no offence and should not therefore be subjected to humiliation. As one said, 'We don't deserve fifteen to twenty years of hardship, do we?' Some were found to be caught in the poverty trap, living on the borderline; surviving on the knife-edge.

Another factor which emerged from these discussions was that while families might accept some temporary stop-gap arrangement for the duration of a short sentence of days, weeks, or even months – the kind of sentences discussed by Morris and Shaw – a life sentence must call for more permanent arrangements. Hence the return by wives to their parents and so on. Life prisoners' wives are faced with very long-term hardship for offences which are not their own, and therefore it ought to be part of the provision of the state that facilities be provided for the small children of these women. This would achieve some very desirable results for the state. For instance, some justice would be done, and be seen to be done, to these women and some of their hardships would be reduced; the investment of resources by the state would be better targeted, and would be more effective; and the measure would provide an opportunity to help care for the children. In Northern Ireland the probation service, NIACRO (Northern Ireland Association for the Care and Resettlement of Offenders), and Prison Link do seek to come to grips with the needs and problems of prisoners, but the demands on the service are very great.

The Black Report (1980) recommended the injection of greater finance into welfare and health care. The recommendation was debunked by Patrick Jenkin and suppressed by the government with the result that the poorest have not kept pace, but have fallen further and further behind the rest of society. Since 1980 the policy has been one of 'cuts' and these have been implemented despite the urgent calls for improved welfare services. Where Black recognized the needs and wanted to end childhood poverty, the government reduced child benefit and abolished free school meals. The interviews indicated that where wives are dependent upon the social services, they suffer from economic hardship as well as the emotional stress caused by their husbands' imprisonment, and that this affects their children. It is difficult to understand how this neglect, and these policies, can possibly be defended.

Another area of concern that needs to be addressed is the extremely high divorce rate among the prison population and its impact upon the children. Many women whose marriages have broken down have said that the life imprisonment was the cause. One said, 'I would have waited maybe a couple of years, but not for life.' Another made the not unreasonable comment: 'I have a life of my own to live.' Added to all that, the deterioration in some prisoners leads to great stress and unhappiness in visits, which usually build up to the point of becoming intolerable, and the relationship breaks down. The major damage is seen to be caused by the long empty years, the loneliness, the problems of coping alone, difficulties with adolescent children, and, above all, the absence of hope.

There is also a need to consider the prisoners' wives' enforced celibacy. The implications are obvious, but some questions need to be clarified. Very few marriages survive a life sentence, but some do. If a woman has her children before her husband is imprisoned she will probably find fulfilment in bringing them up. If, however, the woman is childless when her husband is imprisoned, and she wants to have her family, can it be 'just' that her husband's imprisonment imposes deprivation of children upon her, the innocent party? In fifteen to twenty years when he is released that deprivation will be permanent. His sentence did not include this punishment of her.

Visits are never private – there is always an officer present – and so relationships can only remain superficial and may easily become strained. Prisoners and their families share the perception of Goffman (1961) that 'the phantom of security, and stalling actions in its name, can cause hardships for prisoners and families'. And nowhere is it more seen than in visits. Many families disliked coming to the prison for visits. They are critical of the whole approach of the prison service and complain of the aggressive attitude of some of the staff, their 'coarseness', their 'insensitivity', and of 'being herded like cattle'. One wife said, 'They make you feel as if you are a criminal too'. When children are present, they, naturally, become the centre of attention, and so it is difficult for the spouses to converse meaningfully. The present system appears to be too oppressive and intimidating to most of those who were interviewed. In Maze prison restrictions on visits are exacerbated by the necessary preoccupation with security. It has been said that the mass escape in 1983 has so shocked the administrators of the prison that security has become more of a fetish than a phantom. Goffman's warning is apposite:

> Every institution must not only make some effort to realise its official aims, but must also be protected somehow from the tyranny of a diffuse pursuit of them, lest the exercise of authority be turned into a witch hunt.

One would not deny sympathy to those whose responsibility it is to maintain security. It is rarely the devisers of policies who come to grief when their policies fail; more often the brunt is borne by those at lower levels who are tasked with implementing them. This perception inspires excessive caution which results in excessive pressures on families.

CONCLUSION

What this chapter hopes to do is, by examining the needs and problems of families of life sentence prisoners in a way not done before in Northern Ireland, to discover in what ways changes are necessary, and, if possible, to remove perceived injustices, and to improve effectiveness of this form of punishment.

What then do the submissions imply?

First, that, while punishment has traditionally had to be seen to fit the crime, retribution should not be excessive. Most 'lifers' came into prison in their teens and twenties (Northern Ireland Office 1989). In prison they have matured, become more politically educated, have become disillusioned with paramilitaries, and are no longer likely to re-offend. Thus far none have been re-convicted.

Second, that the best course for such men would be to release them as early as possible. They are actually needed in society because the children of these men are subject to the same influences and pressures as they were. The father at home would be likely to be a strong guiding and deterring influence. His children need him and he should not be detained from them longer than is absolutely necessary. It would be a serious miscalculation to underestimate the value of such men and of such deterrents. It may seem incredible to those who do not know the prison population, but it is a fact that many 'lifers' have been fundamentally changed. The influence of these men in their own areas would be immense and their experience and influence would help to counter corrupting propaganda.

And third, that the cost of imprisonment is so high that it should not be continued beyond the minimum time acceptable, but a higher cost is in the deterioration not only of the men but also of the wives and children too. There comes a point in a life sentence beyond which it is patently pointless. Society has imposed its penalty. The prisoner – in so far as it can ever be done with regard to murder – has paid his debt, and is unlikely any longer to constitute a threat. Why continue the sentence just to satisfy society or the media that he has been in prison for x years? The effects of the ten years to the first review of the sentence are severely affected by the emptiness and lack of purpose and hope in that situation. It became very clear in the interviews that it is crucial that some modification should be made to this procedure, not least to ease the sufferings – and they are seen to be very great sufferings – of the families concerned. It may well be possible to break up this limbo period into a series of progressions within Maze prison, in a way similar to the present policy in the rest of Britain of moving prisoners to various categories of prison. The prisoner, when first sentenced, might be placed in a block where a very strict regime was implemented. Punishment might well be the emphasis at this stage.

The second stage could be a move, after an indefinite period, to a more relaxed regime in another block. The accommodation of the Special Category Prisoners might well be a blueprint for this. Morale is high among them, a fact which may account for the higher success rate of marriages surviving among them than of those in the other H blocks. The prisoner should embark upon the second phase when he is considered ready for it by the highest governor grades but once he does he should not be too readily moved back.

The scheme is an attempt to suggest a modified form of staged sentence tailored to the unique requirements of Northern Ireland, with its high life sentence population. It would aim to minimize the deleterious effects of the long empty years upon families and involve the wives and the families as people with creative roles in the imprisonment and release process. Morris advocated, among other things, better contact between the prisoner and his wife, between them and the social worker, and the involvement of wives in group discussions in the prison. This paper would go a little further by saying that the probation service, already doing excellent work and promoting imaginative schemes, should be given the opportunity to experiment with these ideas.

Families have obviously more than most to contribute to the prisoner's reformation and release, and it is folly not only to exclude them from the opportunity to be involved but actually to contribute unwittingly to their sense of neglect, alienation, and vicarious suffering. The family provides the most sustaining and effective ideology for the prisoner and this should be harnessed to serve towards his rehabilitation and release. Simply locking the prisoner away for many years, with a total neglect of his family, is not really an enlightened or effective way to meet the demands of the situation.

In the second stage of a life sentence – or even of a long determinate sentence – a prisoner's wife, or close family member, should be involved with him in seminars and discussions led by probation officers, chaplains, social workers, and so on. Every encouragement should be given to families to participate. Discussions with prisoners and families indicate that there would be a welcome for such an initiative.

The great virtue of such a scheme would be that something constructive would be seen, at long last, to be in operation. No matter how limited the perceived success might seem to be, the real bonus would be the ending of neglect and alienation of the families, and hence a marked reduction in their suffering.

There would, unfortunately, be exceptions. Some men are psychopathic, recalcitrant, and dangerous, and the prison authorities could not be held responsible if progress towards release for such men should be slow, or even non-existent. Such people can of course never be given up in despair, but neither can they be released into society when they might constitute a danger. They require humane and separate provision.

Let us briefly recall some of the findings listed earlier. The prisoner's wife, who has in no way offended, is faced with a life of loneliness, hardship, difficulty, and deprivation, with no creative role or input into her husband's reformation and release. She is a mere spectator, a passive victim of circumstances. The children must grow up through all their childhood years without their father. The place they could possibly have in the creative process towards his eventual release is denied them. It could rightly be claimed that the role of the children in this is vital, and that few have greater influence upon a man than his children. The research has shown that the present system often erodes the influence of wives and children, who usually grow away from the prisoner. After some years fathers and children no longer know each other. This is often a painful experience when the prisoner comes out on parole. Home leaves during the second stage should be an integral part of the scheme. Christmas paroles have proved they are safe. Of the many who were paroled at Christmas none was in any trouble of any kind, and all returned on time.

It is therefore suggested that a structured life sentence which has home leave schemes built into it (which should occur sufficiently early in the sentence) would reduce the traumatization of families; would contribute towards the reformation and release of prisoners in a constructive way involving prisoners and families; and would contribute towards the reduction of violence. Staged prison sentences in earlier times were usually concerned with the de-criminalization of offenders. Prisoners were prepared for return to society by a programme of hard work, diligent teaching, and moral exhortation, and the thrust was towards making them dutiful, obedient, and useful members of society. The aim here is more 'de-militarization' – the inculcation of the rejection of violence as a means of political or social change. As already stated, very few of the 'lifers' under consideration have any other crime to their discredit than the paramilitary offences for which they have come to prison. The 'macho' image with which they seek to protect themselves from the perceived threats of imprisonment soon disappears, and they begin to doubt their competence more and more as the sentence progresses. Most of them have long ago become disillusioned with paramilitarism.

Once the goal of the imprisonment has been achieved, and retribution has been imposed, punishment inflicted, society's demands met, and so on, it does not seem reasonable that the family should continue to suffer in perpetuity. There must be at some stage a process of damage limitation introduced. The scheme outlined here is an attempt to suggest ways of doing that.

The third and final phase of the life sentence should lead to release, and it is suggested that this could best be conducted in hostel accommodation outside the prison. The prisoner would work during the day and have time off to visit his family, but would live in the hostel. I consider this to be better than the present arrangement whereby a prisoner is confined in Crumlin Road prison with a 'working-out' scheme. The drawback to the present policy is that the prisoner may have come from a regime such as that the Special Category prisoners in Maze enjoy, and in this final stage they must actually revert to the old-style regime. It is arguable that this is hardly the best preparation for release to normal society! In other words, this is an argument for the advancement of the prisoner, rather than his regression.

Forsythe (1987), discussing imprisonment which is preoccupied with custody and security above all else, succinctly comments, and it is a cautionary word:

> Contemporary man, who has known the differing manifestations of the power of evil in Dachau, the Gulag Archipelago, Mackindye Barracks, Arkansas Prison Farm, and amidst the Disappeared Ones, should acknowledge [that] this particular feature of the Reformist work . . . the ideal of social inclusion and the human value of prisoners is of no little importance.

What is being argued in this paper is that prisoners' wives and children, who are victims of a tragedy they did not create, are of the utmost value. They require and deserve the compassion of the society of which they are, and will remain, an integral part. So let them not be pushed out into communities of their own. Retributive and deterrent policies offer no hope to them, but adversely affect them over many years with great suffering falling especially upon the children. Whatever one may say about prisoners bringing trouble upon themselves, their children certainly had no part in creating the suffering visited upon them (Hughes 1989).

REFERENCES

Berger, P. (1985) *Invitation to Sociology*, Harmondsworth: Penguin.
Cohen, S. and Taylor, L. (1972) *Psychological Survival*, Harmondsworth: Penguin.
Forsythe, W. J. (1987) *The Reform of Prisoners 1830–1900*, London: Croom Helm.
Goffman, E. (1961) *Asylums*, New York: Doubleday.
Hughes, W. J. (1989) *The Effects of Life Imprisonment on Prisoners' Families*, Unpublished Thesis, University of Ulster.
Morris, P. (1965) *Prisoners and their Families*, London: Allen & Unwin.
Northern Ireland Office (1989) *Commentary on Northern Ireland Crime Statistics 1988*, Belfast: HMSO.
Shaw, R. G. (1987) *Children of Imprisoned Fathers*, London: Hodder & Stoughton.

12 Prisoners' families
Should the probation service have a role?

Linda Wilson-Croome

A SERVICE FACING CHANGE – WHERE ARE PRISONERS' FAMILIES?

The 1990s promise to be a period of rapid and fundamental change for the probation service in England and Wales – a time when traditional roles and values will come under scrutiny and clarification be sought, most probably from widely different standpoints, about its primary responsibilities and tasks. There has already been a tremendous shift in focus of the service's work with offenders and this will be reinforced with the introduction of major criminal justice legislation following the publication of the government's White Paper *Crime, Justice and Protecting the Public* [CM 965] in February 1990. Furthermore, the service faces critical structural and management changes arising from the Green Paper *Supervision and Punishment in the Community* [CM 966], some of which could enable more effective joint working with other agencies, particularly the independent sector.

Where are prisoners' families in this barrage of change? Certainly, if action is not taken, in danger of being (even more) lost or forgotten. At this watershed of probation service development, I believe that the needs of prisoners' families must be held on to and addressed. The changes that are facing the service provide a fresh opportunity to review present policies and practice in relation to them, but failure to do this in the next couple of years and to do it in a realistic way could seriously impair the potential of effective help and work in the future. The time is ripe for a rethink of the role of the probation service in relation to prisoners' families.

NO STATUTORY OR MANDATORY DUTIES

One of the dilemmas facing the probation service in identifying what its role with prisoners' families should be is that it has no statutory or mandatory responsibilities to assist them. The duties of the service in relation to prisoner throughcare are solely in relation to the supervision of, and the provision of services to, the prisoner or young offender during and following a period in custody. Furthermore, some probation services, in response to the expectations of the Home Office in its *Statement of National Objectives and Priorities for the Probation Service in England and Wales*, issued in 1984, have given throughcare and voluntary after care a lower priority in terms of resource allocation and workload management. At a time of finite resources and competing demands on a busy probation officer's time, the needs of prisoners' families can, therefore, inadvertently get overlooked, unless the local probation service determines the role to be played and adequately resources it.

A FOCUS ON THE OFFENDER

Before addressing the potential role of the probation service in relation to prisoners' families, it is important to acknowledge the major shift of focus that has evolved in the work of the service during the last five years or so, that is, a clearer focus on the offender and his/her offending behaviour. The identification of clearer objectives and priorities for probation services has led to a clarification of function which is now seen as the reduction of crime, particularly through tackling an offender's offending behaviour to reduce the risk of re-offending in the future. This has led to the development of more intensive programmes of supervision, the use of a social skills approach in both individual and group work to address the factors contributing to offending, and the demonstration of effectiveness in terms of reducing offending behaviour. I believe that this significant shift of emphasis, and the cultural shift that has accompanied it, has inevitably led to a diminution in the service's wider work with families and in the community. The next few years will present the service with a particular challenge: how to focus on the offender and achieve the aim to reduce crime while holding on to the social work approach of the service and taking a wider perspective on work in and with the community. Even if you accept, as I do, that the primary role of the probation service must be to focus on the offender, this should not – and cannot – exclude addressing the needs of the family, victims, and the community.

A COMMITMENT TO REDUCE THE USE OF CUSTODY

The probation service now recognizes that it has a major role to play in reducing the number of people sent into custody. The White Paper *Crime, Justice and Protecting the Public*, which will be embodied in legislation later in 1991, sets out a new sentencing framework aimed at increasing the use of community sentences, retaining imprisonment only for those convicted of more serious offences and where it is necessary to protect the public. This will reinforce the key role of the probation service as being to supervise offenders in the community. However, the White Paper contains radical changes to the parole system for those sentenced to custody. It is proposed that all prisoners sentenced to a custodial sentence of one year or more will in future be subject to statutory supervision following release. This has major resource and management implications for the probation service as it will increase the number of prisoners during and after release for whom there will be a statutory responsibility to supervise and assist. This change presents the service with an important opportunity to review its work with prisoners' families, both to ensure that their needs are better addressed and as a means of achieving its aims in the supervision of those on licence.

If the probation service is to achieve its aim of reducing the use of custody, more attention must be given to developing a strategy to offer constructive help to prisoners and their families to cope with the sentence, to tackle the reasons for the offences, prepare for release, and assist in resettlement. With high re-conviction rates following a custodial sentence, prisoners must be at serious risk of a return to custody if this help is not provided. Furthermore, to exclude the family from this assistance would be both inhumane and less effective. However, the probation service cannot, and should not, tackle this alone – it needs to work in partnership with other statutory and voluntary organizations and with families and communities themselves.

THE PROBATION SERVICE IN PARTNERSHIP – A STRATEGIC APPROACH

The primary responsibilities and the shift of focus in the work of the probation service inevitably mean that probation officers will be unable to meet all of the needs of prisoners' families. The imprisonment of a partner and/or parent can have devastating effects: there may be a tremendous sense of loss or grief, deprivation in terms of insufficient money, housing difficulties, lack of support and understanding, and isolation, bewilderment, and loneliness. Children of an imprisoned parent can suffer considerable trauma and their needs are too often ignored. There are not the resources available to allow the probation service to address all of these needs nor, in my view, would probation officers or probation assistants necessarily be the best at doing so. However caring and well-intentioned, the probation officer will have limited time, represents authority, and, with a primary responsibility to the prisoner, may not always be able to hold on to the specific needs of the family. Work with children requires specific skills and not all probation officers would consider themselves equipped to help them. While probation officers should offer help and assistance to prisoners' families – and have a lot to contribute in many instances – they cannot and should not do it all. They should work in partnership with other organizations and community representatives and groups to ensure that the range of facilities necessary is available.

There are many voluntary organizations and groups in the community that can offer advice and help to prisoners' families – women's groups, welfare benefits' advisers, child care providers, citizens' advice bureaux, and groups/organizations catering specifically for ethnic and other minority groups. Indeed, one aspect which is often overlooked is the differing needs of families from Afro-Caribbean, Asian, and other communities. It is crucial that facilities are provided that are relevant and this is likely to be best achieved by joint working with local ethnic groups, including the Black or Afro-Caribbean and Asian initiatives which involve representatives of local communities and probation services, where they exist.

The voluntary sector has a valuable role to play in helping prisoners' families. Voluntary associates, recruited and trained by probation services or by the Society of Voluntary Associates (SOVA) on their behalf, can give of their time, commitment, and expertise to offer help and advice to partners and children of prisoners. Advice about welfare benefits, sources of assistance, child minding, and help with transport to visit the prisoner/young offender are valuable contributions. Those volunteers and workers attached to prison visits centres offer a range of facilities – crèches, child care, refreshments, and help with transport – which can reduce the stress caused by often long and depressing journeys and go some way to make up for usually inadequate facilities in prison visits rooms. The advice and support given by the voluntary organizations set up by interested and concerned individuals to cater specifically for the needs of prisoners' families is a welcome and very relevant contribution. The probation service should work in partnership with these organizations and people to ensure that the necessary range of facilities is provided in each area.

Anyone who is concerned with helping prisoners' families will know of the extreme difficulties that voluntary groups and organizations have in acquiring and retaining adequate financial assistance. The recent commitment of the prison service to the financing of visits centres is welcomed but this cannot meet all of the needs. One major change on the horizon for probation services is the probable introduction of the power to contract out services to the independent sector and, associated with this, grant-aiding powers. Should these be introduced, and in such a way as to allow flexible allocation, it would enable probation services to consider giving financial support to voluntary organizations to provide facilities for prisoners' families as part of a local strategy to reduce/prevent crime and carry out its supervision of offenders effectively. This could be an exciting and enabling development which would allow probation services to give support and encouragement to the provision of a range of facilities for prisoners' families in a helpful, realistic, and tangible way. However, even without these additional powers, the probation service can offer support, encouragement, and advice to facilitate the voluntary sector's contribution to helping prisoners' families and often provide more concrete assistance by the provision of office accommodation, use of telephones, photocopying, etc.

What is needed is a more strategic approach to planning to meet the needs of prisoners' families. While the probation service cannot meet all of the needs of families themselves, working with prisoners and in communities, probation staff should be in an ideal position to assist in the identification of needs and resources, highlight the gaps in provision, take action to fill the gaps, and communicate the sources of help and advice through the prisoners and their community contacts to the families. If the needs of prisoners' families are to be met more consistently and well, this partnership is vital. In April 1990 the government published a discussion document to complement the White and Green Papers entitled *Partnership in Dealing with Offenders in the Community*. This developed in more detail the potential roles for the voluntary and private sectors in work with offenders and put forward options for the management of contracting out of services and grant-aiding powers. In it, the government promoted a strategic, inter-agency approach to reduce crime and proposed the setting up of local committees, where major statutory organizations, local authorities, the voluntary sector, community relations councils, and local businesses would be represented, to analyse crime in their areas and develop a co-ordinated strategy for tackling it. Such a forum would provide an excellent vehicle for considering action required to meet the needs of prisoners' families as part of the overall strategy and enable the harnessing of the range of resources of the statutory, voluntary, and private sectors and the community. Similar groups already exist in some areas through multi-agency groups focusing on young adult offenders or steering groups in the Safer Cities Initiative. There is, therefore, ample scope for the probation service to promote and contribute to a strategy which assists prisoners' families and I would urge probation service managements to explore these options.

A ROLE FOR PROBATION OFFICERS

Good probation practice dictates that work with offenders should be set in the context of their family and community. Action should be taken not only to tackle the offender's reasons for offending but to identity and work with other contributing factors, which could include problems in relationships, housing, and financial difficulties – that is, factors that affect the whole family. Furthermore, unless prisoners' families receive appropriate and sufficient help, not only will they suffer unnecessary hardship but their situation could become untenable, which could lead to family breakdown and even risk of crime.

For these reasons, I believe that probation officers must address the needs of prisoners' families and, where appropriate, work with others to meet them. Both field probation officers in the home area and officers seconded to the institutions can provide a valuable service to prisoners' families. There are some excellent examples of good practice throughout England and Wales but unfortunately there is seldom a consistent approach, backed by policy and good practice guidelines. So what can probation officers contribute?

FIELD (OR HOME) PROBATION OFFICER

Advice and information

The period immediately following sentence is a particularly stressful one for families. They often lack knowledge of the penal system, visiting arrangements, letters, and where to go to for financial assistance, etc. Probation officers should take responsibility to ensure that families are advised of their rights and any queries answered. Direct contact and leaflets can be effective, but to be of help it must be a quick follow-up. Families' organizations and voluntary associates can work with the probation officer on this.

Assess needs and develop a programme to meet them

A home visit specifically to assess the partner's and children's needs – financial, emotional, and situational – should follow sentence. A programme of action should be agreed on how best to deal with the needs identified – by the officer, friend or relative, voluntary associate, or other statutory or voluntary agency – and a level of contact specified. Where children are having particular problems they may need to be referred to a specialist agency, for instance, social services, the child guidance service, a school counsellor, or a suitable voluntary organization, depending on their age, problems, and availability of resources locally. Alternatively, consideration could be given to a referral to the probation civil work team, who have particular expertise in working with children and children's issues and who could provide direct counselling/assistance.

Group support

Many probation services run women's/wives' groups to offer mutual support and an opportunity for social contact. These usually provide crèche and play facilities which can be of immense help to the children, giving them an opportunity to talk and play with others. Probation assistants and voluntary associates play a major role in these.

Keep informed

Families should be kept informed of relevant dates, e.g. home leave, parole, and significant events by or on behalf of the probation officer.

Assist with transport

Although some probation services have to restrict the level of resources for probation staff or voluntary associates to accompany families on visits, each case should be assessed on merit and as part of the overall programme of assistance.

SECONDED PROBATION OFFICERS

Information giving

Leaflets, in a range of relevant languages, can provide families, either directly or via their partner/parent, with useful information about the institution, visiting arrangements, letters, home leave, parole/licence system, etc. Posters in visiting rooms and/or visits centres can be a useful means of communication. Information given via the prisoners at induction groups and reception visits is also important.

Offers of help

Particularly where there is no home probation officer or where a probation service has a policy of low priority to throughcare, direct offers of help and support can be made to the family. Although recognizing the dilemma of offenders being the primary client of the probation service, offers of help to the family should not be determined by the prisoner – this is not always a true reflection of need. Voluntary associates and visits centre staff can help with this.

Provision of visiting/crèche facilities

Prison visiting rooms are not renowned for their good facilities. Probation officers can promote the need for a visits centre or other visiting facilities, e.g. crèches, play areas, refreshments, good waiting areas, and, where appropriate, directly provide them, using voluntary associates and sessional staff.

Link with prisoner/field probation officer/family

The seconded probation officer has a key role to play in maintaining links between the prisoner, his/her family and other community ties, and the field/home probation officer. This role should not be underestimated. Where there is shared working in the institution, the seconded officer has an important role in advising the prison officers of the need and means of achieving this and facilitating these links.

Welfare visits

Supervised visits to work jointly with prisoner and partner/children where there are particular problems are useful. These should be encouraged and used positively as part of the programme of work with the prisoner and the family. Joint work with the field probation officer is also often valuable.

Work with prisoners/young offenders

Prisoners and young offenders in institutions are helped to look at their offending behaviour and other contributing factors, e.g. dysfunctional relationships, alcohol or drug problems, accommodation, or employment issues. Work with them individually or in groups can also aim to improve relationships with family, to help them understand the impact of their offending and the sentence on the family and to bear their needs in mind in planning for release. The video *They Just Don't Think, Do They?* produced by the Lancashire Probation Service, with Lancashire College and the Save the Children Fund, which presents the problems faced by prisoners' wives and children, is an excellent vehicle for dealing with these issues with prisoners.

Availability at visits

Some teams in institutions ensure that a probation officer is available in the visits room to deal with problems arising or answer any queries. A proactive approach by seconded probation officers can be cost-effective and preventive.

FUTURE ROLE OF THE PROBATION SERVICE

In conclusion, therefore, it is important to acknowledge the changing role of the probation service, with its emphasis on tackling offending and supervising offenders in the community. There will be major changes in criminal justice policy and practice over the next few years which will impact on the role of the probation service with prisoners and their families. However, the time is ripe to review service policies and practices in this area. With an anticipated increase in statutory throughcare and the opportunities presented by the powers to contract out services and grant aid, the scope for partnership with voluntary organizations and other groups in the community widens considerably. Probation services should be working with others to develop strategies to meet the needs of prisoners and their families, within which probation officers and other staff will have a vital role to play.

13 A link with normality
The role a school could play to help a prisoner's child in crisis

Stephen Moore

Caroline is 9 years old. You could pick her out if you walked into her classroom. Her mother is having difficulty coping because Dad is away.

> 'He has to live in a home.'
>
> 'Is he poorly?'
>
> 'No but he can't live with us. He has to live in a home. He stayed with us before Christmas for a while but now he has to live in a home. My mum has to manage with me and my brother and baby sister so I have to go at five past three so she can collect us together from the Infants. Is it time yet, Sir? You won't forget will you?'

Every day Caroline misses the last twenty minutes of school so that Mum can cope. In the eyes of other kids she is somehow special. Going home at a different time makes her special. To a teacher Caroline is clinging. She uses her 'special arrangement' to engage you in conversation seemingly just for the sake of being noticed. Walking to the baths, she chooses the company of teacher to talk to. She looks different from the other kids. She looks as if her clothes have come from a jumble sale. Her hair is thin and untidy. She's the one girl in the class who hasn't had her hair styled at all.

I don't know that she's a prisoner's child. I have no means of checking and the family have a right to their privacy. It's nobody's job to tell me, the teacher.

Monger and Pendleton (1981) found that around half the children of imprisoned parents were not told the truth. Some were babes in arms and the question did not arise. Others were too young to understand the actions of the adult world. An older child might find unreasonable gaps in the explanations, plausible to the young mind. Such was the case in the fictitious example of *The Railway Children* (Nesbit 1906). But whether and what a child is told often has more to do with the needs and feelings of the adults around them than with the needs and feelings of the child.

Shaun is seven. His Daddy went off in a space rocket. 'That one over there!' he says looking through the window to a dark stone Victorian folly in the distance, a pointed structure, a local landmark on a hilltop about two miles from the council estate where he lives. He doesn't know when Dad's coming back. He keeps asking his Mum and she tells him to shut up.

His Dad threw his Mum half-way down the stairs once and he saw it. Another time, he and his sister crept downstairs to see what all the noise was and his Dad was hitting his Mum. They were frightened. His Mum called the police. He doesn't like the police coming because he's frightened that they're going to take his Mum and Dad away and then what would he and his sister do? Once when the police came Mum and Dad were hiding under the beds. The worst time of the day is hometime. He is afraid that one day he will go home and nobody will be there.

Shaun's having a lot of problems in school and his headteacher is going to have a word with Mum. His behaviour is not very good at all and it's just got to be sorted out because it's holding back his reading. He doesn't seem able to concentrate for any length of time. They wonder if the educational psychologist can do anything.

Sandra can't concentrate either. In fact she seems to live in a world of her own. She's a thin, sickly looking child. She used to be extremely withdrawn. They couldn't do much with her at all in the Infants. She was a 'pathetic little thing'. Sandra's 10 now and still very quiet but she's starting to join in a bit more. She lives with her Dad and is dressed less fashionably than her classmates. Dad took her on holiday to Paris last year and this year she's going to Disneyland in America!

It has been suggested that if you want to know a child's views you might try asking them. I did.

> 'What's the problem with your reading?'
> 'I can't concentrate.'
> 'Why do you find it difficult to concentrate?'
> 'I keep thinking about my sister. I wonder where she is and what's happened to her.'
> 'Why?'
> 'Because she's dead. I wonder if she's in heaven and whether she can see me. I wonder why it was her and not me.'

She used to live with her Mum and her stepfather. Sandra was one of twins. She and her sister were subjected to physical abuse when she was very young. Her sister was killed. Stepfather was sent to prison. Sandra lived with Mum for a while longer and then went to live with Dad. Mum left town shortly afterwards. She doesn't know where she is.

We agreed she would write the letter that she wanted to write to her mother even though we had no address to send it to. She decided in advance that I could show it to her class teacher and she mentioned it at home. She wanted to take a copy home to show Dad and Grandma who lived round the corner. She wrote the letter looking back to memories of when she was very young. The factual accuracy is not important to me. What is important is that these were the images in her daily preoccupations. Apart from the changed names, this is what she wrote:

Dear Mum,

Why were you so cruel to me? Why did you hit me and kick me in the stomach? What made you swear at me, you and my step-dad? Why did you not give me proper food. Why did I get mash every day, me and my sisters whilst my brother chicken, pies or sausages? Why did you not let me go to school and send me to bed? Why did you keep hitting me and my sisters? Why did we have to go to bed at three in the afternoon? Why were you so cruel to the dogs and cat? Why did you go out so much and leave us on our own? Why would you throw me about on the floor and why did you throw me down the stairs and break my leg? Why did you have more children than you wanted? Why did you drink so much and then batter us? Why did you hit me in the face with a hammer? I had to go to hospital and have an operation on my eye. I was only one year old. Why did you push me outside in cold weather with the dog? You wanted to kill the dog because it bit you to protect me. Why would you bang my head against the wall even when you had not been drinking? Why did my step-dad laugh and tell you to keep doing it to me? He didn't love me. He didn't really like me. He would just keep laughing. Why did you do that to my sisters as well. My baby sister died when you thumped her in the heart and she stopped breathing. You were drunk and started laughing. You were going to set fire to the house till that neighbour stopped you and then the police came. They took baby to hospital but they could not get her a new heart and she died.

I was four when I went to live with my Dad. I remember you. You were called Karen and you had blondish-brown hair. I went to hospital with liver and kidney trouble. I had to have a kidney removed because you would not give me any drink.

You did not love me, did you? Was it because you had too many children and could not cope? The doctor told me you had high blood pressure and stress and that was why you turned on me and my sisters.

How is Emma? My Dad was going to take her. I wish he had. She will be about 16 now. How is she and how is she doing? Emma loved me a lot and so did Debbie. I miss them. I miss both of them. Emma used to try to stop you hitting us.

I don't think you ever loved me after you saw that film about violence to kids. You seemed to decide to do it to us. You used to watch violence films. You used to get videos about them. I heard you laughing at them and saying you would do it to your children. I think the videos and the drink made you like that. You drank too much and you would not stop. The police wanted you to stop it but you wouldn't.

Where are you? I want to know because then I can tell Dad and he'll come round and stop you being cruel to my sister.

I don't like you any more and I don't care about you because you've been so cruel to me. I can't remember a time when I loved you.

At night time I pray that Emma and Debbie were here to love me and to play with and if I was ill they would go to the doctors' and tell them. The doctor would give them a special medicine drink to help me. I wish you would be hung and treated really cruel so you would know what it was like for us. I want to see you locked up. You went to court once and the police told me you'd been telling lies. I can't forgive you for what you did.

You and Dad split up when you were pregnant with us. You used to tell us that you really loved us at first. Then you met my step-dad. He had a wife and three other children elsewhere. He had been cruel to them as well. Emma and I were playing one day and we heard you having a row with him. This is how we found out. You loved us at first. You didn't kick us or hit us or throw us about till he came into your life. I blame him for what happened. When he got sent to prison I didn't think about him but you were still cruel to us and then he came back.

Sandra Connor

It is not my concern as a teacher by whose hand a child has been traumatized. A number of children go through unspeakable experiences. As teachers we don't live through our pupils' nightmares. Yet we have to be the image of normality and stability through whom such children may develop.

Shaw (1987) was concerned to uncover the large number of children who see a parent go to prison at some point in their school career in order to illustrate the need for serious research. When I first looked at the problems faced by the children of prisoners (Moore 1986) I was concerned that schools were unaware of their number, of the problems they faced, and that it was nobody's job to even tell schools of their existence, whereas the children assumed that teachers knew all about them.

Now I am not quite so convinced of the need to know their number as of the need to understand that for some children the problems that occur, associated with the imprisonment of a parent, can be extreme, that information is scant, research almost unknown, and communication discouraged. We need to break the taboo and encourage educators to recognize and respond to the particular needs of prisoners' children.

It has been a long and slow process to get educators to recognize and talk about such things as physical and sexual abuse of children. That children could be traumatized in the events that surround the state's action in arresting their parent or parents or during their parent's imprisonment is still an untold story. I am not concerned to judge whether the disadvantage these children suffer is caused by the behaviour of the parent, of the state, or of others. I am concerned only with the needs of a child at a particular time and the course of their school career. What remains true yet largely ignored is the principle laid down by the Warnock Report (DES 1978) that the needs of a child should be seen

> not in terms of a particular disability which a child may be judged to have, but in relation to everything about him, his abilities as well as his disabilities – indeed all the factors which have a bearing on his educational progress.

In my original work (Moore 1986), I reported that in the small number of cases that schools were aware of, teachers tended to hear about the crime of the parent rather than the condition of the child. Sadly I have found no evidence to alter that view, either in the instance or the relevance of what they hear. Indeed, the situation is compounded by the emerging procedures for dealing with child abuse that aim only to detect the adult. They do not follow through to examine and meet the needs of the child. There is no concept of 'after care'. Without such professional skills, how can teachers fulfil Warnock's principle?

Patrick's dad went to prison three years ago. He's doing life for murder. He was five then and a neighbour assaulted Patrick in the park, placing his hands round his neck and threatening to show him what his Dad had done. Now aged eight, having moved town more than once, he is so traumatized that he soils himself out playing. Mother is trying her best to keep herself and five children under ten together as a family, despite pressures of money and neighbours. The education system makes no special provision for Patrick.

Sheena disrupts every lesson she's in at her comprehensive school. She's twelve and in a special needs group.

'When did you first start hating school?'
'I've always hated it right from when I started when I was seven.'
'Don't you mean five?'
'No I didn't start till I was seven. My Mum wouldn't let me because of the things my Dad was doing to me.'

Father went to prison and Sheena went to live with foster parents. She has had a succession of social workers but no guidance at all concerning the sexual abuse she has been through. Until this conversation with me the school was unaware of her circumstances though they knew she was fostered. Is it the school's job to deal with these matters? Surely they have enough to do delivering the national curriculum? If Sheena continues to sit there making her daily protest, the school will be unable to deliver any curriculum.

Peter is seven. He has moved house several times since his Daddy was imprisoned for armed robbery. One of the moves became necessary after some further trouble involving his Mum's brother with whom they were staying. The police had called in the middle of the night enquiring about some stolen property.

They had moved there after the babysitter's boyfriend had indecently assaulted his 5-year-old sister. When it all came out the boyfriend was jailed but they did not feel they could stay in the neighbourhood. Peter travels ninety miles on the coach with his Mum and his two younger sisters at least once a month to visit his Dad in prison.

He's in his third infant school and the headteacher wants Mum to do something because he keeps being very aggressive in the classroom.

I have been aware of but a few of the children of prisoners that I must have met both in my teaching and in the wider community and can only glimpse their world, perhaps inaccurately, because I can not live through their experiences. Nor can I generalize from such a chance sample, though I am aware that the children I have quoted here have been close to atypically serious crime and often to abnormal behaviours that have occurred in the home. I do not seek to suggest that the children of those imprisoned for any particular crime or type of crime are more likely to have problems than any other. Neither can I conclude that the trauma experienced by an abused child is affected by the subsequent imprisonment of the offender. My evidence is merely gleaned from my *ad hoc* sample and is anecdotal.

Though there may be little positive input from us professionals into the lives of these normal children in abnormal circumstances, there continues to be other input that greatly concerns me. Press headlines at the outbreak of the Strangeways disturbances gave grossly exaggerated stories of death and destruction. What would that do to a child old enough to read a paper or to a younger one hearing such commentary as they watched events unfold on the television? There was little or no provision for adult relatives to be informed of the safety or whereabouts of their loved ones, still less if you are a 7- or 5-year-old. What would be churning round a child's mind as their fertile young imagination tried to come to terms with what was being said?

We adults may have reasonable fear in the light of recent events in several prisons for the future of the prison service and the container operations in police stations. A child may have less well-informed, less rational fears that can be their constant preoccupation.

The circumstances which surround a child are not a feature of the national curriculum. They are not tested for at 7, 11, and 14. There is only provision for excluding children with special needs from parts or all of the national curriculum, an uncomfortable echo of their parents' exclusion from society. Schools that will be judged more and more by result will be less and less willing to have their marks reduced by those with problems. The pressure will grow for segregated provision for children who prove difficult in school, even though we have known since the Warnock Report (DES 1978) that in the past such provision has satisfied administrative convenience rather than the needs of children.

Surely all children have a right of access to education, to physical, intellectual, and social development and to the acquisition of the skills on which their life-chance depends. They can be given that right only if first we adults, especially we teachers who meet them daily, recognize who they are, where they are, and try to understand what impinges on their lives and shapes their outlook.

I still believe that we should listen carefully to what prisoners' children ask of teachers when they say that:

> All children of school age need at least one stable adult figure they feel they can talk to.
>
> Teachers should let their pupils know that they could be approached, if needs be, if the child chooses. This offer should be made to all children. Teachers should not single out the ones they feel may need it. A place and time should be stated away from the attentions of other pupils, when the offer could be taken up.
>
> Practical assistance, such as help in obtaining free dinners, uniforms or maintenance grants, lessens the burden of pressure on the family and therefore the child.

(Moore 1988)

REFERENCES

DES (1978) *Special Educational Needs*, The Warnock Report, London: HMSO.

Monger, M. and Pendleton, J. (1981) *Throughcare With Prisoners' Families*, Nottingham: University of Nottingham.

Moore, S. H. (1986) *Beyond The Stereotype: A Teacher's View of the Problems Faced by the Children of Prisoners*, unpublished dissertation, Manchester Polytechnic.

Moore, S. H. (1988) 'Teachers and prisoners' children', *Childright* 43:16.

Nesbit, E. (1906) *The Railway Children*, London: Wells Gardner, Darton.

Shaw, R. (1987) *Children of Imprisoned Fathers*, London: Hodder & Stoughton.

14 Prisoners' children

The role of prison visitors' centres

Eva Lloyd

INTRODUCTION

The welfare and civil rights of prisoners themselves have long been the concern of independent organizations such as NACRO (and SACRO and NIACRO), the Howard League for Penal Reform, and the Prison Reform Trust. But a voluntary sector interest in the associated needs of prisoners' families, complementary to the limited help given by the probation service, social services departments and NACRO, is more recent (Wilson-Croome 1989).

A growing concern for the needs of prisoners' families has given rise to two movements over the last quarter century. On the one hand, a series of support organizations developed, including self-help groups. These organizations include the Prisoners' Wives and Families Society, HALOW, Prisoners' Wives Service, Black Female Prisoners' Scheme, Women in Prison, the Prisoners' Families Information Centre, and Families Outside (in Scotland).

However, a particular concern also arose about the conditions at most prisons in which visitors had to queue outside the prison walls in all weathers, with nowhere to rest, feed or change babies, get something to eat or drink, or for children to play. These conditions were first described by Vercoe (1968) in a study carried out on behalf of NACRO. This problem was particularly acute in the case of remand prisoners who are entitled to frequent short visits, which puts a heavy burden on visiting relatives with small children.

From this concern came prison visitors' centres, outside the prisons proper and run independently from the prison authorities. The first one was set up at Winson Green prison in Birmingham in 1969, with the probation service in the lead (Clarke 1973). Organizations that followed suit included NACRO, the Society of Friends, and, in the mid-1970s, Save the Children. Also, the Butler Trust and the WRVS developed some crèches in prison visiting areas.

Since then some twenty prison visitors centres have been established in various partnerships between the prison service, local prison authorities, the probation service, and the voluntary sector. Save the Children has been playing a part in four such partnerships in the last decade: at HMP Maze, Belfast, Manchester, and Norwich, and a centre is currently being developed at HMP Holloway.

Some of the organizations involved in prison visitors' centres have got together in the *Association of Prison Visitors' Centres Ltd.* As the Association and several of the prisoners' relatives' support groups identified many common aims and ideas, they have recently initiated the formation of the *Federation of Prisoners' Families Support Groups.*

In December 1989 the Home Office committed itself as from 1990 to establishing a purpose-built visitors' centre at every new or refurbished prison. This official acknowledgement of the need for more substantive support for prisoners' families and friends in relation to prison visits was the culmination of a process set in motion more than twenty years ago.

Other chapters have discussed the experience of imprisonment from the child's perspective. This chapter does not attempt to assess in any analytical way the contribution that prison visitors' centres can make in mediating that experience. It is largely descriptive and focuses on the way in which Save the Children, concerned with the infringement of children's needs and rights, has translated this concern into the approach adopted in its practical work with prisoners' families. This practice draws both on direct child-care experience and on working contacts with other organizations in the same field.

SAVE THE CHILDREN AND PRISON VISITORS' CENTRES: AIMS AND PRACTICE

With other agencies, Save the Children shares a recognition of the multiple disadvantages suffered by prisoners' families and in particular by their children, the 'forgotten victims' (Matthews 1983). It accepts Shaw's (1989: 28) argument that it is 'the *right* of the child to maintain a meaningful relationship with its parent' by means of the opportunity for visiting prison frequently under adequate conditions, 'instead of visits being viewed as the right (or privilege) of the prisoner'.

The aims of Save the Children's work with prisoners' families are therefore threefold (Save the Children 1989). First of all, in its direct work it aims to meet some of the material and emotional needs of this group, who not only tend to come from the least advantaged sections of society, but who are further disadvantaged and discriminated against by having a family member in prison. These needs include the need for child care related to prison visits, for practical advice on benefits and the prison and criminal justice system, and the need for emotional support.

In the second place, Save the Children aims to persuade the statutory authorities and other voluntary organizations to provide visitors' centres which can offer a range of support services for families at all prisons and to establish a code of good practice for such centres.

Third, Save the Children aims to to assist in increasing public understanding that a sentence of imprisonment has punitive repercussions on the whole family and to undertake or promote work designed to throw light on the effect on families of contact with the criminal justice system and how the effect of custodial sentences can adversely affect the whole family.

In accordance with these aims, the Save the Children model of a prison visitors' centre is a dynamic model with the centre as a focus for work with prisoners' families, not only as a source of service provision.

It is argued that these general concerns are best addressed by ensuring that each prison visitors' centre is physically separate from the prison establishment, is independently run, and employs trained staff capable of working in a professional non-judgemental manner. In Northern Ireland the first centre was still located on prison premises, but all these conditions have since been met in the three other centres.

To meet the needs of prisoners' families as defined in its aims, a number of core facilities and services have been considered essential in each centre where Save the Children became a partner agency.

The core facilities should include a supervised play area, canteen facilities, a quiet room where confidential matters can be discussed and where visitors can find some privacy, a comfortable waiting area, toilets and baby changing facilities, and a public telephone.

Among the services provided should be:

a) play matched to the needs of the children, available before and after a visit or when a parent wishes to see his/her partner alone;
b) advice on child development problems and the management of behavioural problems;
c) inexpensive food and drinks;
d) listening, counselling and support for those who need someone to talk to;
e) specialist advice and information on the Benefits and Criminal Justice systems;

f) general information on health, education, prisons, transport, visiting procedures, prisoners' allowances (parcels) etc;

g) a system for linking families with sources of continuing support in their own communities.

(Save the Children 1989)

These objectives have been achieved in each centre, although the premises determine the extent to which certain services can be provided. Moreover, the experience acquired in this area has been translated into a code of practice which is adhered to in Save the Children's work with prisoners' families.

It should be clear from this description that prison visitors' centres should be places which offer shelter in a metaphorical as well as in a literal sense.

SAVE THE CHILDREN AND PRISONERS' FAMILIES IN BELFAST

Save the Children first came into contact with the needs of prisoners' children in relation to prison visits in Belfast. There these needs were taken seriously quite early on and today every prison in Northern Ireland has a prison visitors' centre attached to it. In 1975 Save the Children was asked by the Society of Friends to take on responsibility for child-care provision at a centre on prison premises at the Maze prison. They did so for ten years, until the child-care work was handed on to the Society.

Next, in 1978, came a request from NIACRO to become a partner in a centre serving the needs of visitors to HMP Belfast and the Crown Court, both on the Crumlin Road. Unfortunately, the withdrawal of the building made available by the Northern Ireland Office meant that in 1979 the centre had to close. An opportunity to re-establish it presented itself when a portacabin became available.

In 1982 the Crumlin Road Family Centre opened its doors close to the prison and the court. As before, NIACRO provided the canteen facilities. The probation service provided a good deal of the funding, as it had at the Maze prison. Information about the centre was made available at both prison and court and soon it was being used very heavily, as the families who attended the 'Supergrass Trials' which started around this time were desperate for a place to leave their children while they spent the day in court.

By the end of its first eight months of operation there had been 4,420 visits by children. Since the Supergrass Trials, prisoners' relatives have continued to find their way to the centre, which was due to move into new premises late in 1990.

Child-care advice and emotional support are always on offer for the often extremely young mothers coming in and all workers have counselling skills. Workers make a point of being available for extra support and comfort for those women whose partners have just been remanded or sentenced, or are about to be sentenced (Blake 1990).

From the start, a NIACRO advice worker has been providing information about the benefits and prison system, debt counselling, and organizing referrals to other agencies. In Northern Ireland, where gender roles within the family still tend to be organized along traditional lines, women who suddenly find themselves in charge of the much reduced family finances often require help with contacting agencies like the Housing Executive. Crumlin Road Family Centre distinguishes itself by the extent of the advice work. The project now has its own full-time advice worker.

The centre users form a short-term population. If the workers are to create a bond with the parent in order to help improve life for the children, they must act quickly. It has been found that focusing on the child in discussions with the mother serves this purpose. In consultation with the mother a developmental record is kept on each child attending more than once. If the workers perceive problems, they try to give the child more one-to-one attention and may devise a schedule of activities to promote development. Sometimes children are invited in on Mondays, when the prison is closed and fewer people use the centre, for extra time with the staff.

Behavioural disturbances resulting from the parent's imprisonment may not be easy to spot. Children are often very 'good' at the centre. But mothers may have been overdisciplining their children for fear of them being taken into care. As the project leader remarks, 'We have learned that the child who is quiet is the one to watch.' Sand, water, and drawing materials, for 'therapeutic play', are always available. This allows children to give vent to their feelings of frustration, anger, and fear. One little boy, for instance, built an elaborate sandcastle only to destroy it with a toy car, saying: 'That's the prison, I smashed it to get my dad out.'

No child of any age is ever discouraged from joining in. Generally, they tend to be pre-schoolers from age 2 onwards, but teenagers as old as 17 have been observed playing happily with the sand. According to the principal officer responsible for the project, 'Stress causes regression and even the most well-balanced child is bound to pick up some of the family stress under these circumstances; in this context chronological age does not count.'

A special kind of stress operates for those school-age children, mostly firstborns, who take on parental responsibilities within their families. Crumlin road workers noticed that these 10- to 14-year-olds were at risk of losing out on childhood experiences and organized a residential weekend for them, away from family pressures, on the Save the Children Youth Farm on the outskirts of Belfast.

The centre shares the philosophy of, for instance, the Leicester Prison Visits Centre Trust (1985) that there is a need for support for prisoners' families in their own communities, co-ordinated from the centre. In Leicester this took the form of a home visiting scheme. In Belfast there are various other forms of practical support available. These include the organization of yearly caravan holidays on the coast for prisoners' families, workers taking women under particular stress to court to help them become familiar with the procedures, or to educational establishments to register on training courses, and providing respite care at the centre on Mondays for children whose mothers need an extra break.

One of the principles on which the centre has operated from the start was that it would be non-sectarian and non-political. At the time of the Supergrass Trials it was demonstrated that such a cross-community project was indeed viable in Belfast. While Loyalists and Republicans were united in their hatred of the supergrass system, women on both sides of the divide helped each other with advice and support. This co-operation and mutual tolerance continued beyond the trials, the uniting factor between the women being their status as prisoners' partners and the disadvantages this entails.

How close both sides grew in practice becomes apparent from an incident one Christmas Eve when the bus taking a group of Loyalist women back to Derry broke down and left them stranded at the centre. When the Sinn Fein bus arrived to collect the Republican group also headed for Derry, everyone shared their seats with Loyalists on the return journey.

When Save the Children became involved in setting up a centre at Strangeways prison in Manchester, it drew heavily on the earlier experiences in Northern Ireland.'

SAVE THE CHILDREN AND PRISONERS' FAMILIES IN MANCHESTER

At Strangeways senior probation officers contacted Save the Children in 1984 to discuss possibilities for a visitors' centre near the prison gate. The Manchester Prison Visitors' Centre was opened in December 1986 as a partnership involving seven different agencies. Led by the Selcare Trust, the Greater Manchester Probation Service, the prison authorities, the Manchester Social Services Department, the North Manchester Area Health Authority, and NACRO, as well as Save the Children, were represented on the management board.

Initial funding came from the Greater Manchester Residuary Body, the Home Office, the probation service and Save the Children, who became responsible for child-care provision. Selcare became the managing agent and is taking on responsibility for the services initiated by Save the Children.

Three years after opening, the well-equipped centre, which catered primarily for visitors to remand prisoners, had received well over a quarter of a million visitors. Then the siege at Strangeways took place. At the moment of writing the centre lies idle, as the prison holds only a limited number of convicted prisoners. It is to be hoped that it will be reopened as soon as the need for it arises again. That such a need exists when the prison is fully operational is beyond dispute, as becomes apparent in a quote from Brendan O'Friel, the Strangeways Governor, in the 1990 Centre Report: 'In taking care of the visitors, the Centre provides a most valuable input to our overall aims. It is something we can ill afford to lose now it is so well established.'

From the outset booking in of visits has taken place at the reception desk where visitors are issued with a numbered ticket. Visitors are then allowed to the prison in batches of fifteen or twenty. Unfortunately, they still have to wait there until the inmates they are visiting have been collected and taken to the visiting area. Good working relations with gate and senior prison staff have helped this system here and in Norwich.

Being part of the administrative procedures surrounding the prison visit makes it more likely that staff will get involved in conflicts. Frequently, when a problem arises, they are the ones to cope with the visitors' frustration or distress. Also, the booking-in function may lead visitors to think that the centre is not separate from the prison administration. Generally, tension can be high among the visitors. Staff are prepared to defuse antagonistic situations, but they believe that adequate training is essential for this role and that the use of untrained volunteers for these purposes must be avoided.

Three child-care staff work with the under-2s, the pre-schoolers, and the school-age and older children. They always try to make extra time for one-to-one attention for distressed children and volunteers step in to free staff to do so. The child-care co-ordinator sees dressing-up clothes, of all the available toys, as particularly important in a therapeutic sense. These get used intensively in 'acting out' behaviour, the policeman's hat being the most popular item. The fact that many of the prisoners are remanded on drugs charges is reflected in the way raids are staged very authentically, complete with relevant language and a degree of violence: 'The workers get arrested a lot and bashed about a bit, too.'

It seems that some of the distress seen is in fact due to on-going disadvantage suffered as a result of race, class, and gender issues, rather than directly attributable to the traumatic disappearance of a parent. Another problem the co-ordinator identifies is that some mothers have a problem balancing the needs of their children with those of the man inside. The children's education and health may suffer as a result. For instance, gentle persuasion from staff may be needed to convince a mother who brings in a 10-year-old girl three times a week during school hours to restrict the child's visits to Saturdays and not let her daughter's education suffer.

Health problems, like constant colds in small children, suggested to staff that mothers might benefit from discussing family health with a health visitor. Regular visits to the centre may mean they miss the health visitor calling on them at home, or they may be wary of anyone representing the statutory authorities (Smith 1989: 57). The local health visitor was prepared to do weekly sessions. With the help of a member of staff skilled in easing the initial contact between her and the mothers, this has proved to be a very successful feature.

Poverty – and demands from the prisoner for cigarettes, radio batteries, and newspapers make this even more acute than in other one-parent families – is often responsible for children being inadequately dressed. The centre came up with one solution in the form of a weekly bring-and-buy sale. Welfare advice sessions are also run weekly by a CAB worker seconded from the local office.

The Manchester experience has been put to good use in consultancy work for other prisons in the area interested in setting up a centre. These prisons have included Garth, Redditch, and Risley Remand Centre.

SAVE THE CHILDREN AND PRISONERS' FAMILIES IN NORWICH

The Norwich Prison Visitors' Centre, the most recent of these Save the Children partnership projects to be opened, came about as the result of a shared initiative by the then new prison governor, the senior probation officer and Save the Children Fund. For the first two years the centre had a multi-agency management structure, within which Save the Children was responsible for child-care facilities and workers. Funding for the creation of the project came from Norfolk NACRO, the probation service and Save the Children Fund. Over 3,000 visits from children had been logged within the first year of the centre's operation.

In mid-1989 the Ormiston Trust, an East Anglian child-care charity, took over joint management of the whole centre with Save the Children and a unified staffing structure was created with a full-time project manager post. The extensive employment of voluntary staff was sustained into this new phase through the employment of a part-time reception/volunteer worker co-ordinator, who is currently responsible for over forty volunteer staff.

The Norwich Centre, like the Belfast one, is housed in a portacabin and will eventually move into purpose-built premises. In an evaluation of the child-care provision at Norwich after one year Coulter (1988: 31) concluded that 'Accommodating hundreds of visitors per month, despite its modest size and conditions, the Project is a small but important haven of sympathy in what could be, otherwise, an unremittingly grim situation.'

Administratively, the centre's links with the prison are even closer than in Manchester. Visitors to convicted and remand prisoners in three of the prison's five separate sections book in there. The prison telephones the centre when the inmate being visited has been called to the visiting area inside the prison.

The centre's reception desk is primarily staffed on a voluntary basis; voluntary staff also work daily in the crèche alongside the crèche co-ordinator, playleader and sessional workers. Save the Children's manager sees the development of the centre to date as a start in addressing the central task of countering the disadvantage and discrimination experienced by prisoners' families. The centre provides a suitable environment for intervention to support those families who are unsupported in their home areas and to create links with local sources of support. This is a central purpose of the Save the Children 'model'.

The restricted space limits the provision of certain services. Counselling takes place on an informal basis only, but information and advice about benefits and the prison system are available from the regular centre workers and from leaflets. The play area is smaller than in the other two centres, but there is an outdoor play space.

Children up to the age of 8 can be catered for in the crèche, but facilitier for older children are urgently needed. To compensate for the lack of space the child-care co-ordinator has arranged a 'loan' system of games and drawing materials which older children can use at the tables in the waiting area where the refreshments are served. The crèche co-ordinator tries to have frequent contact with the mothers. While the crèche provides mothers with a choice about leaving or taking their children with them into the prison, staff often help mothers to recognize the importance of the child's link with the father being sustained.

A further issue, that is shared with staff in other visitors' centres, is a concern about how to support parents – already experiencing great stress – in telling their children that their father or mother is in prison. While the parent's wishes are always respected, staff are aware of the additional suffering that children may experience through the parent's secrecy and the potential loss of trust between parent and child if the child were to find out the truth indirectly.

A factor to note is that in Northern Ireland there may be less stigma attached to imprisonment of a parent if this is connected with the political situation. On both the Loyalist and the Republican sides having a father in prison may raise a child's status at school to that of a minor hero.

The 1989 management agreement between the Norwich Prison Governor, the Ormiston Trust, and Save the Children details the exact responsibilities of these parties and of the advisory committee. It provides a working example of the kind of partnership between the prison authorities and voluntary agencies outlined in the Home Office Prison Department *Guidelines* (1989) for governors on the setting up and running of prison visitors' centres by establishments and voluntary organizations. Unlike the Prison Department, Save the Children believes that the responsibility for meeting a consistent commitment to the prison, such as booking-in visits, would make it extremely difficult for a purely volunteer staff to manage the prison/centre relationship.

LESSONS FOR THE FUTURE

It seems likely that the facilities and services described in this chapter will be appropriate in every prison visitors' centre. Nevertheless, no claim is made that the model of a centre as outlined here meets all the visitors' needs in connection with prison visits.

A number of management and development issues arise from the experience that Save the Children and other agencies working in this field have accumulated in prison visitors' centres so far.

Management issues

Lessons learned from Save the Children's experience with prison visitors' centres suggest that there may be some problems in operating with the *Guidelines* issued by the Home Office Prison Department. These problems concern the willingness of local voluntary agencies to become involved, the need for partnerships in the management of these centres, and the employment of volunteer staff.

Voluntary agencies like Save the Children have proved themselves able to act as a catalyst in the development of prison visitors' centres and to 'head up' such partnership projects. However, there will seldom be existing, locally based organizations like the Ormiston Trust willing to take on the management of a prison visitors' centre at a local prison on a continuing basis. The Prison Department's expectation that governors will be able to identify local voluntary organizations and local volunteers to initiate the setting up of such centres, particularly in small towns and rural locations, may prove to be unrealistic. Nor should the time which it takes to set up a management committee capable of running a centre and employing staff be underestimated.

In the management of prison visitors' centres partnerships are preferable to single agency management, as they offer expertise from several disciplines, ensuring the appropriateness of any services provided and securing local commitment to the continuation of successful schemes. The prison authorities must be partners in these projects, particularly if the centre assumes 'prison' functions like booking-in visits. The role and authority of the prison governor in relation to the centre must also be clearly defined. Such partnerships also ought to include the probation and social services and they must operate on the basis of a carefully drafted agreement and a constitution for the management committee. Such a committee needs access to professional support. It is advisable that the total number of agencies involved is limited. More importantly, differences in philosophy and practical approach must be explored at the outset, especially where they pertain to roles and responsibilities of staff.

The Prison Department recommendation for prison visitors' centres to be physically and administratively separate from the prison proper allows for the necessary autonomy as well as making it easier to mobilize support from the community. But such support cannot always be counted on, as many prisons are in isolated locations. Support for prisoners' families should come primarily from their home communities, while the communities surrounding prisons could provide volunteer staff and fund-raising support.

Save the Children shares the view of the Prison Department that volunteers have a valuable and necessary role to play in this work. In their experience, however, some tasks within the centre, like child care and counselling and the co-ordinator's role, require a level of training and skill which is unlikely to be found in someone without professional training. All staff, including volunteers, require practical training in handling people under stress. It must be acknowledged that training volunteers puts additional strain on core staff. High tension among the users of the centre transmits itself to staff, so intensive staff support is also essential.

Development issues

One priority for service development is outreach work to create links with support networks comprising statutory and voluntary agencies in the community where the prisoners' families live. Families come to rely on the facilities and services provided at the centre, leaving a huge gap when the prisoner is transferred. A nationwide database on contact organizations and persons in the statutory and voluntary sector should ideally be set up, to facilitate continued support and more focused referrals.

There are clear unmet needs for facilities in Norwich and Belfast. Both centres are contemplating making their new premises available out of hours for visitors to use for meetings of support systems of their own making, such as self-help groups. Norwich is hoping to extend its advice sessions by bringing in advice workers, and also a health visitor. There is a need for play facilities for older children, and young teenagers.

The views of users themselves should have a major impact in developing the centres' services and facilities. So far, it has been difficult to get anything other than positive feedback from prisoners' families, a problem also noted by Coulter (1988: 33). In Norwich a survey of user views is being organized to guide the provision of more services on new premises. At HMP Holloway a survey of the views of potential users of the planned centre has recently been carried out. By involving users a centre could move some way towards working with people rather than for people.

CONCLUSIONS

Save the Children has now seen some of its aims in its work with prisoners' families partly realized. It has helped raise awareness of their problems, in particular those of their children, and of the need for regular and dignified contact between the prisoners and their families. It has also contributed to the Home Office Prison Department *Guidelines* to governors on prison visitors' centres. Save the Children's experience along with that of others in the field is reflected in these *Guidelines*, although some differences of philosophy and emphasis between Save the Children and the Home Office remain, regarding both the services on offer and the management of these centres.

Much work remains to be done however. It has now been demonstrated that prison visitors' centres relieve some of the worst effects of custody on prisoners' families, by improving the conditions in which they maintain contact with the prisoner. Therefore it is warranted to press for the provision of such centres at all prisons and not just newly built or refurbished ones, and to urge the Home Office to provide secure funding for each one.

The impact of the work of prison visitors' centres with prisoners' families should now be extended to the wider community as well as to the prison community itself. There is a need for support networks in the home communities of the prisoners' families to counter the disadvantage and discrimination they undoubtedly suffer. At the prisons, the conditions in which prisoners meet with their visitors on prison premises must be improved. The problem here is particularly acute for female prisoners, often imprisoned far from home and with infrequent contact with their children (Catan 1988). Not only do prison visiting suites need improving, but appropriate children's areas must be created in each.

However, prison visitors' centres are not the main or only solution to the problems faced by prisoners' families. Other solutions must be found as well. First of all, as far as penal policy is concerned, a reduction in the use of imprisonment and the development of community alternatives to custody are urgently needed. Two other areas for urgent action concern, first, the needs of female prisoners and their children and, second, those of prisoners and their families who belong to ethnic minority groups, including foreign nationals. Save the Children is one of the organizations which are currently becoming involved in these areas of work.

There is also a need for more attention and more support to be given to those groups which speak from direct experience of contact with the prison system. Ultimately, the central issue for Save the Children must remain the need to understand and to reduce the terrible cost to children of having a family member in prison.

ACKNOWLEDGEMENTS

Eva Lloyd gratefully acknowledges the help received in writing this chapter from Save the Children project and managerial staff at Belfast, Manchester, and Norwich as well as at the Save the Children Fund head office in London. Dorothy Elliott, Principal Officer, Northern Ireland, who has been active in Save the Children's work with prisoners' families right from the start, was a special source of information and support.

REFERENCES

Blake, J. (1990) *Sentenced by Association*, London: Save the Children Fund.
Catan, L. (1988) 'The children of women prisoners', in A. Morris and C. Wilkinson (eds) *Women in the Penal System*, Cambridge: Institute of Criminology.
Clarke, A. T. (1973) *Visitors Centres in England*, Hertford: Hertfordshire Probation and After-Care Service.
Coulter, K. S. (1988) *Save the Children Fund H.M. Prison Norwich Visitors' Centre Project*, London: Save the Children Fund.
Home Office Prison Department (1989) *Visitors Centres: Some Guidelines for Establishments and Voluntary Organisations*, London: P3 Division.
Leicester Prison Visits Centre Trust (1985) *Address of the Chairman Annual General Meeting*, 11 September 1985.
Light, R. (ed.) (1989) *Prisoners' Families*, Bristol: Bristol and Bath Centre for Criminal Justice.
Manchester Prison Visitors' Centre (1990) *Five Years On*, Manchester: Save the Children Fund.
Matthews, J. (1983) *Forgotten Victims*, London: NACRO.
Save the Children (1989) *Prison Visitors' Centres: A Response to the Needs of Prisoners' Families*, London: Save the Children Fund.
Shaw, R. (1989) 'Criminal justice and prisoners' children', in R. Light (ed.) *Prisoners' Families*, Bristol: Bristol and Bath Centre for Criminal Justice.
Smith, S. (1989) 'Prisoners' families and the voluntary sector', in R. Light (ed.) *Prisoners' Families*, Bristol: Bristol and Bath Centre for Criminal Justice.
Vercoe, K. (1968) *Helping Prisoners' Families*, London: NACRO.
Wilson-Croome, L. (1989) 'Probation responses', in R. Light (ed.) *Prisoners' Families*, Bristol: Bristol and Bath Centre for Criminal Justice.

15 Conclusion

Politics, policy, and practice

Roger Shaw

DISPENSABLE CHILDREN

It is not the purpose of this short conclusion to list the points raised by previous contributors, but rather to raise issues which encompass those points.

It will be apparent from previous chapters that, although there is now some recognition of the position of prisoners' children, they still remain the Cinderella of the penal system, largely unrecognized and uncared for, and a potential reservoir of future criminality and deviant social behaviour. Such attention as they have received is due to the commitment of individual members of criminal justice, teaching, and health service agencies, charitable bodies, and voluntary groups. Virtually no serious attention has ever been paid to the children of prisoners by government ministers, whatever the complexion of the party in power, and only a little by organizations representing people who work in the justice system.

Many factors, some engineered, others brought about by default, combine to keep the subject hidden. The effect of law and order and crime prevention campaigns produce in the public mind a feeling that dealing with crime and criminals must be uppermost in the order of priorities and any unwanted side effects are inconsequential. Victims of the justice system are thus rendered invisible. Cohen (1972) and Cohen and Young (1981) showed how the manufacture of news distorts public perception of reality. Fishman (1978) noted how particular groups in society charged with social control functions may encourage the perception of a crime wave in order to further their own organizational interests. Thus, unintended side effects of incarceration become submerged by the rhetoric of those concerned with their own agenda, responsibilities, and self-interests. Children of imprisoned parents remain hidden victims of a justice system which, as Shapland *et al*. (1985) have pointed out, pays scant attention to the victims of crime: it pays even less attention to victims resulting from the dispensation of justice. It is as if they are dispensable in the scheme of things. Such support as is offered is on a limited, *ad hoc* basis of chance or favour which reaches only a minority of those in need. This is in spite of a number of imaginative initiatives described in this book.

This neglect is not surprising, even in a country and in an age which subscribes to civilized behaviour and 'the best interests of the child', because any recognition of the plight of these children attacks the major planks on which the justice system is founded. How *can* we lay claim to punishing the guilty and acquitting the innocent when very many prisoners' children not only suffer more than their imprisoned father, but frequently more even than the original victim of the crime (Shaw 1990)? These undesirable consequences of imprisonment are the inevitable effects of a sentencing culture which cannot afford to consider the consequences to innocent parties. Legislators likewise are in a cleft stick. There is thus a conspiracy of silence because the criminal justice system must sacrifice these children, must permit them to become its victims if it is not to question its basis (Shaw 1990). Thus they become dispensable. As Hounslow (1982) and her colleagues in Australia observed:

> Those who uphold the prevailing legal and penal ideology cannot afford to consider what happens to prisoners' children, as any recognition of their plight strikes at the very notions of 'justice', 'innocence' and 'guilt' upon which this ideology is founded.

Politicians are reluctant to touch the subject, in spite of the evidence. As an example one might quote David Mellor (1988), who, when speaking on civil rights in Russia, was at pains to point out that 'Details of one single case show up what's happening better than a whole lot of statistics.' Strange that he should not apply the same criteria to children in his own country – or is it? There are, after all, few votes on the platform of prisoners' children, however great the hardship, however massive the injustice! So a key issue emerges:

Hardship and injustice are insufficient alone to produce change, even in a country which is among the more civilized. These evils must be demonstrated repeatedly. Issues about mother and baby units, the number of mothers who have been imprisoned for relatively petty crimes and fathers incarcerated for non-payment of fines and minor transgressions, and what happens to their children, must be placed firmly in the public domain by organizations such as the Federation

of Prisoners' Families Support Groups, Howard League, NACRO, the Prison Reform Trust, and the media. Then the ignorant, the uninformed and those with vested interests to the contrary, will no longer be able to avoid the issues by saying, 'the criminal should have foreseen the consequences of his or her actions' or hide behind statements professing that a person who has committed a crime is 'always and inevitably a bad parent whom the child would be better without'.

THE PROFLIGATE USE OF CUSTODY BY THE CARCERIAL SOCIETY

Walker (1987) observed that 'The more pessimistic one is about the achievement of positive objectives of custodial sentences, the more one ought to be concerned with the avoidance of unwanted side-effects', adding 'only those who have broken the rules should be punished'. Arguably one of the most serious of the unintended consequences of custody is its effect on prisoners' children. It is ironic, therefore, that, as disillusionment with imprisonment increases and problems within the prison service mount, the proportion of offenders of all ages who receive custodial sentences, as a percentage of those sentenced for indictable offences, rose steadily in the United Kingdom throughout the decade of the 1980s and both the prison population and prison receptions grew (Home Office 1989). Thomas (1988) and Ashworth (1988) both pointed out that average sentence length also increased. Government and penal reformers, no doubt for differing reasons, argue for a reduction in the use of imprisonment. Expense, squalor, and ineffectiveness, though cited as reasons for reducing custody, seem not to have had a significant impact on sentencing culture. Efforts to limit prison use in England and Wales have generally been unsuccessful (Bottoms 1987).

Recently, however, there have been some promising signs of a reduction in the use of custody (Home Office 1990), but there is a long way to go before one can say with honesty that all those in prison need to be there for the good of society as a whole. Currently many men and women are incarcerated for short periods of time which cause major trauma to their families and children but minimal protection to the public (Brody and Tarling 1980). In this respect it is clear that the efforts of the government to reduce the use of imprisonment for less serious offences will, if successful, lessen the number of children suffering the unintended consequences of parental incarceration – even though the government's efforts are motivated by the financial cost of custody rather than the human cost to prisoners' children.

It is of course possible to construct an argument which demonstrates that some criminals are so disruptive that the harm suffered by their children is unavoidable, such is the necessity for their incarceration; but how many such criminals are there? The majority of persons received into British prisons remain there for less than three months and many for only a few days or weeks. They are there as punishment or in an effort to deter and not to protect the public from their activities, the period is too short. One is forced to ask, 'Can the incarceration of these short-sentence prisoners be justified if the children of a significant proportion suffer harm as a result?'

In the autumn of 1989, United Nations member states voted to accept the most comprehensive treaty ever for the protection of children – the Convention on the Rights of the Child. It will become part of international law when twenty countries have signed it. It remains to be seen what effect, if any, it has on the treatment meted out to the children of prisoners but they certainly fall within its remit on the right to be sheltered and protected from, among other things, separation from parents. The issue is thus self evident:

> **At any one time there are more than half a million children in England and Wales alone who have experience of parental imprisonment. This figure is kept topped up by more than 30,000 children annually experiencing this for the first time. The number is too high and unmanageable because of the profligate use of custody as a punishment. Does the state have a right morally – as practice shows it has legally – to strip a child of its parent because that parent has offended, although the crime may have been less harmful to the victim than imprisonment of the offender is to his or her child? Does not the child have a right to uninterrupted parenting at least equal to the right of the state to punish? The profligate use of custody must be markedly reduced – not because of the high cost and overcrowding in prisons which are separate issues – but because of the undesirable consequences which a penal policy based on extensive use of the ultimate sanction, even for trivial offenders, is having on an unacceptably high proportion of the nation's children.**

PARENTS – THE CHILD'S RIGHT

Even in an enlightened society which reserves custody for those people whose behaviour is so damaging that they must be taken out of circulation – and there will likely always be some of these – the problem of how to minimize the harm to their children will remain to be addressed. Much of what goes on within prisons has as its rationale 'good order and discipline', 'security and control'. It is not surprising, therefore, that visits are seen as the right (or privilege) of the inmate; never as the right of the child to maintain a relationship with its father or mother. This is in marked contrast to divorce where the child's access to the parent who does not have custody is seen as the child's right and generally in the child's interest.

NASPO (1982) observed how prison staff become conditioned to 'think within the walls' because of the pressures on them to run a secure, escape-free establishment with the minimum of publicity and fuss. What happens to the inmate when he or she is released is of negligible importance when compared to the repercussions if something goes wrong within the prison, for instance the much publicized incidents of violence and escape – Hughes, Prosser, the Maze, Blake – and hostage situations and major disturbances in the prison systems of Scotland, Northern Ireland, and England and Wales. The situation of the inmate's family and children is generally even less relevant to the prison priorities. This is not a criticism of prison staff, but rather a comment on the carcerial society, a reflection of society's attitudes to 'justice' and its unpreparedness to consider the unintended and undesirable effects of imprisonment. Nevertheless, contributors to this book have shown that there are some promising moves in prisons in some parts of the United Kingdom and it is clearly possible to address some of the needs of children from within the institution – given the political will.

None of the several major enquiries into United Kingdom prison systems during the past few decades addressed prisoners' families until the Lord Justice Woolf (1991) inquiry which received submissions relating to dependents and reported as this chapter was being written. A main recommendation was: 'Better prospects for prisoners to maintain their links with families and the community through more visits and home leaves and through being located in community prisons as near to their homes as possible'. The extent to which government implements the spirit of this recommendation will be highly significant. If it responds by only tinkering with the system and, for instance, more telephones and improved home leave for low security groups – which in a modern civilized society should be happening already – the message will be clear: prisoners' children remain a low priority.

The United Kingdom compares unfavourably with most other European countries in relation to home leave (NACRO 1985, 1988, 1989). The Control Review Committee (1984) observed in its report, 'Home leave is, in fact, a matter on which the practices in this country are markedly more cautious than in the rest of Europe.' Six years have passed and practices remain 'markedly more cautious'. Yet it is abundantly clear that there is an overwhelming need for the children of incarcerated parents to maintain a meaningful relationship with their imprisoned parent. Two issues arise from this:

i) **How to achieve a more humane and responsible balance between the rights of the prisoner and the need for security on the one side and the rights and needs of the child for a meaningful relationship with the imprisoned mother or father on the other.**
ii) **How to develop a planned approach to home leave so that it really does provide a mechanism for maintaining family links, which it fails to do at present when it is generally granted only towards the end of the sentence. Regular home leave could provide benchmarks in a long sentence and help maintain the parent/child relationship. It would have the benefit of not presenting logistic difficulties and pressure on space as would for example a big expansion of visits or the introduction of conjugal visits.**

THE REDUCTION OF HARM

There is much which can be done to reduce the harm currently suffered by prisoners' children and contributors to a number of chapters in this book have shown that clearly. The development of visits centres offering support, advice, and help – not just a place to move the queue away from the front of the prison and out of view of the public – is to be applauded as is the wide range of local organizations, national charities, and individals involved in this development and the interest of the Home Office. The need for a strong national voice which has both experience and credibility is apparent and the Federation of Prisoners' Families' Support Groups could provide this. Schools have a major role but, because crime and victimization tend to cluster in districts of poverty, the pressure falls on teachers in schools with poor catchment areas who are already under considerable strain from a great mix of social problems.

Although positive movements are happening, there is a long, long way yet to go and there is much change in the *opposite* direction too. Elsewhere in this book contributors have shown how difficult it is for a woman to survive the economic problems presented by the imprisonment of her partner and the difficulties she herself encounters when released from custody. Recent changes in social security legislation hit hardest at those at the very bottom of the social ladder and cuts in family planning, infant welfare foods, health visiting services, to name but a few, have very serious implications for families and again hit hardest at those on the bottom line – and that means the majority of prisoners' children. The rest of society is also hit when it has to pick up the pieces. The problems faced by single parents have been described on many occasions and Phillips (1985) gave a particularly graphic account of how disadvantaged individuals are shunted from one ignorant or indifferent official to another as they struggle to obtain, for example, medical attention. Prisoners' families are temporarily deprived of one parent and fall into Phillips' category while at the same time being additionally disadvantaged by stigmatization and almost always at the bottom of the economic, social, and educational ladder.

It is not only for humanitarian reasons that the United Kingdom, and indeed all nations purporting to be civilized, must address this issue. These children are mostly from the poorest and most disadvantaged families. Farrington (1989), commenting on a thirty-two-year follow-up of boys from an Inner London Borough observed (and it constitutes a fundamental issue in regard to prisoners' children)

> children from poorer families are more likely to offend because they are less able to achieve their goals legally and because they value some goals (eg excitement) especially highly. . . . Children who are exposed to poor parental child-rearing behaviour, disharmony or separation are likely to offend because they do not build up internal controls over socially disapproved behaviour, while children from criminal families and those with delinquent friends tend to build up anti-establishment attitudes and the belief that offending is justifiable. The whole process is self perpetuating. . . . The major policy implications of the Cambridge study are that potential offenders can be identified at an early age and that offending might be prevented by training parents in effective child-rearing methods, pre-school intellectual enrichment programmes, giving more economic resources to poor parents. . . . Because of the link between crime and many other social problems, any measure that succeeds in preventing offending will probably have benefits that go far beyond crime. . . . More resources need to be directed toward the early social prevention of crime.

He is not alone in this conclusion: Graham (1989) reviewed the findings of research on the role of the family in general, and parenting skills in particular, in the later occurrence of delinquency. He concluded that to improve cost effectiveness, resources should best be targeted at multi-problem families and lone teenage mothers. A crime prevention policy such as that advocated by Farrington would automatically have the twin advantages of attending to the tens of thousands of neglected prisoners' children, who represent one of the great social injustices of our day, while aiming to reduce crime at its origin instead of spending vast sums of money dealing with its aftermath.

REFERENCES

Ashworth, A. (1988) 'Crime and Punishment: towards a national sentencing policy', *New Law Journal*, 138:6377.
Bottoms, A. E. (1987) 'Limiting prison use: experience in England & Wales', *Howard Journal* 26:117.
Brody, S. R. and Tarling, R. (1980) *Taking Offenders Out of Circulation*, Home Office Research Study No. 64, London: HMSO.
Cohen, S. (1972) *Folk Devils and Moral Panics*, London: MacGibbon & Kee.
Cohen, S. and Young, J. (1981) *The Manufacture of News*, London: Constable.
Control Review Committee (1984) *Managing the Long-Term Prison System*, London: HMSO.
Farrington, D. (1989) 'The origins of crime: the Cambridge study in delinquent development', *Home Office Research Bulletin* No. 27, London: HMSO.
Fishman, M. (1978) 'Crime waves as ideology', *Social Problems* 25:531.
Graham, J. (1989) 'Families, parenting skills and delinquency', *Home Office Research Bulletin* No. 26, London: HMSO.
Home Office (1989) *Prison Statistics, England & Wales*, 1988, London: HMSO.
Home Office (1990) *Statistical Bulletin* 20/90, London: Home Office.
Hounslow, B., Stephenson, A., Stewart, J., and Crancher, J. (1982) *Children of Imprisoned Parents*, The Family & Children's Services Agency, Ministry of Youth & Community Services of New South Wales, Australia.
Mellor, D. (1988) 'Today', *BBC Radio 4*, interviewed by Bill Frost on civil rights in Russia. 15 April.
NACRO (1985) 'Home leave', *NACRO briefing*, July.
NACRO (1988) 'Home leave', *NACRO briefing*, October.
NACRO (1989) *Prisoners' Opportunities for Contact with the Outside World*, March.
NASPO (1982) *Probation Officers in Prison Department Establishments*, National Association of Senior Probation Officers, Professional Committee Paper Number 2, *NASPO News* 4.
Phillips, K. (1985) 'Into the poverty trap', *Nursing Mirror* 160 (10):18.
Shapland, J., Willmore, J., and Duff, P. (1985) *Victims in the Criminal Justice System*, Aldershot: Gower.
Shaw, R. G. (1990) 'Prisoners' children and politics: an aetiology of victimisation', *Children and Society*, 4:3315.
Thomas, D. (1988) 'Is now the time to make time shorter?', Legal Brief, *The Times* 9 August.

Walker, N. (1987) *Crime and Criminality: A Critical Introduction*, Oxford: Oxford University Press.
Woolf, Lord Justice and Tumin, His Honour Judge Stephen (1991) *Prison Disturbances 1990* (cmnd 1456) London: HMSO.

Name index

Genovese, E.D. 93
Gibbs, C. 24, 29, 30, 32, 34, 38n, 39n
Gilroy, P. 93
Glendenning, C. 75
Goffman, E. 156
Goldfarb, W. 16
Graham, H. 75
Graham, J. 198
Griffiths, C. 93
Griffiths, R. 15, 18
Gutteridge, S. 32, 33, 34, 35, 36, 38n

Hall, S. 90, 93
Hamnett, C. 75
Hansard 65
Hansberry, L. 94
Heidensohn, F. 30
Henriques, Z.W. 32, 33, 36, 37
Hetherington, E.M. 5
Hickling, D. 109–10
Hoghughi, M. 25
Home Office 14, 30, 31, 44, 45, 56, 69, 72, 114–15, 116, 118, 132, 156, 162, 187, 188, 190, 194
Hope, J. 147
Hounslow, B. 111, 193
Hughes, W.J. 160
Hurd, D. 46

Jenkin, P. 155

King, R.D. 54, 61
Kozol, V. 89

Lakes, G. 69
Land, H. 75
Lane, Lord 103, 104
Lea, J. 149
Leicester Prison Visitors' Centre Trust 183
Light, R. 4, 39n, 48, 75, 76
Lipton, R.C. 16
Lowe, N.V. 101

McDermott, K. 54, 61, 86, 90, 91, 93
McGowan, B.G. 35
Maclean, M. 6, 128, 129

McPherson, S. 74
McTaggart, M. 134
Maidment, S. 101
Matthews, J. 4, 48, 179
Matthews, R. 115
Mellor, D. 193
Millar, J. 75
Monger, M. 46, 170
Moore, S. 39n, 174
Morris, P. 4, 46, 48, 153, 154

NACRO (National Association for the Care and Resettlement of Offenders) 31, 46, 96, 178, 196
Nadin-Davis, R.P. 104
NAPO (National Association of Prison Officers) 13
NASPO (National Association of Senior Probation Officers) 196
Nesbit, E. 170
Nooney, K. 13, 30
Northern Ireland Office 149
Norz, F. 110, 111

O'Friel, B. 184
Open University 128, 130–2
Ormrod, R. 5, 9

Pahl, J. 75
Pendleton, J. 46, 170
Phillips, K. 198
Player, E. 86
Plotnikoff, J. 50, 106
Pond, C. 75
Popay, J. 75
Posen, I. 24, 32, 35, 39n
Prison Reform Trust (PRT) 57, 65, 97, 125
Provence, S. 16

Quinton, D. 25

Ray, I. 13, 30
Read, D. 142
Richards, M.P.M. 5, 9
Rose, H. 75
Rutter, M. 4, 6, 11, 25, 26
Ruxton, S. 64, 65

SACRO (Scottish Association
for the Care and Resettlement
of Offenders) 145
Save the Children 178–91 *passim*
Schupak, T.L. 110, 111
Scottish Home and Health
Department 45
Scottish Office 143–6
Shapland, J. 193
Shaw, R. 4, 29–41 *passim*, 44,
45, 46, 47, 48, 67, 86, 149, 153,
154, 174, 179, 193
Skeels, H.M. 16
Slipman, S. 74
Smith, S. 74–5, 185
Sparks, R.F. 45
Spitz, R.A. 14, 16
Stanton, A.M. 29, 31, 34, 37, 38,
39n

Tarling, R. 194
Taylor, L. 147
Thomas, D. 104, 194
Totterman, N. 8
Train, C. 50

Treverton-Jones, G.D. 106, 107

United States Department of Justice
69

Vercoe, K. 178

Wadsworth, M.E.J. 6
Walker, N. 194
Warnock Report 174, 176
Waters, E. 3
West, D. 26
Widgery, Lord 103
Wilkinson, C. 24, 29, 32, 33, 34, 36,
37
Williams, M. 115
Wilmer, 46
Wilson-Croome, L. 178
Women's Equality Group (WEG)
31

Young, J. 149
Young, J. 192

Zalba, S.R. 32, 33, 34, 38, 39n

Subject index

For Product Safety Concerns and Information please contact our EU
representative GPSR@taylorandfrancis.com
Taylor & Francis Verlag GmbH, Kaufingerstraße 24, 80331 München, Germany

www.ingramcontent.com/pod-product-compliance
Lightning Source LLC
Chambersburg PA
CBHW050429280326
41932CB00013BA/2041

* 9 7 8 1 0 3 2 5 7 2 8 6 4 *